KB201432

English Worship Song

영어찬양

English & Korean

BEST 450

CcM²u

As the deer pants for the water
So my soul longs after you
You alone are my heart's desire
And I long to worship you
You alone are my strength, my shield
To you alone will my spirit yield
You alone are my hearts desire
And I long to worship you

As the deer by Martin Nystrom
영어찬양 No.64

목차

A

B

J

M

N

O

U

목차

Alleluia

(예수 사랑해요)

Jude Del Hierro

1

C

Je - sus I lo - ve You I bow down be - fore You
예 – 수 사 랑 해 요 나 주 앞 에 엎 드 려

Prai - ses and wor - ship to our King
경 – 배 와 찬 – 양 왕 께 드 리 네

Al - le - lu – ia Al - le - lu – ia
알 – 렐 루 – 야 알 렐 루 – 야

Al - le - lu – ia Al - le - lu
알 – 렐 루 – 야 알 렐 – 루

2 All The Heavens
(거룩하신 하나님)

Reuben Morgan

Ho - ly, ho - ly are You Lord The whole earth is filled with Your
거 룩 하 - 신 하 나 - 님 - - 온 세 상 - 주 의 - 영 - - 광

glo - ry. Let the na - tions rise to - give
가 득 - 해 열 방 들 - 아 일 어 나 -

Hon - or and praise to Your name Let Your face
경 배 - 와 찬 - 양 - - 드 - 려 - 주 얼 - 굴

shine on us And the world will know You live All the heav
비 출 - 때 - 주 사 심 - 모 두 - 알 리 - - 온 하 늘

- - ens shout Your praise Beau - ti - ful is our God, the
- - 찬 양 하 네 아 름 다 - 우 신 - 주 - 온

u - ni - verse will sing "Hal - le - lu - jah!" to You, our King!
우 주 찬 - 양 해 - 할 렐 루 - 야 - 우 리 왕 - - 께 -

Words and Music by Reuben Morgan
© 2002 Hillsong Music Publishing Australia (admin in Korea by Universal Music Publishing/ CAIOS)

All We Like Sheep

(우리 모두 양과 같이)

3

C

Don Moen

All Things Are Possible

(모든 것 가능해)

Darlene Zschech

All Things Are Possible

C

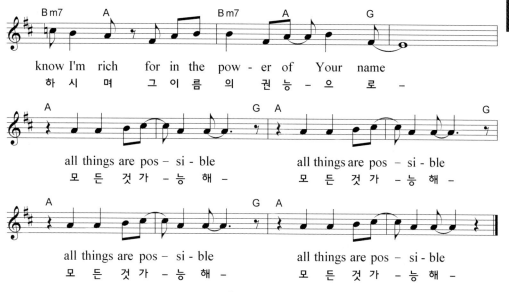

know I'm rich   for in the pow - er of   Your   name
하 시   며   그 이 름 의   권 능 - 으   로 -

all things are pos – si - ble   all things are pos – si - ble
모 든 것 가 - 능 해 -   모 든 것 가 - 능 해 -

all things are pos – si - ble   all things are pos – si - ble
모 든 것 가 - 능 해 -   모 든 것 가 - 능 해 -

5 Blessed Be The Lord God Almighty

(사랑하는 나의 아버지)

Robert D Fitts

Fa-ther in heaven how we love You,   we lift Your name in all the earth.
사 랑 하 는 나의 – 아 버 – 지   이 름 높 여 – 드 립 니 다

MayYour king-dom beest-ab-lish'd in our prai-ses,   as Your people declare Your migh-ty works.
주 의 나 라 찬 양 속 에임 – 하 시 – 니   능 력 의 주 께 찬 송 – 하 네

Blessed be the Lord God Al-migh-ty,   who was and is and is to come,
전 능 하 – 신 하 나 님 찬 – 양   언 제 나동 – 일 하 신 주 – –

bless-ed be the Lord God Al-migh-ty,   who reigns for-e-ver more.
전 능 하 – 신 하 나 님 찬 – 양   영 원 히 다 스 리 네

Fine

나 주 의 이 름 높 이 리   나 주 의 이 름 높 – 이 리 – – –

하 늘 높 이 들 린 깃 – 발 – 처 럼 – – –   주 의 이 름 높 – 이 리 전 능 하 – 신

D.S.

Cares Chorus

(모든 근심을 주께)

Kelly Willard

Change My Heart Oh God

(항상 진실케)

Eddie Espinosa

Change my heart, oh, God, make it ev-er true.
항 상 진 실 케 - 내 맘 바 꾸 사 -

Change my heart, oh God, may I be like You
하 나 님 닮 게 - 하 여 주 소 서 -

Fine

You are the Pot - ter I am the clay
주 는 토 기 장 이 나 는 진 흙

Mold me and make me, this is what I pray.
날 빚 으 소 - 서 기 도 하 오 니

D.C.

Christ In Me

(내 안에 사는 이)

Gary Garcia

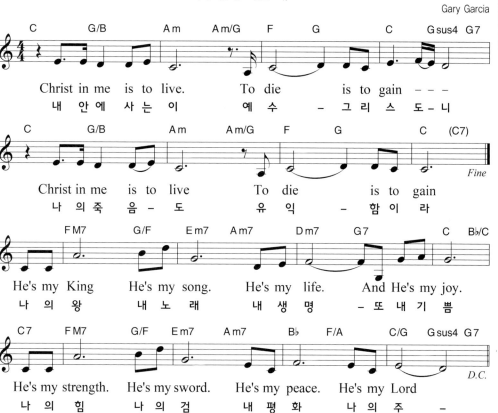

8

C

C · G/B · Am · Am/G · F · G · C · Gsus4 · G7

Christ in me is to live. To die is to gain - - -
내 안에 사 는 이 예 수 – 그 리 스 도 - 니

C · G/B · Am · Am/G · F · G · C · (C7)

Christ in me is to live To die is to gain
나 의 죽 음 – 도 유 익 – 함 이 라

Fine

FM7 · G/F · Em7 · Am7 · Dm7 · G7 · C · Bb/C

He's my King He's my song. He's my life. And He's my joy.
나 의 왕 내 노 래 내 생 명 – 또 내 기 쁨

C7 · FM7 · G/F · Em7 · Am7 · Bb · F/A · C/G · Gsus4 · G7

He's my strength. He's my sword. He's my peace. He's my Lord
나 의 힘 나 의 검 내 평 화 나 의 주 –

D.C.

Emmanuel

(임마누엘)

Bob McGee

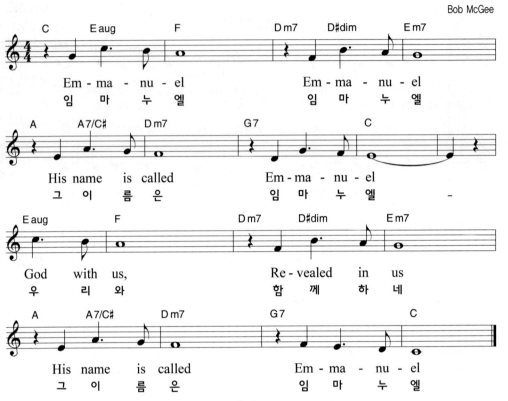

Em - ma - nu - el　　　Em - ma - nu - el
임　마　누　엘　　　임　마　누　엘

His name　is called　　Em - ma - nu - el　-
그　이　름　은　　　임　마　누　엘

God　with　us,　　　Re - vealed　in　us
우　리　와　　　함　께　하　네

His　name　is called　　Em - ma - nu - el
그　이　름　은　　　임　마　누　엘

Great And Mighty Is He

(광대하신 주님)

Todd Pettygrove

Great and migh - ty is He, great and migh - ty is He;
광 대 하 – 신 주 님 전 능 하 – 신 주 님

clothed in glo - ry, ar-rayed in splen - dor, great and migh - ty is He.
찬 란 하 – 게 빛 난 영 광 – 으 로 옷 입 으 – 신 주 님

Let us lift His name up high, ce - le-brate His grace;
주 의 이 름 높 – 이 며 – 주 은 혜 찬 양 –

for He has re-deemed our lives and He reigns on high.
우 릴 구 원 하 – 신 주 – 통 치 하 – 시 네 –

great and migh - ty is, great and migh-ty is, great and migh-ty is He!
광 대 하 – 신 주 전 능 하 – 신 주 광 대 하 – 신 주 님

Forever Reign

(영원히 다스리네)

Reuben Morgan & Jason Ingram

11

1.You are good, You are good, when there's no-thing good in me. You are
peace, You are peace, when my fear is crip-pl-ing. You are
more, You are more, than my words will e-ver say. You are

1.좋 으 신 하 나 님 선 한 것 나 없 지 만 사 랑
의 하 나 님 내 가 두 려 워 할 때 진 리
신 하 나 님 말 로 다 표 현 못 해 나 의

love, You are love, on dis-play for all to see. You are light, You are light, when the
true, You are true, e-ven in my wan-de-ring. You are joy, You are joy, You're the
Lord, You are Lord, all cre-a-tion will pro-claim. You are here, You are here, in Your

의 하 나 님 온 세 상 보 게 되 리 빛 되 신 하 나 님 어 둠
의 하 나 님 내 가 방 황 할 때 도 기 쁨 의 하 나 님 노 래
주 하 나 님 만 물 이 선 포 하 네 이 땅 의 하 나 님 주 안

dark-ness clo-ses in. You are hope, You have hope, You have co-vered all my sin.
rea-son that I sing. You are life, You are life, in You
pre-sence I'm made whole. You are God, You are God, of all

은 사 라 지 네 소 망 의 하 나 님 나 의 죄 덮 으 셨 네 —
할 이 유 있 네 생 명 의 하 나 님 사 망
에 나 완 전 해 당 신 은 하 나 님 내 모

2.You are death has lost its sting.
else I'm let-ting go.

2.평 강 권 세 이 겼 네 — —
든 것 드 리 리 — —

Oh, I'm run-ning to Your arms, I'm run-ning to Your arms. the ri-ches of Your
오 나 달 려 가 리 라 주 님 의 품 으 로 그 넘 치 는 사

Forever Reign

love will al-ways be e-nough No-thing com-pares to Your em-brace.
랑 늘 충 만 하 리 라 주 님 같 은 – 분 은 – 없 네

Light of the world, for-e-ver reign.
– 주 영 원 히 – 다 스 – 리 네 – 3.그 크

I'm run-ning to Your arms, I'm run-ning to Your arms. The ri-ches of Your
– 나 달 려 가 리 라 주 님 의 품 으 로 그 넘 치 는 사

love will al-ways be e-nough. No-thing com-pares to Your em-brace.
랑 늘 충 만 하 리 라 주 님 같 은 – 분 은 – 없 네

Light of the world, for-e-ver reign.
– 주 영 원 히 – 다 스 – 리 네 –

My heart will sing, no o-ther Name. Je-sus. Je-sus.
그 이 름 만 나 찬 양 해 예 – 수 예 – 수 – –

Written by Jason Ingram, Reuben Morgan
© 2009 Hillsong Music Publishing Australia (admin in Korea by Universal Music Publishing/ CAIOS)

12 For You Are Glorious

(주를 보라)

David W. Morris & Mike Massa

We see Je - sus   For His suffer-ing crown-ed with glory and with praise
주 를 보 라 고 난 으 로 면 류 관 을 쓰 시 고

Tas - ting   death   for   all   men   by   God's   grace
만 민 위 해 죽 임 당 하 사

Gi-ven power to put all things in place   -   -   And we see Je - sus
모 든 만 물 회 복 하 셨 네 - - 주 예 수 보 라

Sea-ted at the right hand of the throne   Ma-king in-ter-ces-sion for His own
보 좌 오른 편 에 앉 으 사 우 리 위 해 기 도 하 시 고

Up hold - ing all things by his word a - lone   -   -   -   -
그 말 씀 만 물 다 스 리 시 네 - - - -

For you are glo-ri-ous Shin-ing vic-to-ri-ous Over powers and prin-ci-pa-li-ties
영 광 의 주 예 수 - 승 리 의 하 나 님 모 든 권 세 이 기 - 셨 네 -

For you are glo-ri-ous   Shin-ing vic-to-ri-ous Dis-arm-ing all your e-ne-mies
영 광 의 주 예 수 - 승 리 의 하 나 님 원 수 를 정 복 하 - 셨 네 -

For You Are Glorious

G#dim Am   Em7

The rul - ers of this world   Be - neath your feet are hurled
이 세 상 권 – 세 를 – 그 발 아 래 – 두 신 –

Dm7   G   G7sus4   C

As you reign, our con - quer - ing King!
왕 되 신 주 통 치 – 하 네   –

13 From The Inside Out

(내 안의 중심이 주를 찬양)

Joel Huston

From The Inside Out

yond all fame.　　In my heart, in my soul,　　Lord, I give You con-trol.
가 득 해　　　　　내 맘 과 영 혼 –　　　모 두 드 리 리

Con - sume me from the in - side out, Lord　　Let jus-tice and praise
– 성 령 의 불 로 태 우 소 서　　　　주 님 의 의 로

be-come my em - brace,　　to love You from the in - side out
– 날 감 싸 소 서 –　　　주 를 더 사 랑 하 도 록

in - side out. E-ver - las – ting, Your light will shine when all else fades. Ne-ver-en
하 도 록 변 함 없 – 는 주 님 의 빛 비 추 시 네 영 원 하

– ding, Your glo - ry goes be - yond all fame. And the cry
– 신 주 영 광 온 땅 가 득 해 내 맘 의

of my heart is to bring You praise, from the in – side out. Lord my soul
– 소 망 은 – 주 님 을 – 찬 양 내 안 의 – 중 심 이 주 를

cries out. E - ver - las cries out Lord.
– 찬 양 변 함 없 – 찬 양 해 –

Words and Music by Joel Houston
© 2005 Hillsong Music Publishing Australia (admin in Korea by Universal Music Publishing/ CAIOS)

14 Happy Day
(오 기쁜 날)

Tim Hughes & Ben Cantelon

The great-est day in his - to - ry, death is beat-ten, You
When I stand in that place free at last, meet
위 대 한 구 원 - 의 날 죽 음 이 기 고
주 앞 에 - 서 - 는 날 주 얼 굴 - 바

have res - cued me. Sing it out, Je - sus is a - live.
- ing face to face I am yours. Je - sus You are mine.
- 날 구 - 했 네 찬 양 해 예 - 수 사 - 셨 네 -
- 라 보 - 는 날 주 님 은 나 - 의 모 - 든 것 -

The emp-ty cross, the emp - ty grave, life e - ter-nal, you
End-less joy per - fect peace earth - ly pain fi
그 십 자 가 텅 빈 - 무 덤 영 원 한 승 리
영 원 한 기 쁨 - 평 화 세 상 고 통 모

have won the day. Shout it out, Je - sus is a - live,
- nal - ly will cease. Cel - e - brate, Je - sus is a - live,
- 의 날 - 주 네 소 리 쳐 예 - 수 사 - 셨 네 -
- 두 사 - 라 져 찬 양 해 예 - 수 사 - 셨 네 -

He's a - live! And Oh, hap-py day, hap-py day,
사 셨 네 - - 오 오 - 기 쁜 날 - 기 쁜 날

You washed my sin a-way. Oh, hap-py day, hap-py day,
- 주 내 - 죄 씻 었 네 오 기 쁜 날 - 기 쁜 날

Happy Day

C

15 Hear Our Praises

(거리마다 기쁨으로)

Reuben Morgan

May our homes be filled with danc - ing,
May our light shine in the dark - ness,
거 리 마 - 다 기 - 쁨 으 - 로 -
십 자 가 - 앞 에 - 행 할 - 때 -

may our streets be filled with joy;
as we walk be - fore the cross;
춤 을 추 - 게 하 - 시 고 -
주 의 빛 - 비 추 - 시 고 -

may in - jus - tice bow to Je - sus
may your glo - ry fill the whole earth
주 의 백 - 성 기 - 도 할 - 때 -
물 이 바 - 다 덮 - 음 같 - 이 -

as the peo - ple turn and pray. From the
as the wa - ter over the seas. From the
이 땅 회 - 복 하 - 소 서 - 산 위
주 영 광 - 채 우 - 소 서 -

moun - tain to the vall - ey, hear our prai - ses
에 서 - 계 곡 까 지 - 우 리 찬 양 -

rise to you. From the hea - vens to the na - tions,
울 리 네 하 늘 에 서 - 열 방 까 지 -

Hear Our Praises

hear our sing - ing   fill the air.
우 리 노 래 –   가 득 하 네   –

air From the   Hal - le - lu - jah!
네 산 위   할 렐 루 야 –

Hal - le - lu - jah!   Hal - le - lu - jah!   Hal - le -
할 렐 루 – 야 –   할 렐 루 야 –   할 렐

lu - jah!   Hal - le   From the air.
루 야 – – 할 렐 – 산 위 네 – –

Words and Music by Reuben Morgan
© 1998 Hillsong Music Publishing Australia (admin in Korea by Universal Music Publishing/ CAIOS)

16 He Is Able

(능력 위에 능력으로)

Rory J. Noland & Gregory F. Ferguson

He is a - ble more than a - ble to ac-com-plish what con-cerns me today
능력위 - 에 능 력으 - 로 - 나를 향한 주 뜻이 - 루 시 고

He is a - ble more than a - ble to han-dle a-ny-thing that comes my
- - 능력위 - 에 능 력으 - 로 - 내 앞의일을주 - 관하시

way He is a - ble, more than a - ble to
네 - 능력위 - 에 능 력으로 - 내

do much more than I could e - ver dream, He is a - ble, more than a -
생 각 보 다 더 - 크 신 - - 주 님 - 능력위 - 에 능 력으

ble to make me what He wants me to be.
- 로 - 주 뜻 대 로 날 빛 - 으 소 서 -

O.T. : He Is Able / O.W. : Gregory F. Ferguson, Rory J. Noland
O.P. : Universal Music – Brentwood Benson Publ. / S.P. : Universal Music Publishing Korea, CAIOS
Adm. : Capitol CMG Publishing / All rights reserved. Used by permission.

Holy Spirit We Welcome You

(거룩하신 성령이여)

Chris Bowater

Ho - ly Spi - rit we wel - come You
거 룩 하 신 – 성 령 이 여 – – –
우 리 에 게 – 임 하 소 서 –

Move a - mong us with ho - ly fire
Let the breeze of Your pre - sence blow
please a - ccom - plish in me to - day
성 령 의 – 불 – 로 오 셔 서 –

As we lay a - side all earth - ly de - sire,
That Your child - ren here might tru - ly know
Some new work of lo - ving grace I pray
세 상 헛 된 마 음 태 우 소 서 –

Hands reach out and our hearts as - pire
How to move in the spi - rit's flow
Un - re - ser – ve - dly have Your way
손 들 고 – 주 를 바 랄 때 –

Ho - ly Spi - rit Ho - ly Spi - rit
성 령 이 여 – – 성 령 이 여 – –

Ho - ly Spi - rit we wel - come You
성 령 이 여 – – 임 하 소 서 –

18 If Were A Butterfly

(내가 만약 나비라면)

Brian Howard

If I were a bu-tter-fly   I'd thank You Lord for giv-ing me wings
If I were an e-le-phant   I'd thank you Lord by rai-sing my trunk
I'd I were a wi-ggl-y worm   I'd thank you Lord that I could squirm
내 가 만 약 나 비 라 면 -   내 날 개 주 신 주 께 감 사 -
내 가 코 끼 리 라 면 -   내 코 를 들 어 주 께 감 사 -
내 가 지 렁 이 라 면 -   난 땅 을 기 며 주 께 감 사 -

If I were a ro-bin in a tree   I'd thank You Lord that I could sing
If I were a kang - ga - roo   You know I'd hop right up to you
If I were a fu-zzy wu-zzy bear   I'd thank you Lord for fuzzy wuzzy hait
또 내 가 나 무 위 의 새 라 면   난 지 저 귀 며 찬 양 해 -
또 내 가 캥 거 루 - - 라 면   난 높 이 뛰 며 찬 양 해 -
또 내 가 만 약 악 어 - 라 면   내 큰 입 으 로 찬 양 해 -

If I were a fish in the sea   I'd wig-gle my rail and I'd gig-gle with glee
If I were an oc-to-pu-s   I'd thank you Lor-d for my fi-ne looks
If i were a croco-di-le   I'd thank you Lor-d for my great smile
또 내 가 바 다 고 기 라 면 -   꼬 리 를 치 며 기 쁨 으 로 찬 양 -
또 내 가 만 약 문 어 라 면 -   내 팔 을 들 고 기 쁨 으 로 찬 양 -
또 내 가 만 약 곰 이 라 면 -   따 뜻 한 별 을 주 신 주 를 찬 양 -

But I just thank You Fa-ther for mak-ing me   me   For you
감 사 드 리 세 날 만 드 신 주 를   찬   양   내 게

gave me hea-rt   and you ga-ve me a smile   You gave me Je-sus and you
즐 거 움 과 - 기 쁨 주 시 었 네 -   하 나 님 자 녀 삼 아

made me your child   And I just thank you Fa-ther for mak-ing me   me
주 시 었 네 -   감 사 드 리 세 날 만 드 신 주 를   찬   양

I Have Decided To Follow Jesus

(주님 뜻대로)

Norman Johnson

I have de - ci - ded to fol-low Je - sus　I have de - ci - ded to fol-low Je-sus
The world be-hind me the cross be-fore me　The world be-hind me the cross be-fore me
Tho' none go with me still I will fol - low　Tho' none go with me stll I will fol-low
Will you de - cide now to fol-low Je - sus?　Will you de-cide now to fol-low Je-sus?
We de-ci - ded to fol-low Je - sus　we de-ci-ded to fol-low Je-sus

주 님 뜻 대 로 　살 기 로 했 네 　주 님 뜻 대 로 　살 기 로 했 네
이 세 상 사 람 　날 몰 라 줘 도 　이 세 상 사 람 　날 몰 라 줘 도
세 상 등 지 고 　십 자 가 보 네 　세 상 등 지 고 　십 자 가 보 네

I have de - ci - ded to fol-low Je - sus Noturn-ing back No turn - ing back
The world be-hind me the cross be - fore me Noturn-ing back No turn - ing back
Tho' none go with me still I will fol - low Noturn-ing back No turn - ing back
Will you de - cide now to fol-low Je - sus? Noturn-ing back No turn - ing back
We de-ci - ded to fol-low Je - sus Notrun-ing back No turn - ing back

주 님 뜻 대 로 　살 기 로 했 네 　뒤 돌 아 서 　지 않 겠 네
이 세 상 사 람 　날 몰 라 줘 도 　뒤 돌 아 서 　지 않 겠 네
세 상 등 지 고 　십 자 가 보 네 　뒤 돌 아 서 　지 않 겠 네

20 In These Dark Days

(괴로울 때 주님의 얼굴 보라)

Harry John Bollback

In these dark days lift up your eyes to Je - sus lift up your
괴 로 울 때 주 님 의 얼 굴 보 라 평 화 의
힘 이 없 고 내 마 음 연 약 할 때 능 력 의

eyes He's still up - on the throne And come what may, He ne - ver will for-
주 님 바 라 보 아 라 세 상 에 서 시 달 린 친 구
주 님 바 라 보 아 라 주 의 이 름 부 르 는 모 든

sake you For He is God to Him all things are known Lift up your
들 아 위 로 의 주 님 바 라 보 아 라 눈 을 들
자 는 힘 주 시 며 늘 지 켜 주 시 리

eyes He still is there be not dis-mayed He knows your weight of
어 - 주 를 보 라 - 네 모 든 염 려 주 께 맡 겨

care In these dark days lift up your eyes to
라 슬 플 때 에 주 님 의 얼 굴

Je - sus And trust in Him He will your bur - den bear
보 라 사 랑 의 주 님 안 식 주 리 라

O.T. : In These Dark Days / O.W. : Harry John Bollback
O.P. : New Spring Publishing Inc. / S.P. : Universal Music Publishing Korea, CAIOS
Adm. : Capitol CMG Publishing / All rights reserved. Used by permission.

Into Your Presence Lord

(찬양을 드리며)

Richard Oddie

21

C

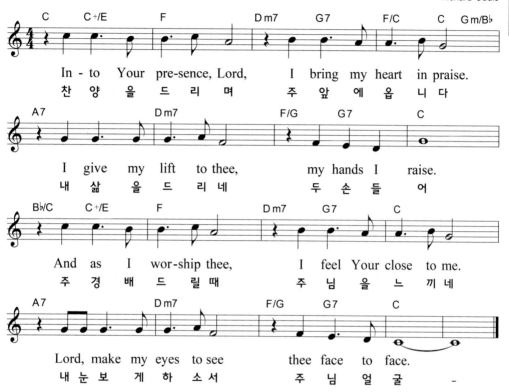

In - to Your pre-sence, Lord, I bring my heart in praise.
찬 양 을 드 리 며 주 앞 에 옵 니 다

I give my lift to thee, my hands I raise.
내 삶 을 드 리 네 두 손 들 어

And as I wor-ship thee, I feel Your close to me.
주 경 배 드 릴 때 주 님 을 느 끼 네

Lord, make my eyes to see thee face to face.
내 눈 보 게 하 소 서 주 님 얼 굴 -

22 I Simply Live For You
(주만 위해 살리)

Russell Fragar

Say the word, and I will sing for You. O-ver o-ceans deep, I will
주 위 해 -나 노래 하리 라 - 깊은 바 다 라 도 - 주 -를

fol - low If each star was a song. and every breath of wind praise It would
따 르 리 - 하 늘 에 별 들 도 - - 부 는 바 - 람 도 - 내 안

still fail by far to say All my heart con-tains I sim-ply live,
의 주 님 을 - 모 두 - 노 래 할 수 없 네 주 를 위 해 -

I sim-ply live for You. Say the As the
주 만 위 해 - 살 리 - 주 위 - 주 의

glo - ry of Your pres-ence now fills this place, in
임 재 안 - 에 영 광 이 가 득 해 - 예

wor-ship we will meet You face to face. - - - - There is
배 안 에 - 서 주 얼 굴 보 네 - - - - 세 상

noth-ing in this world to which You can be com-pared,
무 엇 과 - 도 비 교 할 수 없 - 으 리 -

I Simply Live For You

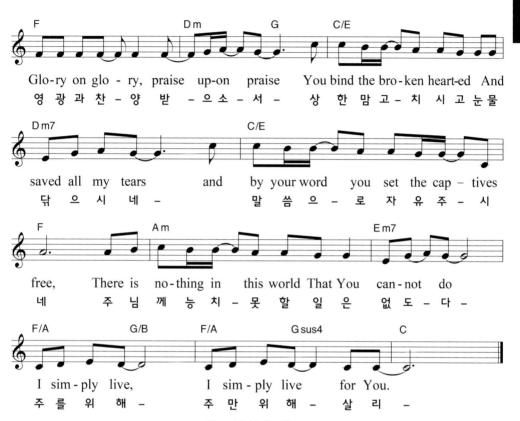

Glo-ry on glo - ry, praise up-on praise You bind the bro-ken heart-ed And
영광과 찬 – 양 받 –으소 – 서 – 상 한 맘 고 – 치 시 고 눈물

saved all my tears and by your word you set the cap – tives
닦 으 시 네 – 말 씀 으 – 로 자 유 주 – 시

free, There is no-thing in this world That You can-not do
네 주 님 께 능 치 – 못 할 일 은 없 도 – 다 –

I sim-ply live, I sim-ply live for You.
주 를 위 해 – 주 만 위 해 – 살 리 –

Words and Music by Russell Fragar

23 I Will Come And Bow Down

(주께 와 엎드려)

Martin J. Nystrom

I will come and bow down at Your feet, Lord Je-sus.
주 께 와 엎 드 려 경 배 드 립 니 다

In Your pres-ence is full-ness of joy.
주 계 신 곳 엔 기 쁨 가 득 　

There is noth-ing there is no one who com-pares with You.
무 엇 과 도 누 구 와 도 바 꿀 수 없 네

I take pleas-ure in wor-ship-ing You, Lord.
예 배 드 림 이 기 쁨 됩 니 다 　

Fine

Heav-en is Your throne and the earth is Your foot stool

Je-sus I come to bow down at Your feet

O, how I love just to wor-ship be-fore You in Your

D.S. al Fine

pres-ence my joy is com-plete so, I will
주 께

I Will Lift My Hands

(나의 손 들고)

Bruce Ellis

24 C

I will wor - ship You, Wor-ship and a - dore You.
경 배 합 – 니 다 – 오 직 주 – 만 높 – 여

I will wor - ship You Lay my life be - fore You. I'll
경 배 합 – 니 다 – 나 의 삶 – 을 드 – 려 주

bow my head be-fore Your glo - ry, Wor-ship at Your feet, And
영 광 앞 – 에 머 – 리 숙 – 여 – 엎 드 립 니 다 –

I'll de-clare that You are wor-thy, I'll set my eyes on You a-lone and
선 포 해 – 존 귀 – 하 신 – 주 난 오 직 한 – 분 주 님 을 보 – 네

I will lift my hands to You, Say-ing "Fa-ther I love You, Fa-ther I need You."
나 의 손 – 들 고 – 주 께 – 사 랑 해 – 요 아 버 – 지 주 님 필 요 해 – 요

I will lift my voice and sing, I will sing of Your glo-ry, the glo-ry of my King.
나 의 목 – 소 리 – 높 여 – 찬 양 해 – 주 의 영 – 광 나 의 왕 – 주 께 –

25 Jesus Your Name

(능력의 이름 예수)

Claire Cloninger & Morris Chapman

Je - sus, Your name is pow - er
healing
ho - ly,

능 력 의 이 - 름 예 - 수
치 유 의 이 - 름 예 - 수
거 룩 한 이 - 름 예 - 수

Je - sus, Your name is might.
give sight.
brings light

권 능 의 이 름 예 수 -
용 서 의 이 름 예 수 -
빛 을 주 는 - 예 수 -

Je - sus, Your name will break ev - 'ry strong hold
will free ev - 'ry cap - tive
a - bove ev - 'ry oth - er,

모 든 강 력 - - 을 - 파 하 는 예 - 수 -
자 유 주 시 - - 는 - 그 이 름 예 - 수 -
모 든 이 름 - - 위 에 뛰 어 난 예 - 수 -

Je - sus, Your name is life.

생 명 되 신 - 예 수 -

Joy Joy Down In My Heart

(주 예수 사랑 기쁨)

26

David Clydesdale & PD. George W.Cooke

I've got the joy, joy, joy, joy, down in my heart Down in my heart
주 예 수 사 랑 기 쁨 내 마 음 속 에 내 마 음 속 에
이 제 는 정 죄 없 네 예 수 안 에 서 예 수 안 에 서
이 제 는 해 방 됐 네 예 수 안 에 서 예 수 안 에 서

Down in my heart I've got the joy, joy, joy, joy, down in my heart
내 마 음 속 에 주 예 수 사 랑 기 쁨 내 마 음 속 에
예 수 안 에 서 이 제 는 정 죄 없 네 예 수 안 에 서
예 수 안 에 서 이 제 는 해 방 됐 네 예 수 안 에 서

Down in my heart to stay. And I'm so hap-py, so ve-ry hap-py I've
내 마 음 속 에 있 네 나 는 기 뻐 요 정 말 기 뻐 요 주
예 수 안 에 서 없 네
예 수 안 에 서 해 방

1. G
got the love of Je-sus in my heart And I'm so
예 수 사 랑 기 쁨 내 맘 에 나 는 기

2. G
got the love of Je-sus in my heart.
예 수 사 랑 기 쁨 내 맘 에

27 Knowing You

(나의 만족과 유익을 위해)

Graham Kendrick

All I once held dear built my lift up on All this
Now my heart's de - sire is to know You more To be
O, to know the power of Your ri - sen life And to
나 의 만 족 과 유 익 을 위 - 해 가 지
부 활 의 능 력 체 험 하 면 - 서 주 의

world re - veres and wars to own All I once thought gain I have
found in You and known as Yours To poss - ess by faith what I
know You in Your suff - er - ings To be - come like You in Your
려 했 던 세 상 일 들 이 젠 모 두 다 해 로
고 난 에 동 참 하 고 주 의 죽 으 심 본 을

coun - ted loss, spent and worth - less now com - pared to this
could not earn, all - sur - pa - ssing gift of right - eous - ness
death, my Lord, So with You to live and ne - ver die
여 기 - 고 주 님 을 위 해 다 버 리 네
받 아 - 서 그 의 생 명 에 참 예 하 네

Know - ing You, Je - sus know - ing You there is no great - ter thing You're my
내 안 에 가 장 귀 한 것 주 님 을 앎 이 라 모 든

all You're the best You're my joy, my right - ous - ness and I love You Lord
것 되 시 며 - 의 와 기 쁨 되 신 주 사 랑 합 니 다

love You Lord love You Lord
합 니 다 - 나 의 주 -

Mighty Is Our God

(광대하신 주)

Eugene Greco/Gerrit Gustafson & Don Moen

Migh-ty is our God, Migh-ty is our King,
광 대 하 – 신 주 – 전 능 하 – 신 왕 –

Migh-ty is our Lord, ru-ler of eve - ry-thing
전 능 하 – 신 주 – 만 물 의 주 – 관 자 –

glo-ry to our God, glo-ry to our King
하 나 님 께 – 영 광 – 우 리 왕 께 – 영 광 –

glo-ry to our Lord ru-ler of eve - ry - thing
주 님 께 – 영 광 – 만 물 의 주 – 관 자

His name is high - er high-er than a - ny o - ther name
온 세 상 위 – 에 – 가 장 높 으 – 신 그 – 이 름

His power is great-er for he has cre - a - ted ev - 'ry - thing
그 능 력 크 도 다 – 만 물 을 창 조 – 하 셨 – – 네

29 Living Hope
(주 예수 내 산 소망)

Phil Wickham & Brian Johnson

Living Hope

30 Lord Reign In Me

(오셔서 다스리소서)

Brenton Brown

so won't You reign in me a-gain? so won't You
오 셔 서 다 스 리 소 서 - 오 셔 서

reign in me a-gain? So won't You reign in me a-gain?
다 스 리 소 서 - 오 셔 서 다 스 리 소 서 -

O Give Thanks To The Lord

(주께 감사하세)

31

Brent Chambers

O give thanks to the Lord, for He is good,
주 께 감 사 하 세 그 는 선 하 시 며

for His stead - fast love en - dures for - e - - - ver
인 자 하 심 이 영 원 함 이 라

O give thanks to the Lord for He is good
주 께 감 사 하 세 그 는 선 하 시 며

For His stead - fast love en - dures for - e - - - ver
인 자 하 심 이 영 원 함 이 라

32 Made Me Glad

(내 기쁨 되신 주)

Miriam Webster

I will bless the Lord for-e-ver
주 － － 를 － 영 원 히 － 송 축 － 해 － －

I will trust Him at all times
항 － － 상 － 주 의 지 － 하 리 － － － － －

He has de-liver-ed me from all fear
Whom have - - - I in hea-ven but You
두 － － 렴 － 속 에 서 날 － 건 지 － 사 － － 네 －
내 － － 가 － 사 모 할 자 － 오 직 － 주 － －

He has set my feet u-pon a rock
There's - - none I de-sire be-sides You
반 － － 석 － 위 에 날 － 세 우 셨 － 네 －
주 － － 와 － 같 은 분 － 없 으 리 － － －

And I will not be moved And
And You have made me glad.
－ 요 동 하 지 － 않 － 고 － － 주
－ 내 기 쁨 되 － 시 － 는 －

I'll say of the Lord You are my shield, my strength,
를 고 백 － 하 리 － 나 의 － 방 패 － － 힘 － 과

Made Me Glad

my por - tion, de - li - ver - er my shel
- - 내 - 기 - 업 - 구 - 원 - - 자 - 피 - 난

- ter strong to - wer. My ve - ry pre - sent help
- 처 - 강 한 성 - 루 - 언 - 제 - 나 나 - 의 도

in time of need.
- 움 되 - 시 네 -

33

Made To Worship
(예배하기 위해)

Chris Tomlin, Stephan Sharp, Ed Cash

Be-fore the day, be-fore the light, be-fore the world re-volved a-round the sun.
빛 이 있기 - 이 전 부 터 - 세 상 이 운 - 행 하 - 기 도 - 전 에

God on high stepped down in - to time, and wrote the sto-
- 하 나 님 이 땅 에 - 계 셔 - 우 릴 위 한

ry of His love for ev - 'ry - one. He has filled our
- 사 랑 - 이 야 - 기 쓰 - 셨 네 - 주 가 주 신

hearts with won-der, so that we al - ways re - mem - ber.
경 이 로 움 우 린 항 상 기 억 하 네

You and I are made to wor - ship, you and I are called to love,
주 를 예 - 배 하 - - 기 위 - 해 우 린 지 - 음 받 - - 았 네 -

You and I are for-giv-en and free. When you and I em-brace sur-ren-der,when
주 님 우 - 릴 자 유 케 했 네 - 주 님 께 기 - 쁘 게 - - 엎 드 - 려 순

1. G7   last time to Coda

you and I choose to be-lieve,then you and I will see who we were meant to be.
종 하 며 - 주 믿 - - 을 때 - 우 리 는 보 리 라 - 주 님 - 의 부 - 르 심

Made To Worship

All we are and all we have, is
내 모습 – 나 가 진것 – 모

all a gift from God that we re-ceive. Brought to life we o-pen up
두 주가–주 신–선물–이네 – 새 생명 – 내 눈을 열

our eyes, to see the maj-es-ty and glo-ry of the King
– 어–서 – 주 님의 영 –광과위 엄–을 보 겠네 –

who we were meant to be. E-ven the rocks cry out, e-ven the heav-ens shout,
– 주 님–의 부–르 심 – 바 위도 소–리 쳐 – 하 늘도 노–래 해

at the sound of His Ho-ly name. So let ev-'ry voice sing out
– 주 님–의 음 성 들 을–때 – – – 온 열 방 들 노 –래 해

let ev-'ry knee bow down, He's wor-thy of all our praise.
– 모 두 무릎–꿇고 – 주 님 께 찬 양 드–려 – – –

O. We were meant to be.
– 오 – – 주 –의 부–르 심 –

O.T. : Made To Worship / O.W. : Chris Tomlin, Ed Cash, Stephan Sharp
O.P. : worshiptogether.com Songs, sixsteps Music, Vamos Publishing, New Spring Publishing Inc., Stenpan Music / S.P. : Universal Music Publishing Korea, CAIOS
Adm. : Capitol CMG Publishing / All rights reserved, Used by permission,

34 My Best Friend

(예수 좋은 내 친구)

Joel Houston & Marty sampson

Have you heard of the One called Sa-viour?   Have you heard of His per-fect love?
I be - lieve in the One called Sa-viour.   I be - lieve He's the Ri - sen One,
완 전 한 사 랑 보 여 주 신 – 구 세 주 그 분 아 나 요
구 원 하 신 주 나 는 믿 네 – 부 활 하 신 주 나 믿 네

Have you heard of the One in hea-ven?   Have you heard how He gave His son?
I be - lieve that I'll live for-e - ver   I be - lieve that the King will come.
그 아 들 우 리 에 게 주 신 – 하 나 님 그 분 아 나 요
다 시 오 실 왕 나 는 믿 네 – 그 분 과 영 원 히 살 리

Cause I have found this love,   and I be - lieve in the son
그 사 랑 알 – 기 에 –   그 아 들 나 – 는 믿 – 네

Show me your way – –   Je - sus You are my best friend
날 이 끄 소 – 서   예 수 좋 은 내 – 친 구

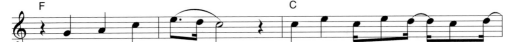

You will al - ways be   and no-thing will e - ver change that
내 곁 에 계 – 시 네 – 영 원 히 변 – 치 않 – 네 –

Je-sus You are my best friend   You will al - ways be   and no-thing will e-
예 수 좋 은 내 – 친 구 –   내 곁 에 계 – 시 네 – 영 원 히 변

My Best Friend

Words and Music by Joel Houston, Marty Sampson
© 2000 Hillsong Music Publishing Australia (admin in Korea by Universal Music Publishing/ CAIOS)

35 My Love And My Light
(주님은 나의 사랑)

Don Moen

You are my love and my light,　You are my pur-pose for liv - ing;
주 님은 나 - 의 사 랑 -　내 삶 의 이 - 유 되 시 - 며

You are my hope in the night,　my rea-son for sing - ing
어 둠 속 에 - 내 소 망 -　내 노 래 되 시 - 네 -

You bring a joy　to my life,　and You're mak - ing it bet - ter and bet-
주 님 이 주 - 신 기 쁨 -　날 이 갈 수 록 커 - 져 가 리

- ter;　And I will give thanks　for - ev - er and
- 라 -　영 원 영 원 히 -　감 사 를 드

1. ev　 - 　er.
리 　리 -

2, 3. ev　 - 　er.
리 　리 -

Will we ev - er know　what we have been gi - ven?
We will bless Your name　for al - ways and ev - er;
주 님 주 - 신 것 -　다 알 수 가 없 - 네 -
주 의 이 - 름 을 -　영 원 히 높 이 - 며 -

He has cho - sen us　and called us His own.
And of - fer up the sac - ri - fic - es of praise.
우 릴 선 택 해 - 불 러 주 - 셨 네
찬 양 의 제 사 주 - 께 드 리 - 리 라

My Love And My Light

Flow-ing from His throne, there is a riv - er.
Teach us, Load, we pray, to live in Your pres - ence;
보 좌 로 – 부 터 – 생 명 과 강 건 – 함 –
주 계 신 – 곳 에 – 나 살 기 원 하 – 니 –

Bring -ing life and health wher - ev - er He goes.
Make us more and more like You ev - ery day.
어 느 곳 에 나 – 흘 러 넘 – 치 네
주 님 닮 도 록 – 날 빛 으 – 소 서

– ev – er.
– 리 – 리 –

36 None but Jesus

(오직 주 예수만이)

Brooke Ligertwood

None but Jesus

C

All my de-light　　is in　You Lord
주 님 만 - 이 　- 나의 - 기 - 쁨

All of my hope　　all of my　strength　　All my de-light
- 나 의 능 - 력 - 　나 의 소 - 망 - - 　주 님 만 이

is in　You Lord　　For-e-ver-more
- 나 의 - 기 - 쁨 - 　영 원 토 록 -

Words and Music by Brooke Ligertwood
© 2007 Hillsong Music Publishing Australia (admin in Korea by Universal Music Publishing/ CAIOS)

37 O Lord, Your Tenderness

(주의 온유하심)

Graham Kendrick

O Lord, Your tend-er-ness melt-ing all my bit-ter-ness O
주 의 온 유 하 심 - 나 의 아 픔 녹 이 시 네 주 님

Lord, I re-ceive Your Love O Lord, Your
의 사 랑 받 았 네 - 주 의 크

love-li-ness chang-ing all my ug-li-ness O Lord, I re-
신 사 랑 이 가 치 없 이 연 약 한 - 나 를 변 화

ceive Your love O Lord, I re-ceive Your
시 키 - 네 - 주 님 의 사 랑 받 았

Love O Lord, I re-ceive Your love
네 - 주 님 의 사 랑 받 았 - 네 -

Only By Grace
(은혜로만 들어가네)

Gerrit Gustafson

On-ly by grace can we en - ter, on-ly by grace can we stand,
은 혜 로 만 - 들 어 가 - 네 - 은 혜 로 만 - 선 다 네 -

Not by our hu - man en-dea - vour, but by the blood of the Lamb.
우 리 의 노 - 력 이 아 - 닌 - 어 린 양 의 - 보 혈 로 -

In - to Your pres - ence you call us, You call us to come.
그 분 의 임 - 재 가 운 - 데 - 오 라 - 하 시 네 -

In - to Your pre - sence You draw us and now by Your grace we come,
우 리 를 부 - 르 신 그 - 곳 - 은 혜 로 들 어 - 가 네 -

now by Your grace we come,
주 님 의 그 - 은 혜 -

Lord, if You mark our trans-gres - sions, who would stand?
범 죄 한 우 - 리 가 어 - 찌 서 리 요

Thanks to Your grace we are cleansed by the blood of the Lamb.
어 린 양 의 - 보 혈 이 - 깨 끗 케 - 하 시 네 -

1. Bm7(♭5) E7
2. F/G G

D.C. al Coda

now by Your grace we come.
주 님 의 그 - 은 혜 -

Our God Reigns

(주 다스리시네)

Leonard E Jnr. Smith

How lo-ve-ly on the mount-ains are the feet of him
복음들고 산 을 넘 는 자 들 의 발길

who b-rings good news good news
- 아름답고도 - 아름답도다

an noun-cing peace, pro-claim - ing news of happi-ness
평화전하며 복 된 소 식 을 외치네 -

our God reigns, our God reigns, our God reigns, our God
주 다 스 - 리시 네 - 주 다 스 - 리 시

reigns, our God reigns, our God reigns.
네 - 주 다 스 - - - - - 리 시 네

Psalm 19
(시편 19편)

Terry Butler

40

C

41 People Need The Lord
(주가 필요해)

Phil McHugh & Greg Nelson

Ev-'ry day they pass me by
We are called to take His light
매 일 스 치 는 사 람 들
캄 캄 한 – 세 상 에 서

I can see it
to a world where
내 게 무 얼
빛 으 로 부

in their eyes;
wrong seems right
원 하 나 –
름 받 아 –

emp-ty peo-ple filled with care,
What could be too great a cost
공 허 한 그 눈 빛 은
잃 어 버 린 자 들 과

head-ed who knows where
for shar-ing life with lost
무 엇 으 로 채 우 나
나 누 라 고 하 시 네

on they go through
Through His love our
모 두 자 기
주 의 사 랑

pri - vate pain
hearts can feel
고 통 과
으 로 만

liv - ing fear to fear
all the grief they bear
두 려 움 – 가 득
사 랑 할 수 있 네

Laugh-ter hides the si - lent cries;
They must hear the words of life;
감 춰 진 울 음 소 리
우 리 가 나 눌 때 에

on-ly Je - sus hears.
on-ly we can share.
주 님 들 으 시 네 – –
그 들 알 – 겠 네 – –

People Need The Lord

peo-ple need the Lord   peo ple need the Lord.
그 들 은 모 두 –   주 가 필 요 해 –

At the end   of bro-ken dreams,   He's the o-pen   door.
깨 지 고   상 한 마 음   주 가 여 시   네

peo-ple need the Lord   peo ple need the Lord
그 들 은 모 두 –   주 가 필 요 해 –

Whenwill we re - al-ize that   peo - ple need the Lord.
모 두 알 게 되 리 –   사 랑 의 주 님

O.T. : People Need The Lord / O.W. : Greg Nelson, Phill Mchugh
O.P. : Shepherd's Fold Music, River Oaks Music Company / S.P. : Universal Music Publishing Korea, CAIOS
Adm. : Capitol CMG Publishing / All rights reserved, Used by permission.

42 Send Your Rain

(메마른 우리 마음)

Don Dalton & Valerie Dalton

Our hearts are dry and thirs-ty our land is parched and bare Give us
메 마 른우 - 리 마 - 음- 황 폐 한 이 - 땅 에 - 강 물

riv-ers in the de - sert let them o - ver flow
같 은주 - 의은 - 혜 부 어 주 소 서

Come and rain up on us wish us with your wa - ter
성 령 의 - 비 내 - 려 - 우 리 를 씻 - 으 소 - 서 -

Give us life a new 'til our hearts are owned by You
우 리 마 음 을 - 새 롭 게 하 소 서

Send Your rain send Your rain Pour
- 성 령 의 - 단 비 를 - - - 온

out your Spi-rit water all the ear-th send Your rain
세 계 위 에 부 어 주 - 소 서 - - 성 령 의

send Your rain Fill us with Your pow-er
- 단 비 로 - - - 주 의 빛 과 능 력

flood us with Your light Send Your rain
넘 쳐 나 - 도 록 - - 하 소 서 -

Fine

Send Your Rain

C

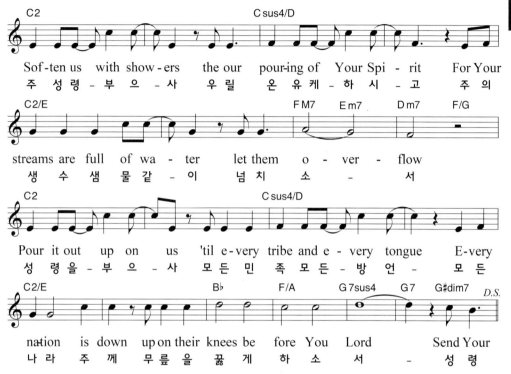

C2

Sof-ten us with show-ers the our pour-ing of Your Spi - rit For Your
주 성령 – 부 으 – 사 우 릴 온 유 케 – 하 시 – 고 주 의

C sus4/D

C2/E

streams are full of wa - ter let them o - ver - flow
생 수 샘 물 같 – 이 넘 치 소 – 서

FM7 Em7 Dm7 F/G

C2

Pour it out up on us 'til e-very tribe and e - very tongue E-very
성 령 을 – 부 으 – 사 모 든 민 족 모 든 – 방 언 – 모 든

C sus4/D

C2/E

nation is down up on their knees be fore You Lord Send Your
나 라 주 께 무 릎 을 꿇 게 하 소 서 – 성 령

B♭ F/A G 7sus4 G7 G#dim7 D.S.

See His Glory

(눈을 들어 주를 보라)

Chris Bowater

See His glo - ly see His glo - ly see His glo - ry now ap - pear
눈 을 들 – 어 주 를 보 – 라 주 의 영 광 을 보 라

See His glo - ly See His glo - ly see His glo - ry now ap - pear
눈 을 들 – 어 주 를 보 – 라 주 의 영 광 을 보 라

God of light Ho - li - ness and truth Power and might See His
주 는 빛 – 거 룩 과 진 리 능 력 의 – 주 의

glo - ry see it now ap - pear Now we de - clare our God is
영 광 나 타 나 셨 네 – 선 포 – 하 라 선 하 – 신

good and His mer - ci - es en - dure for - ev – er Now we de -
주 주 의 인 자 는 영 원 함 이 – 라 선 포 – 하

clare our God is good and His mer - ci - es en - dure for - ev – er
라 선 하 – 신 주 주 의 인 자 는 영 원 함 이 – 라

Shout To The Lord

(내 구주 예수님)

Darlene Zschech

45 Shout Your Fame

(나는 외치리)

Jonas Myrin/Natasha Bedingfield &
Gio Galanti/Paul Nevison

Some say You're just a good man,　Some say You were kind,
Some say You're just a pro - phet,　Some say You were wise,
예 수 는 선한사 –람–　친 절 했 지 만
예 수 는 선지 – –자–　지 혜 롭던 한 사람

Some say You are in the grave,　I say You're a - live.
Some say You were just a man,　I say you are
무 덤 에 묻 힌 자 라 – – –　But 사 람 들 말 하 –죠–
사 람 들 말 하 지 만 – – –　주 는 살 아 계

God, You are my God.　I will shout Your fame to all　the earth, I will lift
–신– 주 하 나 –님–　나 는 외 치 리 –주의 –위 엄–세 상 모

Your Name on high.　And the world will know Your great – – ness.
I will show the world Your good – – ness.
–두 듣–도 록 –　홀 로 위 –대 하 –신 주 –이 름 –

You are my God I will shout Your fame.　I know You're the Mes-
As I live a life that shouts Your fame.
세 상 향 해 나 는 외 치 리 –　예 수 는 메 시

si - ah;　You gave Your life for me　I know You're the
–아 –　생 명 을 주 신 분　길 과 진 리

Shout Your Fame

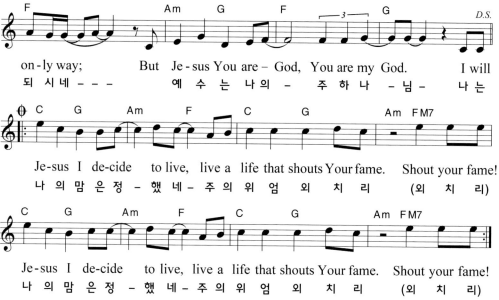

on-ly way; But Je-sus You are – God, You are my God. I will
되 시 네 - - - 예 수 는 나의 – 주 하 나 –님– 나는

Je-sus I de-cide to live, live a life that shouts Your fame. Shout your fame!
나 의 맘 은 정 – 했 네 – 주 의 위 엄 외 치 리 (외 치 리)

Je-sus I de-cide to live, live a life that shouts Your fame. Shout your fame!
나 의 맘 은 정 – 했 네 – 주 의 위 엄 외 치 리 (외 치 리)

Words and Music by Gio Galanti, Jonas Myrin, Natasha Myrin, Paul Nevison
© 2003 Hillsong Music Publishing Australia (admin in Korea by Universal Music Publishing/ CAIOS)

46

Spirit Of The Living God
(살아계신 성령님)

Paul Armstrong

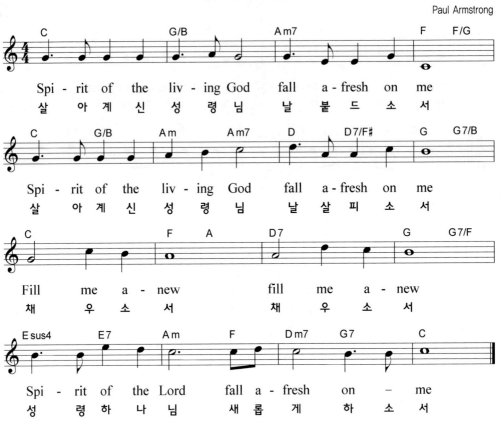

Spi - rit of the liv - ing God fall a - fresh on me
살 아 계 신 성 령 님 날 붙 드 소 서

Spi - rit of the liv - ing God fall a - fresh on me
살 아 계 신 성 령 님 날 살 피 소 서

Fill me a - new fill me a - new
채 우 소 서 채 우 소 서

Spi - rit of the Lord fall a - fresh on — me
성 령 하 나 님 새 롭 게 하 소 서

Still

(주 품에)

Reuben Morgan

Hide me now un-der Your wings
Find rest my soul, in Christ a - lone
주 품에 품으소서
주님 안에 나 거하리

co-ver me with-in Your mighy-y hand When the o-ceans
Know His power, In qui-et-ness and trust
능력의 팔로 덮으소서 거친 파도
주 능력 나 잠잠히 믿네

rise and thun-ders roar I will soar with you, a-bove the storm Fa-ther You are
날 향해 와도 주와 함께 날아오르리 폭풍 가운

King o-ver the flood I will be still, and know You are God
데 나의 영혼 잠잠하게 주를 보리라

48 Stronger

(강하신 주)

Reuben Morgan & Ben Fielding

There is Love, that came for us. Hum-bled to a sin-ner's cross. You broke my
우리를 위한 사 - 랑 겸손히 죽으셨 - 네 내 수치

shame, and sin - ful - ness. You rose a - gain, vic - to - ri - ous.
와 죄 거 두 - 신 승 리 하 신 부 활 의 주

Faith - ful - ness none can de-
폭 풍 과 불 속 에

- ny. Through the storm, and through the fire. There is truth that sets me
- 도 신 실 한 우 리 주 - 님 자 유 케 한 그 진

free. Je - sus Christ who lives in me. You are
- 리 내 안 에 계 신 예 수 강 하

stron - ger You are stron - ger. sin is bro - ken, You have saved me. It is
신 주 강 하 신 주 죄 사 하 고 구 하 셨 네 말 씀

writ - ten, Christ is ri - sen. Je - sus You are Lord of all.
대 로 부 활 하 신 예 수 는 만 유 의 - 주 -

No be - gin - ning, and no
주 는 소 망 과 요

Stronger

Words and Music by Ben Fielding, Reuben Morgan © 2007 Hillsong Music Publishing Australia (admin in Korea by Universal Music Publishing/ CAIOS)

49 Thank You For The Blood

(예수 감사하리 주의 보혈)

Matt Redman

Thank you, thank You for the blood that You shed
Thank you, thank You for the bat - tle You won,
예 수 감 사 하 리 주 의 보 혈 –
예 수 감 사 하 리 주 의 승 리 –

Stand-ing in its bless-ing, we sing these free – dom songs,
Stand-ing in Your victo-ry, we sing sal - va – tion songs,
축 복 속 에 우 린 자 유 – 를 노 – 래 해 –
승 리 안 에 우 린 구 원 – 을 노 – 래 해

we sing sal - va – tion's song, You have
– 구 원 – 을 노 – 래 – 해 – 새 롭

o - pened a way to the Fa - ther where be fore we could nev - er have
고 산 길 이 되 신 예 수 길 과 진 리 생 명 되 셨

come. Je - sus count us as Yours now for - ev - er as we sing
네 우 릴 주 의 자 녀 삼 으 셨 네 자 유 를

these free – dom songs, We
– 노 래 – 할 – 때 – 주

sing of all You've done, We sing of all You've done
행 한 일 – 찬 양 – 주 행 한 일 – 찬 양

Thank You For The Blood

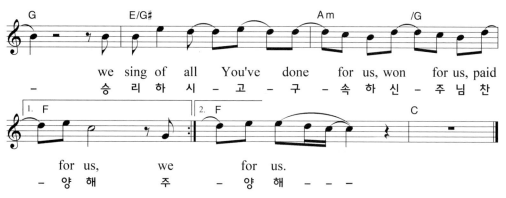

we	sing of all You've	done	for us, won	for us, paid
– 승	리 하 시 – 고 – 구	– 속 하 신 –	주	님 찬

for us,	we	for us.
– 양 해	주 – 양	해 – – –

Within The Veil
(휘장안에 들어가리)

50

With - in	the	veil	I	now would come
휘 장	안	에	들	어 가 리

In - to Thy	Ho - ly place	to look	up - on	Thy face
주 얼 굴	뵈 오 리	거 룩	한 곳	으 로

I see such beau - ty there	none oth - er	can com - pare
거 기 아 름 다 움	비 할 데	없 으 리

I wor - ship Thee my Lord	with - in	the veil
나 주 를 경 배 해	휘 장	안 에

51 Today Is The Day
(주가 지으신 이 날에)

Paul Baloche & Lincoln Brewster

Today Is The Day

to-day is the day
주 님 의 날 에 –

to-day is the day
주 님 의 날 에 – – –

2.I'm put-ting my fears
내 두 렴 내 려

I
주

will stand u –pon Your truth (I will stand u-pon Your truth) And all
– 진 리 – 위 – 에 – 서 리 – 주 진 리 – 위 에 – 서 리 – 내 평

my days I'll live for You (All my days I'll live for You) And I
– 생 을 – 주 – 를 – 위 해 – – 평 – 생 을 – 주 를 – 위 해 – 나 주
주

my days
– 님 을 – 위 해 – – –

to-day is the day
주 가 지 으 신 –

I won't wor – ry about
난 내 – 일 을 – 염 려 하

to-mor – row Giv – ing You my fears and sor – rows Where You lead me I
– 지 않 – 네 내 두 – 렴 과 – 슬 픔 – 맡 기 – 니 주 – 인 도 – 해 난

will fol – low I'm trust-ing in what You say to-day is the day
– 따 르 – 리 주 의 말 씀 신 – 뢰 해 – 주 님 의 날 에 –

to-day is the day
주 님 의 날 에 –

52 We Exalt Your Name

(거룩하신 주님)

Andy Park

You are the ho - ly one　The Lord mo-st high
거 룩 하 신 주 님　지 존 하 신 분

You reign in ma - jes-ty　You reign on high
하 늘 의 위 엄 으 로　다 스 리 네

You are the wor - thy one　Lamb that was slain
You are the king of kings　The Lord of Lords
존 귀 한 어 린 양　죽 임 당 하 사
만 왕 의 왕 예 수　만 주 의 - 주

You bought us with Your blood　And with You we'll reign
All men will bow to You　Be - fore your thr - one
그 피 로 우 리 를　구 속 하 셨 네
보 좌 에 엎 드 려　경 - 배 하 네

We ex-alt Your name　high and migh - ty one of Is - ra - el
주 이 름 찬 양　크 신 이 스 라 엘 의 전 능 - 자

We ex-alt Your name　Lead us on to war in the power of Your name
주 이 름 찬 양　주 의 이 름 권 세 로 인 도 하 네

We ex-alt Your name　The name abo-ve all names our vic-tori-ous king
모 든 이 름 중　가 장 높 으 신 이 름 승 리 의 왕 께

1. A
We ex - alt Your name
경 배 드 리 세

2. A
name
세

What The Lord Has Done In Me

(약한 나로 강하게)

53

C

Reuben Morgan

54 When I Look Into Your Holiness

(주의 거룩하심 생각할 때)

Cathy Perrin & Wayne Perrin

When I look in-to Your ho - li - ness, When I gaze in-to your love - li - ness,
주의 거룩하심생 각 할때– 주의 크신사랑느 낄때

When all things that sur-round be-come sha-dows in the light of You;
주의 영광의빛 나의 생활 비춰주 실 때 –

when I've found the joy of reach-ing Your heart, when my will be-comes en-thralled in Your love,
주가 주신 기쁨맛볼 때 에– – 주의 사랑 속에 나 잠길 때

when all things that surround be-come sha-dows in the light of You,
주의 영광의빛 나의 생활 비춰주 실 때 –

I wor - ship You, I wor-ship You,
경 배 하 리 – 경 배 하 리 –

the rea - son I live is to wor-ship You
나 사 는 동 안 주 께 경 배 해 – –

I wor - ship You. I wor-ship You,
경 배 하 리 – 경 배 하 리 –

the rea - son I live is to wor-ship You.
나 사 는 동 안 주 께 경 배 해 –

Where Could I Go From Your Spirit?

(주의 신을 내가 떠나)

Kelly Willard

55
C

56 You Raise Me Up

(날 세우시네)

Brendan Graham & Rolf Lovla

When I am down and, oh my soul, so wea-ry when trou-bles
내 영혼 지 – 치 고 피 곤 할 때 에 근 심 걱

come and my heart burd-ened be Then, I am still and wait here in the
정 내 맘 짓 – 누 를 때 난 잠 잠 히 – 주 님 을 기 다

si – lence Un – til you come and sit a-while with me You raise me
리 네 주 님 내 곁 에 오 실 때 – 까 지 주 날 일

up so I can stand on moun – tains You raise me
으 켜 산 위 에 세 우 네 거 친 바

up, to walk on stor-my seas I am strong When I am on your
다 위 걷 게 하 시 – 네 주 만 의 지 할 때 강 함

shoul – ders You raise me up to more than I can be
주 네 크 신 능 력 내게 부 어 주 – 시 네

You Sat Down

(하나님 오른편에 앉아 계신)

Mark Altrogge

You sat down at the right hand of the Fa - ther in maj-es - ty,
하 나 님 오 른 편 – 에 – 앉 아 계 – 신 – 영 광 의 주

You sat down at the right hand of the Fa - ther in maj-es - ty;
하 나 님 오 른 편 – 에 – 앉 아 계 – 신 – 영 광 의 주

You are crowned Lord of all, You are faith-ful and right-eous and true,
왕 의 왕 주 의 주 – 의 와 진 리 신 실 하 신 주

You're my mas - ter, You're my own - er, and I love serv-ing You.
나 의 주 – 님 – 나 의 생 – 명 – 영 원 히 섬 기 리

58 Let It Rain
(성령의 비가 내리네)

Michael Farren

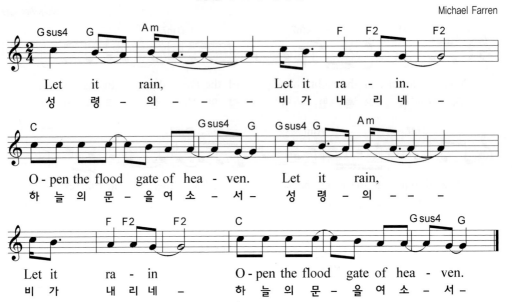

Let it rain, Let it ra - in.
성 령 - 의 - - - - 비가 내 리 네 -

O - pen the flood gate of hea - ven. Let it rain,
하 늘 의 문 - 을 여 소 - 서 - 성 령 - 의 - - -

Let it ra - in O - pen the flood gate of hea - ven.
비 가 내 리 네 - 하 늘 의 문 - 을 여 소 - 서 -

You Are My Hiding Place

(피난처 되신 주)

Michael James Lender

59

C

You are my hid - ing place,   You al - ways fill   my heart with
피   난   처   되   신   주   구   원   의   노   래   로   내

songs   of   de - liv - er - ance When-ever   I   am   a - fraid, I will trust   in
맘   채   워   주   시   네   두   려   움   있   을   때   주   를   의   지

Fine

You.   I will trust   in   You.   Let the weak   say,
해   주   를   의   지   해   내   가   약   할

D.C. al Fine

"I   am   strong   in   the   strength   of   the   Lord!"
때   강   함   주   시   는   나   의   주

60

Ah, Lord God

(주께 능치 못할 일 없네)

Kay Chance

Ah, Lord God, Thou hast made the heavens and the earth by Thy great pow-er
아 주님 크 - 신 권능으로 하늘과 땅 만드 셨네 -

Ah, Lord God, Thou hast made the heavens and the earth by Thine out-stretched arm.
아 주님 그 - 의 펴신 팔로 하늘과 땅 만드 셨네 네

Noth-ing is too dif-fi-cult for Thee   Noth-ing is too dif-fi-cult for Thee
주께 능치 못할 일 - 없 네 - -   주께 능치 못할 일 - 없 네 - -

great and might-y God,   great in coun-sel and might-y in deed.
위 대 하 신 주   크 고 놀 라 운 모 든 일 들

Noth-ing, noth-ing abso-lute-ly noth-ing, noth-ing is too dif-fi-cult for Thee.
없 네 없 네 능 치 못 함 없 네 주 께 능 치 못 할 일 - 없 네 - -

All The Earth

61

(주님 궁정으로 들어가리)

Andrew Ulugia & Jack Hayford/Wayne Huirua

D

62 And In The Fullness Of Time

(때가 차매)

Tom Fettke

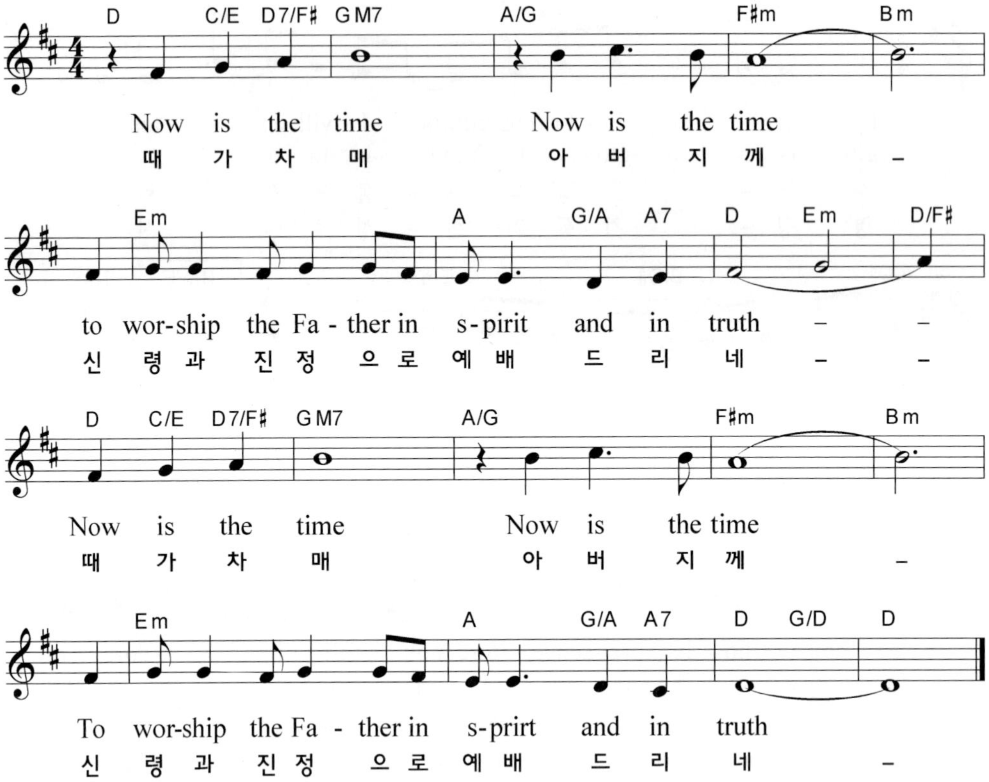

D C/E D7/F♯ GM7 A/G F♯m Bm
Now is the time Now is the time
때 가 차 매 아 버 지 께 –
Em A G/A A7 D Em D/F♯
to wor-ship the Fa - ther in s-pirit and in truth – –
신 령 과 진 정 으 로 예 배 드 리 네 – –
D C/E D7/F♯ GM7 A/G F♯m Bm
Now is the time Now is the time
때 가 차 매 아 버 지 께 –
Em A G/A A7 D G/D D
To wor-ship the Fa - ther in s-prirt and in truth
신 령 과 진 정 으 로 예 배 드 리 네 –

As For Me

(나는 믿음으로)

Daniel Dee Marks

D

As for me, I will be hold Thy face in right-eous-ness I will be
나 - 는 믿 음 으 로 주 얼 굴 보 리 니 - 아 침 에

satis - fied when I a - wake with Thy like - ness I want to
깰 때 에 주 형 상 에 만 족 하 - 리 나 주 님

be just like you Lord So as for me, I will be
알 기 원 하 네 믿 음 으 로 주 얼 굴

hold Thy face As for face so as for
보 리 라 - 나 - 라 - 믿 음 으

me, I will be hold Thy face
로 주 얼 굴 보 리 라 -

64

As The Deer
(목마른 사슴)

Martin J. Nystrom

As the deer pant-eth for the wa-ter so my soul longeth af-ter Thee.
I want You more than gold or sil-ver; on-ly You can sat-is-fy.
You're my friend and You are my broth-er e-ven though You are a King.

목 마 른 사 슴 시 냇 물 을 찾 아 헤 매 이 듯 이
금 보 다 귀 한 나 의 주 님 내 게 만 족 주 신 주

You a-lone are my heart's de-sire and I long to wor-ship Thee.
You a-lone are the real joy gi-ver and the ap-ple of my eye.
I love You more than an-y oth-er, so much more than an-y-thing.

내 영 혼 주 를 찾 기 에 – 갈 급 하 – 나 이 다
당 신 만 이 – 나 의 기 쁨 또 한 나 의 참 보 배

You a-lone are my strength, my shield. To You a-lone may my spir-it yield.

주 님 만 이 – 나 의 힘 나 의 방 패 나 의 참 소 망

You a-lone are my heart's de-sire and I long to wor-ship Thee.

나 의 몸 정 성 다 바 쳐 서 주 님 경 배 합 니 다

O.T. : As The Deer / O.W. : Martin J. Nystrom
O.P. : Universal Music – Brentwood Benson Publ. / S.P. : Universal Music Publishing Korea, CAIOS
Adm. : Capitol CMG Publishing / All rights reserved. Used by permission.

As We Gather

(우리 모일 때 주 성령 임하리)

Michael Fay & Thomas W. Coomes

D

As we gath-er, may Your Spir-it work with in us.
우 리 모 일 때 – 주 성 령 임 – 하 리

As we gath-er, may we glo-ri-fy Your name.
우 리 모 일 때 – 주 이 름 높 이 리

Know-ing well that as our heart be-gin to wor-ship
우 리 마 음 모 – 아 주 를 경 배 할 때

We'll be blessed be-cause we came
주 님 축 복 하 – 시 리 – –

we'll be blessed be-cause we came.
주 님 축 복 하 – 시 리

66 Awakening

(깨우소서)

Chris Tomlin & Reuben Morgan

Awakening

O.T. : Awakening / O.W. : Chris Tomlin, Reuben Morgan
O.P. : Rising Springs Music, Hillsong Music Publishing, worshiptogether.com Songs, Vamos Publishing /S.P. : Universal Music Publishing Korea, CAIOS
Adm. : Capitol CMG Publishing / All rights reserved, Used by permission.

67 Beautiful One

(놀라운 주의 사랑)

Tim Hughes

Won-der-ful, so won-der-ful is Your un-fail-ing love Your
Po-wer-ful, so po-wer-ful Your glo-ry fills the skies Your
놀 라 운 주 의 사 랑 영 원 하 시 도 — 다 십 자
주 님 의 크 신 영 광 온 하 늘 을 덮 — 고 만

cross has spo-ken mer-cy o-ver me No eye has seen, no
migh-ty works dis-played for all to see The beau-ty of Your
가 자 비 로 나 타 내 셨 네 그 누 구 도 그
물 이 주 의 능 력 을 보 네 아 름 다 운 주

ear has heard No heart could ful-ly know How glo-ri-ous, how
ma-jes-ty A-wakes my heart to sing How mar-vel-ous, how
무 엇 도 깨 달 지 못 하 — 리 아 름 답 고 영
의 위 엄 내 영 혼 깨 어 — 서 노 래 하 네 놀

beau-ti-ful You are Beau-ti-ful One I love You Beau-ti-ful
won-der-ful You are
화 로 우 신 주 아 름 다 우 신 주 — 사 랑 하
라 우 신 주 를

One I a-dore Beau-ti-ful One my soul must — — sing
고 경 배 해 멈 출 수 없 는 내 노 — — 래

1. 2. 3.
Last time to Fine
Beau-ti-ful you O-pened my eyes to Your won-
아 름 다 주 를 — — 향 해 — 내 눈 여

Beautiful One

ders a   new   You cap - tured my heart with this   love   'cause noth-
– 셨 네 – 날 붙 – 드 시 는 – 그 사 – 랑   그 어

- ing on earth is a beau - ti - ful   as You
– 느 누 가 – 내 주 – 와 같 – 으 리 –

ing on earth is as   beau-
– 느 주 가 – 내 주

- ti - ful   as You
– 와 같 – 으 리 –

Beau - ti - ful
아 름 다

My soul
내 영

my soul must sing
– 노 래 – 하 리 –

My soul   my soul must sing
내 영 – 노 래 – 하 리 –

My soul
내 영

my soul must sing
– 노 래 – 하 리 –

Beau - ti - ful One
예 수 님 께 – –

Beau - ti - ful
아 름 다

O.T. : Beautiful One / O.W. : Tim Hughes
O.P. : Thankyou Music Ltd / S.P. : Universal Music Publishing Korea, CAIOS
Adm. : Capitol CMG Publishing / All rights reserved, Used by permission.

68 Before The Throne Of God Above

(주님의 보좌 앞에서)

Bancrof & Vikki Cook

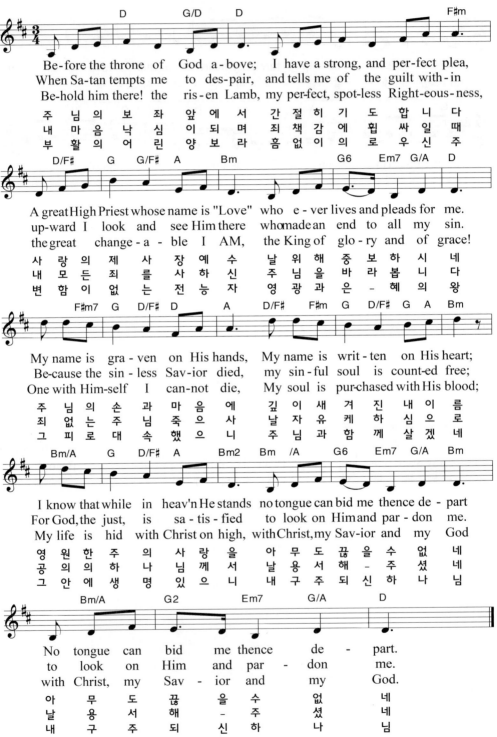

Be-fore the throne of God a-bove; I have a strong, and per-fect plea,
When Sa-tan tempts me to des-pair, and tells me of the guilt with-in
Be-hold him there! the ris-en Lamb, my per-fect, spot-less Right-eous-ness,

주 님 의 보 좌 앞 에 서 간 절 히 기 도 합 니 다
내 마 음 낙 심 이 되 며 죄 책 감 에 휩 싸 일 때
부 활 의 어 린 양 보 라 흠 없 이 의 로 우 신 주

A great High Priest whose name is "Love" who e - ver lives and pleads for me.
up-ward I look and see Him there whom made an end to all my sin.
the great change - a - ble I AM, the King of glo - ry and of grace!

사 랑 의 제 사 장 예 수 날 위 해 중 보 하 시 네
내 모 든 죄 를 사 하 신 주 님 을 바 라 봅 니 다
변 함 이 없 는 전 능 자 영 광 과 은 - 혜 의 왕

My name is gra - ven on His hands, My name is writ - ten on His heart;
Be-cause the sin - less Sav-ior died, my sin - ful soul is count-ed free;
One with Him-self I can-not die, My soul is pur-chased with His blood;

주 님 의 손 과 마 음 에 깊 이 새 겨 진 내 이 름
죄 없 는 주 님 죽 으 사 날 자 유 케 하 심 으 로
그 피 로 대 속 했 으 니 주 님 과 함 께 살 겠 네

I know that while in heav'n He stands no tongue can bid me thence de - part
For God, the just, is sa - tis - fied to look on Him and par - don me.
My life is hid with Christ on high, with Christ, my Sav-ior and my God

영 원 한 주 의 사 랑 을 아 무 도 끊 을 수 없 네
공 의 의 하 나 님 께 서 날 용 서 해 - 주 셨 네
그 안 에 생 명 있 으 니 내 구 주 되 신 하 나 님

No tongue can bid me thence de - part.
to look on Him and par - don me.
with Christ, my Sav - ior and my God.

아 무 도 끊 을 수 없 네
날 용 서 해 - 주 셨 네
내 구 주 되 신 하 나 님

Be Still

(주의 임재 앞에 잠잠해)

David Evans

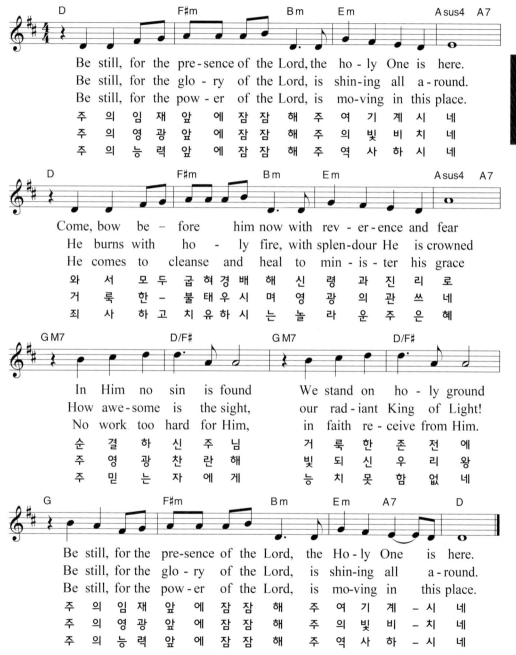

Be still, for the pre-sence of the Lord, the ho-ly One is here.
Be still, for the glo-ry of the Lord, is shin-ing all a-round.
Be still, for the pow-er of the Lord, is mo-ving in this place.

주 의 임 재 앞 에 잠 잠 해 주 여 기 계 시 네
주 의 영 광 앞 에 잠 잠 해 주 의 빛 비 치 네
주 의 능 력 앞 에 잠 잠 해 주 역 사 하 시 네

Come, bow be – fore him now with rev - er - ence and fear
He burns with ho - ly fire, with splen-dour He is crowned
He comes to cleanse and heal to min - is - ter his grace

와 서 모 두 굽 혀 경 배 해 신 령 과 진 리 로
거 룩 한 – 불 태 우 시 며 영 광 의 관 쓰 네
죄 사 하 고 치 유 하 시 는 놀 라 운 주 은 혜

In Him no sin is found We stand on ho - ly ground
How awe-some is the sight, our rad - iant King of Light!
No work too hard for Him, in faith re - ceive from Him.

순 결 하 신 주 님 거 룩 한 존 전 에
주 영 광 찬 란 해 빛 되 신 우 리 왕
주 믿 는 자 에 게 능 치 못 함 없 네

Be still, for the pre-sence of the Lord, the Ho-ly One is here.
Be still, for the glo-ry of the Lord, is shin-ing all a-round.
Be still, for the pow-er of the Lord, is mo-ving in this place.

주 의 임 재 앞 에 잠 잠 해 주 여 기 계 – 시 네
주 의 영 광 앞 에 잠 잠 해 주 의 빛 비 – 치 네
주 의 능 력 앞 에 잠 잠 해 주 역 사 하 – 시 네

70 Blessed

(주의 집에 거하는 자)

Darlene Zschech & Reuben Morgan

Blessed are those who dwell in your House. They are e - ver
주 의 집 에 거 하 는 자 - - 항 상 주 찬

prai - sing You Blessed are those whose strength is in You
성 하 리 - - 시 온 의 대 로 가 있 - 고 -

whose hearts are set on our God Blessed are those who
- 힘 얻 는 - 자 - 복 있 네 - 주 의 집 에

We will go from strength to strength, 'til we see You face to face
- 주 얼 굴 볼 때 까 지 - 힘 을 더 얻 어 가 리 -

Hear our prayer Oh Lord God Al - migh - - ty
들 으 소 - 서 - - 만 군 의 - 주 - 하 나 - - 님

come bless our land, as we seek You wor - ship You
구 하 오 니 - - 이 땅 축 - 복 - 하 - 소 서 - - -

Fine

- ship You
- 소 서 - - -

D.S.

Blessed

71

Be The Centre

(예수 내 삶의 중심)

Michael Frye

Je - sus, be the cen - ter, be my source,
Je - sus, be the cen - ter, be my hope,
Je - sus, be my vi - sion, be my path,
예 수 내 삶의 중 - 심 삶의 근 원
예 수 내 삶의 중 - 심 나의 희 망
예 수 내 꿈과 소 - 망 내 가는 길

be my light, Je - sus,
be my song Je - sus,
be my guide Je - sus,
－ 빛 되 신 － 예 수 님 －
－ 내 노 래 － 예 수 님 －
－ 인 도 자 － 예 수 님

Be the fire in my heart, Be the wind
주 － 의 성 － 령 내 맘 에 － 새 힘 을

in these sails, Be the rea - son that I live,
－ 주 시 네 － 내 － 가 사 － 는 이 유 는

Je - - sus, Je - sus,
－ 예 － 수 님 － 예 수 님 －

Come And Let Us Go

(오라 우리가)

Bill Quigley & Mary Anne Quigley

72

D

Come and let us go up to the moun-tain of the Lord and
오 라 우리 - 가 - 여 호 와 의 산 에 올 라 - 하

to the house of our God of our God
나 님 의 전 에 이 르 - 자 - - 에 이 르 - 자 - -

And He will teach us of His ways.
주 님 의 도 를 배 우 - 고 - -

And we will walk in His paths
주 님 의 길 로 행 하 - 리 - -

And the low shall go forth from Zi - - - on
이 는 율 법 이 시 온 에 서 나 오 고

And the word of the Lord from Je - ru - sa - lem
주 의 말 씀 은 예 루 살 렘 에 서 -

O.T. : Come And Let Us Go / O.W. : Bill Quigley, Mary Anne Quigley
O.P. : Universal Music – Brentwood Benson Publ. / S.P. : Universal Music Publishing Korea, CAIOS
Adm. : Capitol CMG Publishing / All rights reserved. Used by permission.

73 Come Let Us Worship And Bow Down

(주님께 경배 드리세)

David J. Doherty

come, let us wor-ship and bow down, let us
주 님 께 경 배 드 - 리 세 주 님

kneel be-fore the Lord, our God, our mak - er.
앞 에 나 와 모 두 무 릎 꿇 - 고

come, let us wor-ship and bow down, let us
주 님 께 경 배 드 - 리 세 주 님

kneel be fore the Lord,our God,our mak - er. For He - - is our
앞 에 나 와 모 두 무 릎 꿇 - 고 그 는 우 리 하 나

God, and we are the peo-ple of His pas - ture, and the
님 우 린 그 의 기 르 시 는 백 - 성 그 의

sheep - - of His hand, just the sheep - - of His hand.
손 - 의 양 이 라 그 의 손 - 의 양 이 라

Come Now Is The Time To Worship

(주께 경배 드리세)

74

Brian Doerksen

Come, now is the time to wor – – ship
Come, 주 께 경 배 – 드 리 – – 세 –

Come, now is the time to give your heart
Come, 우 리 의 마 음 을 다 – – – 해 –

Come, just as you are to wor – ship
Come, 우 리 하 나 – 님 앞 – – 에 –

2nd time to Coda

Come, just as you are be-fore your God
Come, 겸 손 히 무 – 룹 꿇 – – 고 –

Fine

Come.
Come.

One day eve - ry tongue will con - fess
모 든 이 가 주 라 시 인

you are God One day eve - ry knee will bow.
– 하 겠 네 – 주 께 무 룹 꿇 – 겠 네 –

Still, the great-est trea - sure re - main for those who gla
기 쁨 으 로 선 택 하 는 – 우 리 – 앞 에 주

2nd time D.C.

– dy choose You now
– 상 급 – 있 네 –

Come.   Come.   Come.

75 Cover The Earth

(덮으소서)

Meleasa Houghton & Israel Houghton, Cindy Cruse

Cover The Earth

Co-ver the earth with the sound of hea - ven Co-ver the earth
덮 으소서 천 국 의 – 소 리 – 로 – 덮 으 소 서 –

Bridge

O-pen up the hea-ven-lies Let a new sound be re-leased
천 국 열 어 주 소 서 새 노 래 퍼 지 도 록

As the wa-ters co-ver the see Co-ver the earth
물 이 바 다 덮 음 같 이 덮 으 소 서 – –

O-pen up the hea-ven-lies Let a new sound be re-leased
천 국 열 어 주 소 서 새 노 래 퍼 지 도 록

As the wa-ters co-ver the sea Co-ver the earth
물 이 바 다 덮 음 같 이 덮 으 소 서 – – –

76 Dancing Generation

(춤추는 세대)

Matt Redman

Your mer - cy taught us how to dance to ce - le - brate with
주 자 비 춤 추 게 하 네 - 모 든 것 다 해

all we have and we'll dance to thank You for mer - cy
찬 양 해 - 춤 - 을 추 - 며 자 - 비 감 사 - 해

Your glo - ry taught us how to shout we'll lift Your name in
주 영 광 외 치 게 하 네 - 온 땅 에 서 주

all the earth and we'll shout to the praise of Your glo - ry
높 이 며 - 주 - 의 영 - 광 소 리 - 쳐 찬 양 - 해

It's the o - ver-flow of a for - gin - en soul
넘 - 쳐 흐 르 는 용 서 받 은 영 혼

and now we've seen You God Our hearts can - not stay si
이 제 주 를 보 네 우 린 - 멈 출 - 수 없

- lent And we'll be a dan-cing ge - ne - ra - tion dan-cing be-cause of Your
- 어 우 리 는 춤 추 는 세 대 되 - 리 주 크 신 자 비 로

great mer - cy Lord Your great mer - cy Lord
- 춤 추 리 라 - - 주 - 의 자 - 비 로 -

Dancing Generation

and we'll be a shou-ting ge - ne - ra - tion shou-ting be-cause of Your
주 영 광 외 치 는 세 대 되 - 리 놀 라 운 주 영 광

great glo - ry Lord You great glo - ry Lord
- 외 치 리 라 - - 주 - 의 영 - 광 을 -

O.T. : Dancing Generation / O.W. : Matt Redman
O.P. : Thankyou Music Ltd / S.P. : Universal Music Publishing Korea, CAIOS
Adm. : Capitol CMG Publishing / All rights reserved. Used by permission.

D

Deep In My Heart

(내 맘 깊은 곳)

77

Deep in my heart There's a song for Je - sus
내 맘 깊 은 - 곳 주 께 노 래 하 네
내 맘 깊 은 - 곳 주 를 찬 양 하 네
새 로 운 노 래 로 주 를 찬 양 하 세
할 렐 - 루 - 야 할 - 렐 루 야 -

Deep in my heart There's a song for Him.
내 맘 깊 은 - 곳 주 께 노 래 해
내 맘 깊 은 - 곳 주 를 찬 양 해
새 로 운 노 래 로 주 를 찬 양 해
할 렐 - 루 - 야 할 - 렐 루 야

78 Did You Feel The Mountains Tremble

(높은 산들 흔들리고)

Martin Smith

Did you feel the moun-tains trem-ble?　Did you hear the o-ceans roar
Did you feel the peo-ple trem-ble?　Did you hear the sing-ers roar
Do you feel the dark-ness trem-ble　when all the saints join in one song,

높 은 산 들 흔 들 리 고 ─　대 양 은 춤 을 추 네
사 람 들 의 함 성 소 리 ─　거 센 함 성 들 나 요
어 두 움 은 물 러 가 네 ─　성 도 들 찬 양 할 때

when the peo-ple rose to sing of　Je-sus Christ, the ris-en One?
when the lost be-gan to sing of　Je-sus Christ, the sav-ing One?
and all the streams flow as one riv-er　to wash a-way our bro-ken-ness?

모 든 사 람 하 나 되 어 ─　예 수 이 름 부 를 때 ─
가 난 한 자 노 래 하 며 ─　구 원 의 주 맞 이 하 리
그 찬 양 이 강 같 이 넘 쳐 ─　죄 악 의 줄 을 끊 게 되 리

And we can see that, God You're mov-ing, a might-y

오 주 님 당 신 의 오 심 ─ 은 ─ ─ 거 친
오 주 님 당 신 이 오 실 ─ 때 ─ ─ 희 년 의

riv-er through the na-tions; and young and old will turn to Je-sus.

바 다 처 럼 흘 ─ 러 모 든 나 라 에 넘 치 ─ 니
나 팔 은 울 리 ─ 고 청 년 과 노 인 이 다 나 ─ 와

Fling-wide, you heav-en-ly gates; pre-pare the way of the ri-sen Lord.

천 국 의 문 을 열 어 우 리 주 의 길 ─ 예 비 하 세

Did You Feel The Mountains Tremble

O - pen up the doors. Let the mu - sic play.
벽 을 - 넘 - 어 서 목 소 - 리 - 높 여

Let the streets re-sound with sing-ing; songs that bring Your hope,
거 리 - 마 다 - 부 르 는 노 래 - 소 망 - 의 - 노 래

songs that bring Your joy,- danc-ers who dance up-on in-jus - tice.
기 쁨 - 의 - 노 래 - 공 의 - 안 에 - 춤 추 는 노 - 래

79 Cry Of My Heart

(내 마음 간절하게)

Terry Butler

It is the cry of my heart to fol-low You it is the cry of my heart
내 마 음 간 절 하 게 주 따 - 르 며 주 께 가 까 이 가 길

to be close to You it is the cry of my heart to fol-low
원 - 합 - 니 다 나 의 삶 다 하 도 록 간 절 - 하 게

all of the days of my life
주 님 을 따 - 라 가 리 -   -

Teach me Your ho-ly ways,
주 의 길 가 르 치
나 의 눈 열 어 주

oh Lord. So I can walk in Your truth.
- 소 서 - 진 리 안 에 서 도 록 -
- 소 서 - 주 님 의 뜻 알 도 록 -

Teach me Your ho-ly ways.
주 의 길 가 르 치
나 의 눈 열 어 주

oh Lord and make me whol-ly de-vot- ed to You
- 소 서 나 주 께 온 전 히 드 - 리 도 록
- 소 서 나 주 께 온 전 히 드 - 리 도 록

All of the days of my life
주 님 을 따 - 라 가 리

All of the days of my life.
주 님 을 따 - 라 가 리

Faithful One

(신실한 나의 하나님)

80

Brian Doerksen

81 Forever
(영원히)

Marty Sampson

I'll wor-ship at Your throne Whis-per my own love song With all my heart I'll sing
사 랑 의 노 래 로　　　주 님 을 경 배 해 –　　　내 마 음 다 하 여

for You my Dad and King I'll live for all my days to put a smile on Your face
왕 되 신 아 버 지　　　주 님 을 기 쁘 게 –　　　내 모 든 삶 드 리 – 네

And when we fi-nally meet it-'ll be for e-ter-ni-ty And oh
그 날 에 만 나 면　　　영 원 히 함 께 하 리 라 –　나 주

how wide You o-pen up Your arms when I need Your love
– 의 사 – 랑 필 – 요 로　– 할 때 –　안 아 주 – 시 네

And how far You would come if e-ver I – was lost
– – 나 방 황 할 – 때 도 –　– 주 찾 아 오 – 시 네

You said that all You feel for me is un-dy-ing love
– – 나 를 위 한 – 영 원 – 한 주 –　사 랑 십 자 가

that You showed me through the cross.
– 에 서 보 여 주 – 셨 네 – – – –

Forever

I'll worship You, my God I'll worship You, my God. I love You,
주님을 경배해 주님을 경배 – 해 – – 사 랑 – 해

I love You. for-ev-er I will sing for-ev-er I will be
주 님 – 을 영원히노래해 영원히주님과

with You, be with You.
– 함께 – 주 – 함께 – –

Words and Music by Marty Sampson
© 2000 Hillsong Music Publishing Australia (admin in Korea by Universal Music Publishing/ CAIOS)

D

82 God Of Glory, We Exalt Your Name
(영광의 주)

David Fellingham

God of glo - ry we ex - alt Your name You who
영 광 의 - 주 이름 높 이 세 전 능

reign in maj-est-y. We lift our hearts to You and we will
의 - 왕 되신 주 - 우 리 정 성 - 바 쳐 - -경 배 하

wor-ship, praise and mag-ni-fy Your ho - ly name In power res
며 섬 기 리 주의이름 찬 양 하 리 - 빛 나 는

In power res-plen - dent You reign in glo - ry,
빛 나 는 보 - 좌 - 다 스 리 시 는 -

plen - dent You reign in glo - ry, e - ter-nal
보 좌 - 다 스 리 시 는 - 영 원 한

e - ter-nal King, Your reign for - ev - er
영 원 한 왕 나 의 - - 하 나 님 -

King, You reign for - ev - er Your words is
왕 - 나 의 하 나 님 -능 력 의

God Of Glory, We Exalt Your Name

D

Your word is might - y, re - leas - ing cap - tives,
능력의 말 씀 - 자 유 주 시 네 -

might - y, re - leas - ing cap - tives, Your love is
말 씀 - 자 유 주 시 네 - 넘 치 는

Your love is gra-cious, You are my God.
넘 치 는 사 랑 주 - 하 나 님 -

gra - cious, You are my God.
사 랑 - 주 하 나 님 -

O.T. : God Of Glory, We Exalt Your Name / O.W. : David Fellingham
O.P. : Thankyou Music Ltd / S.P. : Universal Music Publishing Korea, CAIOS
Adm. : Capitol CMG Publishing / All rights reserved, Used by permission,

83 God Of This City

(주는 이 도시의 주)

Lan Jordan, Prter Comfort, Richard Bleakley &
Aaron Boyd, Peter Kernaghan, Andrew McCann

You're the God of this cit-y You're the king of these
주 는 이 도 시 - 의 주 - 주 는 이 백 성

peo-ple You're the Lord of this na-tion You are
- 의 왕 - 이 나 라 의 주 - 되 신 주 님

You're the light in this dark-ness You're the hope to the
- 주 는 어 둠 속 - 의 빛 절 망 가 운 데

hope-less You're the peace to the rest-less You are
- 소 망 - 참 된 평 화 되 - 시 는 주 님 -

There is no one like our God. There is no one like our
주 - 와 같 은 분 - 없 - 네 주 - 와 같 은 분 - 없

God. great-er things have yet to come and
- 네 더 위 대 한 일 이 땅 에 더

great-er things have still to be done in this city
놀 라 운 일 이 도 시 에 이 뤄 - 지 리 - - - - -

God Of This City

great - er things have yet to come and
위 대 한 일 이 땅 에 더

great-er things have sill to be done in this city
놀 라 운 일 이 도 시 에 이 뤄 – 지 리 – – – – – –

great-er things are sill to be done here
놀 라 운 일 주 행 하 시 리 – –

84 Grace Flows Down
(놀라우신 주의 은혜)

David Bell/Loule Giglio & Rod Pageant

O.T. : Grace Flows Down / O.W. : Louie Giglio, David Bell, Rod Padgett
O.P. : worshiptogether.com Songs, sixsteps Music / S.P. : Universal Music Publishing Korea, CAIOS

He That Is In Us

(내 안에 계신 주)

Graham Kendrick

85

D

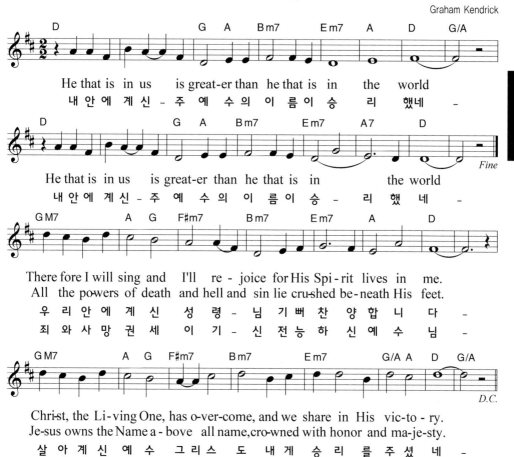

He that is in us   is great-er than he that is in   the world
내 안에 계신 – 주 예 수 의 이 름 이 승   리   했네 –

He that is in us   is great-er than he that is in   the world
내 안에 계신 – 주 예 수 의 이 름 이 승 –   리 했 네 –

Fine

There fore I will sing and   I'll re - joice for His Spi - rit lives in   me.
All   the po-wers of death and hell and sin lie cru-shed be-neath His   feet.
우 리 안 에 계 신   성 령 – 님 기 뻐 찬 양 합 니   다 –
죄 와 사 망 권 세   이 기 – 신 전 능 하 신 예 수   님 –

Chri-st, the Li-ving One, has o-ver-come, and we share in His vic-to - ry.
Je-sus owns the Name a - bove all name,cro-wned with honor and ma-je-sty.
살 아 계 신 예 수 그 리 스 도 내 게 승 리 를 주 셨   네 –
모 든 이 름 위 에 뛰 – 어 난 주 의 영 광 을 찬 양   해 –

D.C.

86 He Touched Me

(험한 세상 나그네 길)

William J. Gaither

Shack - led by a heav - y bur-den   'Neath a load of
Since I met this bless - ed Sav - ior   Since He cleansed and
험 한 세 상 나 그 네 길 - 나 의 맘 이
죄 와 수 치 무 거 운 짐 - 괴 롬 슬 픔

guilt and shame   Then the hand of Je - sus touched me
made me whole   I will nev - er cease to lraise Him
곤 할 때 - 사 랑 스 런 주 의 손 길
당 할 때 - 그 때 예 수 손 내 미 사

and now I am no long - er the same
I'll shout it while e - ter - ni - ty rolls
- 내 맘 을 항 상 두 드 리 네 -
- 오 늘 라 운 구 원 주 셨 네 -

He touched me   O He touched me   and O the
주 붙드네 오 날 붙 드 네 - 넘 치 는

joy that floods my soul   some-thing a hap-pened and now I
기 쁨 내 맘 에 - 근 심 - 걱 정 나 없 겠

know He touched me and made me whole
네 날 언 제 나 붙 드 시 네 -

O.T. : He Touched Me / O.W. : William J. Gaither
O.P. : Hanna Street Music / S.P. : Universal Music Publishing Korea, CAIOS
Adm. : Capitol CMG Publishing / All rights reserved. Used by permission.

I Am Free
(나는 자유해)

Jon Egan

Through You the bl - ind will see　　Through You the mute
눈 먼 - 자 보 - 게 해 -　　갇 힌 - 자 노

will sing　　Through You the dead will rise
- 래 해 -　　죽 은 - 자 일 - 어 나 -

Through You all hearts will praise　　Through You the dark
모 든 - 맘 찬 - 양 해 -　　어 둠 - 이 걷

- ness flees　　Through You my heart screams I am free
- 히 고 -　　내 영 - 혼 외 - 쳐 자 유 해 -

I am freee to run I am
나 는 자 - - 유 해 나 는

free to run I am free to dance I am free to dance
자 - - 유 해 나 는 춤 - - 추 네 나 는 춤 - - 추 네

I am free to live for You　　I am free to live for You
주 님 만 위 해 - 살 리　　주 님 만 위 해 - 살 리

I am free I am free I am free I am free
자 유 해 자 유 해 자 유 해 자 유 해 -

88 I Never Want Anything

(나 무엇과도 주님을)

Wes Sutton

I ne-ver want a-ny-thing in my life to take You place
나 무엇 과 - 도 주 님 을 바 - 꾸 지 - 않 으 리 -

I ne-ver want to live by a-ny o - ther grace. My
다 른 어 떤 - 은 혜 - 구 하 지 않 - 으 리 - 오 직

long-ing and my heart's de-sire is to see Your face, O Lord,
주 님 만 - 이 내 삶 에 - 도 움 이 - 시 니 - 주 의

and be-come a friend of God. I love You day and night,
- 얼 굴 보 기 - 원 합 니 다 - 주 님 사 랑 해 요

I love You all my life, I love You, Lord,
- 온 맘 과 정 성 다 해 - 하 나 님 - - 의

heart and soul, I long to be a friend of God.
신 실 - 한 친 구 되 기 - 원 합 니 다 -

In His Time

(주님의 시간에)

Linda Diane Ball

D

In His time, In His time.
In your time, In your time.
주 님 의 – 시 간 에 –
기 다 려 – 그 때 를 –

He makes all things beau-ti-ful, in his time.
You make all things beau-ti-ful, in your time
그 의 뜻 이 뤄 지 리 기 다 려 –
그 의 뜻 이 뤄 지 리 기 다 려 –

Lord, please show me ev-'ry day, as You're tea-ching me your way,
Lord, my life to you I bring, May each song I have to sing,
하 루 하 루 살 동 안 주 님 인 도 하 시 니
주 의 뜻 이 뤄 질 때 우 리 들 의 모 든 것

that you do just what you say, in your time.
be to you a love-ly thing, in your time.
주 뜻 이 룰 때 까 지 기 다 려 –
아 름 답 게 변 하 리 기 다 려 –

90 In Moments Like These

(이와 같은 때엔)

David Graham

In mo - ments like these, I sing out a song. I
이 와 같 은 때 엔 난 노 래 하 네 사

sing out a love song to Je - sus. In mo - ments like
랑 을 노 래 하 네 주 님 께 이 와 같 은 때

these, I lift up my hands. I lift up my hands to the
엔 손 높 이 드 네 손 높 이 드 네 주 님

Lord. Sing - ing I love you, Lord.
께 ― 주 님 사 랑 해 요 ―

I love You, Lord I love You,
사 랑 해 요 ― 사 랑 해

Lord. O I love You, Lord.
요 주 님 사 랑 해 요 ―

I See The Lord

(보좌 위에 앉으신 주님)

Chris Falson

91

D

I see the Lord seat-ed on the throne ex - al - ted And the
보 좌 위 에 - 앉 으신 - 주 님 - 바 라 보니 성 전

train of His robe fills the tem - ple with glo - ry And the
안 을 두 른 - 그 옷 자 - 락 과 영 광 온 땅

whole earth is filled the whole earth is filled with His glo - ry
가 득 - - 한 - 온 땅 가 득 - 한 - - 주 의 영 광

Ho - ly ho - ly ho - ly ho - ly ho - ly
거 룩 - 거 룩 - 거 룩 - 거 룩 - 거 - 룩

is the Lord Lord of Lord
하 신 주 - 주 의 주

92 I See The Lord

(눈을 들어 주 봅니다)

John Chisum & Don Moen

I see the Lord　I see the Lord　Ex-alt-ed
눈을 들어　주 봅 니 다　땅 위 의

high up-on　the wor-ship　of the peo-ple of　the earth　I see the
모 든 백 - 성 주 - 를 -　높 여 경 배 드 - 리 네 - 눈 을 들

Lord　I see the Lord　My eyes have been　the King　The
어　주 봅 니 다 -　보 좌 위 어 - 린 양 -　영

Lamb up-on　the throne　who reigns for - e　- ver more
원 한 통 - 치 자 -　왕 되 신 주 -　보 네

The train of　His robe　Fills the tem - ple　A
성 전 가 - 득 한　그 옷 자 - 락 -　보

cloud of heaven - ly　wor-ship-ers　Sur-roun-ding His throne　We
좌 를 두 - 른 천 사 들 -　주 경 배 - 하 네　우

join with them now cry - ing Ho - ly　ho - ly is the
리 도 - 함 께 찬 양 거 룩　거 룩 하 신 주

Lamb　The Lamb　a - lone　I see the
-　어 린 양 께 -　눈 을 들

I'm In Love With You

(사랑합니다 나를 자녀 삼으신 주)

Danny Daniels

D

I'm in love with You. for You have called me
사 랑 합 니 다 – 나를 자 녀 삼 으 신

child. I'm in love with You for
주 – 사 랑 합 니 다 – 나를

You have called me child. You reached out and
자 녀 삼 으 신 주 – 내 부 르 짖 음

touched me. You heard my lone - ly cry. I will
들 으 시 고 감 싸 주 시 - 는 – 영 원

praise Your name for - ev - er, and give You all my life.
히 주 찬 양 합 니 다 내 삶 을 다 해 –

Jesus Is Alive

(할렐루야 살아계신 주)

Ron Kenoly

Just The Mention Of Your Name

(주의 이름 부를 때)

Chris Bowater

95

D

Just the men-tion of Your name
주 의 이름 부를 때

Cau-ses me to fall be-fore You,
– 주 님 앞에 엎 드 리 어

Te-ars flow as I a-dore You,
– 눈 물 속에 경배 하 네

At the men-tion of Your name,
– 주의 이 름 부 를 때

Just the men-tion of Your name.
주 의 이 름 부를 때

Just the man-tion of Your name,
주 의 이 름 부를 때

Re-a - ffirms the love that holds me,
– 나를 붙 드 시 는 사 랑

Speaks once more of love that knows me
그 사 랑 을 확 인 하 네

At the men-tion of Your name,
주 의 이 름 부를 때

Just the men-tion of Your name.
주 의 이 름 부를 때

Je - sus, Je - sus, Je - sus, Je - sus,
예 수 예 수 예 수 예 수

At the men-tion of Your name,
주 의 이 름 부를 때

I wor-ship.
– – 주 경 배 – –

96 King Of Kings
(지극히 높으신 주)

Jason Ingram, Scott Ligertwood & Brooke Ligertwood

In the dark - ness, we were wait-ing with-out hope, with-out light, 'til from hea
소 망 없 - 고 - 빛 도 없 - 는 어 두 운 - 세 상 을 - 하 나 님

- ven You came run - ning; there was mer - cy in Your eyes. To ful-fill
- 이 사 - 랑 하 - 사 우 리 에 - 게 오 - 셨 네 - 예 언 하

the law and proph - ets, to a vir - gin came the Word, from a throne
- 신 약 - 속 대 - 로 말 씀 이 - 육 신 - 되 어 - 하 늘 영

of end - less glo - ry to a cra - dle in the dirt.
- 광 버 - 리 시 - 고 이 땅 으 - 로 오 - 셨 네 -

Praise the Fa - ther, praise the Son, praise the Spir - it
찬 양 하 세 우 리 주 삼 위 일 체

Three in One. God of glo - ry, maj - es - ty, praise for - ev-er to the
하 나 님 지 극 히 높 으 신 주 영 원 토 록 찬 양

King of kings. To re-veal the king-dom com-ing and to rec
합 니 다 주 - 가 - 지 으 - 신 모 - 든 세 상 을

on-cile the lost, to re-deem the whole cre - a - tion, You did not
- 구 원 - 하 려 - 영 광 의 - 주 예 - 수 님 - 이 죽 음 을

King Of Kings

D

King Of Kings

Written by Jason Ingram, Scott Ligertwood, Brooke Ligertwood
© 2019 Hillsong Music Publishing Australia (admin in Korea by Universal Music Publishing / CAIOS)

Lamb Of God

(죄 없으신 주 독생자)

Twila Paris

Your on - ly son no sin to hide but You have
Your gift of love they cru - ci - fied They laughed and
I was so lost I should have died but you have

죄 없 으 신 주 독 생 자 하 나 님
겸 손 하 신 왕 주 예 수 사 람 들
죽 어 야 할 이 죄 인 을 주 님 께

sent Him from your side to walk up - on this guilt - y
scorned Him as He died The him - ble king they named a
brought me to your side to be led by your staff and

보 좌 를 떠 – 나 죄 악 된 땅 에 오 셨
은 조 롱 했 – 네 우 리 를 사 랑 하 신
로 이 끄 셨 – 네 주 지 팡 이 막 대 기

sod and to be - come the Lamb of God O Lamb of
fraud And sa - cri - ficed the Lamb of God
rod and to be called a Lamb of God

네 세 상 죄 지 신 어 린 양 오 – 어 – 린 –
주 십 자 가 에 못 박 았 네
로 어 린 양 인 도 하 시 네

God sweet Lamb of God I love the ho ly Lamb of
양 귀 한 어 린 양 주 님 을 사 랑 합 니 –

God O wash me in your pre-cious blood my Je - sus
다 주 보 혈 – 로 씻 으 소 서 예 수 님

Christ the Lamb of God
귀 한 어 린 – 양 –

98

Light Of The world

(나를 세상의 빛으로)

Scott Brenner

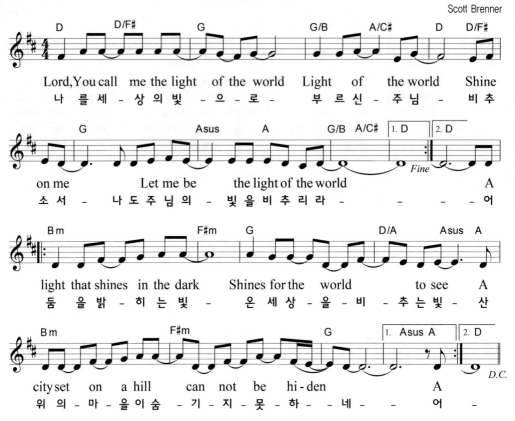

Lord, You call me the light of the world   Light   of   the world   Shine
나 를 세 - 상 의 빛 - 으 - 로 - 부 르 신 - 주 님 - 비 추

on me   Let me be   the light of the world   A
소 서 -   나 도 주 님 의 -   빛 을 비 추 리 라 -   -   - - 어

light that shines in the dark   Shines for the   world   to see   A
둠 을 밝 - 히 는 빛 -   온 세 상 - 을 비 - 추 는 빛 - 산

city set   on   a hill   can not be hi-den   A
위 의 - 마 - 을 이 숨 - 기 - 지 - 못 - 하 - - 네 - - 어 -

Lord Of My Heart

(나의 예수)

99

Scott Brenner

Je-sus my Lord　　Lord of my heart　　I give You my love
나 의 예 수 - 　온 맘 다 해 - 　사 랑 해 요 -

Je-sus my Lord　　Lord of my strength　　I give You my praise
나 의 예 수 - 　온 맘 다 해 - 　경 배 해 요 -

Je-sus my Lord　　Lord of my soul　　I give You my life
예 수 님 께 - 　온 맘 다 해 - 　순 복 해 요 -

Lord of my love　　Lord of my life　　Lord of my all
영 원 토 록 - 　찬 양 을 - 　드 립 니 다 -

Fine

You are pure　　You are fa - ir　　You are love - ly be-yond com-pa-re
당 신 은 - 순 결 하 고 - 　아 름 다 -운 주 이 십 니 다 -

Clothed in holi - ness, crown-ed in　　glo-ry For-e-ver wor-thy to be　exa - lt - ed
거 룩 하 - 고 사 랑 스 -러 운 능 력 과 영 -광 의 주 - 이 십 - 니 다

Hea-ven and ear - th sing Your pra-ise　　The King of glory the An-cient of Days
하 늘 과 땅 -이 주 찬 양 해 - 　영 광 의 왕 -을 영 원 한 주 를 -

D.S.

Prince of pea-ce　　Lord of　　all Now and for-ev - er Lord, be exa - alted Je-sus my Lord
평 화 의 왕 - 자 모 든 만 물 -의 주 영 원 영 원 - 토 록 주 님 을 높 - 이 세 나 의 예 수

100 Lord You Are The Author Of My Life

(주 내 삶의 주인 되시고)

Judy Pruett

Mercy Is Falling

(주의 자비가 내려와)

David Ruis

101

D

Mer - cy is fal - ing, is fal - lig, is fal - ling.
주 의 자 비 – 가 내 려 – 와 내 려 – 와 –

Mer - cy is falls like a sweet spring rain.
주 의 자 비 – 가 봄 비 같 이

Mer - cy is fal - ling, is fal - ling all o - ver me.
주 의 자 비 가 내 려 – 와 나 를 덮 네 –

Hey Ho I re - cei - ve Your mer - cy Hey Ho I re - ceive Your grace.
헤이 호 – 주 의 자 비 하 심 과 헤이 호 – 주 의 은 혜 로

Hey Ho I will dan - ce for - e - ver more.
헤이 호 – 나 는 영 원 히 춤 추 리 –

102 My Heart Your Home

(나의 맘 받으소서)

Nathan Nockels & Christy Nockels

Come and make my heart Your home Come and be
나의 맘 받으 - 소 서 - - - 오 셔서

ev-'ry-thing I am and all I know Search me through and through
주님의 - 처소삼으 - 소서 - 나의 - 전부이 - 신

'til my heart be-comes a home for You Come and make
주 여 내 맘 을 - 받 아 주 소 - 서 - 나 의 맘

A home for You Lord a home for You Lord
- 오 나 의 맘 을 - - - - 주 님 께 열 었 - - - 으 니

Let ev-'ry-thing I do o-pen up a door for You to come through
- 주 여 내 게 - 오 - 셔 서 - 내 맘 에 - 거 하 - 여 주 - 옵 소 - 서

And then my heart will be a place where You want to be Come and make
주 가 기 뻐 하 는 - 주 의 성 전 되 게 하 소 서 나 의 맘

'til my heart be-comes a home for You
- 주 여 내 맘 을 - 받 아 주 소 - 서

'til my heart be-comes a home for You
- 주 여 내 맘 을 - 받 아 주 소 - 서 -

My Peace I Give Unto You

(평안을 너에게 주노라)

Keith Routlege

103

D

My peace I give un-to you.
평안을 너에게 주노라 –

it's a peace that the world can-not give;
세상이 줄 – 수 없 – 는 –

it's a peace that the world can-not un – der-stand,
세상이 알수도 없는평 – 안

peace to know, peace to live.
평 – – 안 평 – – 안

My peace I give un-to you.
평안을 네게 주노라 –

104

No Other Name

(오직 예수 다른 이름은 없네)

Robert Gay

No oth-er name but the name of Je-sus No oth-er
오 직 예 수 다 른 이 름 은 없 네 주 이 름

name but the name of the Lord, No oth-er name but the name of
만 우 리 에 게 주 셨 네 오 직 예 수 다 른 이 름

Je - - sus is wor - thy of glo-ry and wor - thy of hon-or and
없 - - 네 오 영 - 광 과 존 귀 권 세 - - 와 찬 양 받

wor - thy of pow-er and all praise No oth-er praise His
으 - 실 분 오 직 주 예 수 오 직 예 수 온

name is ex-alt - ed far a - bove the earth His
땅 위 에 홀 - 로 높 으 신 - 이 름 - 하

name is high a-bove the hea - vens His name is ex-alt - ed
늘 위 높 이 들 - 리 셨 - 네 - 온 땅 위 에 홀 - 로

far a-bove the earth Give glo-ry and ho-nor and praise un - to His name
높 으 신 - 이 름 - 영 광 과 존 귀 와 찬 양 드 리 세

D.S. al Coda
No oth - er wor - thy of pow-er and all praise
오 직 예 으 - 실 분 오 직 주 예 수

Pass It On

(작은 불꽃 하나가)

Kurt Kaiser

105

It on-ly takes a spark to get a fire go-ing
작은 불 꽃 하 나 가 큰 불 을 일 으 키 - 어 - -
이 돋 아 나 며 새 들 은 지 저 귀 - 고 - -
구 여 당 신 께 이 행 복 전 하 고 싶 소 - -

And soon all those a-round can warm up to its glow-ing
곧 주 위 사 람 들 그 불 에 몸 녹 이 듯 이 - -
꽃 들 은 피 어 나 화 창 한 봄 날 이 라 네 - -
내 주 는 당 신 의 의 지 할 구 세 주 라 오 - -

That's how it is with God's love Once you've ex-peri-enced it
주 님 의 사 랑 이 같 이 한 번 경 험 하 면 -
주 님 의 사 랑 이 같 이 한 번 경 험 하 면 -
산 위 에 올 라 가 - 서 세 상 에 외 치 리 -

You spread His love to ev-ry one; You want to pass it on
그 의 사 랑 모 두 에 게 전 하 고 싶 으 리 - - 새 싹
봄 과 같 은 새 희 망 을 전 하 고 싶 으 리 - - 친 -
내 게 임 한 주 의 사 랑 전 하 기 원 하 네 - -

I'll shout it from the mountain top I want my world to know, The
- 산 위 에 올 라 가 서 세 상 에 외 치 리 - 내

Lord of love has come to me, I want to pass it on.
게 임 한 주 의 사 랑 전 하 기 원 하 네 - -

106
Sanctuary
(주여 나를 주님의)

John Thompson & Randy Scruggs

Lord, pre-pare me to be a sanc-tu-ar-y, pure and ho-ly tried and true;
주 여 나를 주님의 성전 으로 – 준 비시 켜 주시 고 – – – –

With thanks-giv-ing I'll be a liv-ing sanctu-ar-y for You.
순 결 함 과 감 사 한 마 음 – 넘 치 도 록 하 소 – 서

107
Savior, Like A Shepherd Lead Us
(선한 목자 되신 우리 주)

D. A. Thrupp & W. B. Bradbury

Sa-vior like a shep-herd lead us Much we need Thy ten-der care
선 한 목자 되신 우리 주 – 항 상 인 도 하 시 고

In Thy pleasant pas-tures feed us For our use Thy folds pre-pare
푸 른 풀밭 좋은 곳 에 서 – 우 리 먹 여 주 소 서

Bless-ed Je - sus Bless-ed Je - sus Thou hast bought us, Thine we are
선 한 목 자 구 세 주 여 항 상 인 도 하 소 서

Bless-ed Je - sus Bless-ed Je - sus Thou hast bought us, Thine we are
선 한 목 자 구 세 주 여 항 상 인 도 하 소 서

Seek Ye First

(먼저 그 나라와 의를 구하라)

Karen Lafferty

108

Seek ye first the King – dom of God, And His righ - teous - ness
Man shall not live by bread a - lone, but by ev - ry word
Ask, and it shall be gi - ven un - to You, seek, and ye shall find

먼 저 그 나 라 와 의 를 구 하 라 그 나 라 와 그 의 를
사 람 이 떡 으 로 만 살 것 아 니 요 하 나 님 말 씀 으 로
구 하 라 그 리 하 면 주 실 것 이 요 찾 으 라 찾 을 것 이 요

And all these things shall be ad - ded un - to You Al - le - lu, Al - le - lu - ia
That pro - ceeds from the mouth of God Al - le - lu, Al - le - lu - ia
Knock, and the door shall be op-ened un - to You Al - le - lu, Al - le - lu - ia

그 리 하 면 이 모 든 것 을 너 희 에 게 더 하 시 리 라
그 리 하 면 이 모 든 것 을 너 희 에 게 더 하 시 리 라
두 드 리 라 문 이 열 릴 것 이 니 할 렐 루 할 렐 루 야

Hal - le - lu - jah, Hal - le - lu - jah,
할 렐 루 야 할 렐 루 야

Hal - le - lu - jah, Hal - le - lu, Hal - le - lu - jah
할 렐 루 야 할 렐 루 할 렐 루 야

O.T. : Seek Ye First / O.W. : Karen Lafferty
O.P. : Cccm Music, Universal Music–Brentwood Benson Publ, / S.P. : Universal Music Publishing Korea, CAIOS
Adm. : Capitol CMG Publishing / All rights reserved, Used by permission,

D

109 Shepherd Of My Soul

(선하신 목자)

Martin J. Nystrom

She - pherd of my soul I give You full con - trol, Wher-
선 하신 - 목자 - 날 사 랑 하 - 는 분 - 주

ev - er You may lead I will fol - - low.
인 도 하 - 는 곳 - 따 라 가 - - 리

I have made the choice to lis - ten for Your voice Wher-
주 의 말 - 씀 을 - 나 듣 기 위 - 하 여 - 주

ev - er You may lead I will go. go. Be it
인 도 하 - 는 - 곳 가 려 네 네 나 를

in a qui - et pas - ture or by a gen - tle stream, The
푸른초 - 장 과 - - 쉴 만 한 물 - 가 로 - 내

Shep - herd of my soul is by my side Should I
선 하 신 - 목 자 - 날 인 - 도 해 - 험 한

face a might - y moun - tain or a val - ley dark and deep The
산 과 골 - 짜 기 - 로 내 가 다 닐 찌 - 라 도 - 내

Shep - herd of my soul will be my guide
선 하 신 - 목 자 - 날 인 - 도 해 -

Soften My Heart, Lord

(온유한 맘을 주옵소서)

Graham Kendrick

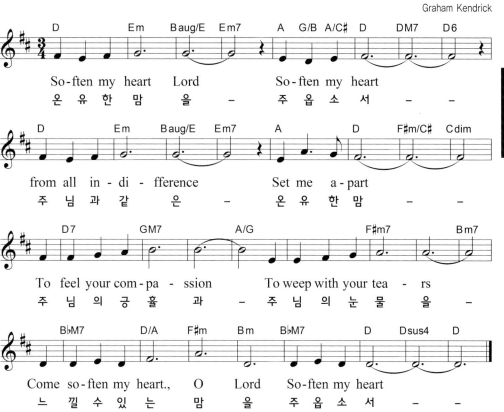

So-ften my heart Lord So-ften my heart
온 유 한 맘 을 – 주 옵 소 서 – –

from all in - di - fference Set me a - part
주 님 과 같 은 – 온 유 한 맘 – –

To feel your com - pa - ssion To weep with your tea - rs
주 님 의 긍 휼 과 – 주 님 의 눈 물 을 –

Come so-ften my heart., O Lord So-ften my heart
느 낄 수 있 는 맘 을 주 옵 소 서 – –

111 So Good To Me

(주님 내게 선하신 분)

Darrell Evans & Matt Jones

O God You've been so good to me You
주 님 내 게 선 하 신 분 — and

came and found this or-phan and You brought me right in-to Your fa-mi-ly;
Eve-ry day I wake up, I breathe an-oth-er breath of Your mer-cy;
고 아 같 은 나 를 구 해 주 의 자 녀 — 삼 아 주 셨 네
매 일 아 침 마 다 주 의 — 자 비 로 새 생 명 주 네 —

O God You've been so good to me;
주 님 내 게 선 하 신 분

You threw a-way my past and You ne-ver count my sins a-gainst me.
My de-light is in You' cause I know that Your hand is up-on me.
내 과 거 를 던 지 — 시 고 내 죄 세 지 않 으 시 — 네
주 의 손 이 내 게 계 셔 내 기 쁨 이 주 께 있 — 네

You got me dan-cing; And now I'm shout-ing;
나 춤 을 추 네 나 주 께 외 쳐 —

You got me leap-ing; and now I'm spin-ning, hal-le-lu-jah.
나 주 께 뛰 네 뛰 어 돌 며 할 렐 루 야 —

You're so good to me, You're so good to me, You're so good to me,
선 하 신 분 — 선 하 신 분 — 선 하 신 분

So Good To Me

O
Je-sus, You're the One
- 주 오 직 주 - 님 이 -

Who saved my - self from me; So I will be
나 를 구 하 - 셨 네 - 나 거 리 에

the one to praise You in the streets.
- 서 도 - 찬 양 을 드 - 리 리

D.S. al Coda

You're so good to me. You're so good to me.
선 하 신 분 - 선 하 신 분 -

D

112

Spirit Song
(오 나의 자비로운 주여)

John Wimber

O let the Son of God en-fold You with His Spi-rit and His love
O come and sing this song with glad-ness as your hearts are filled with joy
오 나 의 자 비 로 운 주 여 나 의 몸 과 영 혼 을
모 여 라 주 께 찬 양 하 라 나 의 귀 한 친 구 야

Let Him fill your heart and sa-tis-fy your soul
Lift your hands in sweet sur-ren-der to His name
주 님 은 혜 로 다 채 워 주 – 소 서
주 이 름 앞 에 너 두 손 모 – 으 고

O let Him have those things that hold you and His Spi-rit like a-dove
O give Him all your tears and sad-ness Give Him all your years of pain
이 세 상 괴 롬 걱 정 근 심 주 여 받 아 주 시 고
오 너 의 슬 픔 세 상 눈 물 너 의 쌓 인 아 픔 을

will des-cend up-on your life and make you whole
and you'll en-ter in-to life in Je-sus name
험 한 세 상 에 서 인 도 하 소 서 –
십 자 가 앞 에 너 모 두 버 리 고 –

Je - sus O Je-sus come and fill your lambs
예 수 오 예 수 지 금 오 셔 서 –

Je - sus O Je-sus come and fill your lambs.
예 수 오 예 수 채 워 주 소 서

Thank You Lord Thank You Jesus For Your 113

(감사해요 주님의 사랑)

Allison Revell Huntley

D

Thank You Je - sus for Your love to me
감 사 해 요 주 님 의 사 랑

Thank you Je - sus for Your grace so free.
감 사 해 요 주 님 의 은 혜

I'll lift my voice to praise Your name,
목 소 리 높 여 주 님 을

Praise You a - gain and a - gain You are ev' - ry things
영 원 히 감 사 해 요 나 의 전 부 이 신

You are my Lord
나 의 주 님

114

Take My Life
(나의 생명 드리니)

Louie Giglio & Chris Tomlin

Take my life and let it be con - se - crat - ed, Lord, to Thee.
Take my voice and let me sing al - ways, on - ly, for my King.
Take my will and make it Thine, it shall be no long - er mine.
나 의 생 - 명 드 - 리 - 니 - 거 - 룩 하 - 게 하 - 시 고 -
나 의 음 - 성 드 - 리 - 니 - 주 - 만 노 - 래 하 - 도 록 -
나 의 모 - 든 생 - 각 - 이 - 주 - 뜻 되 - 게 하 - 시 고 -

Take my mo - ments and my days, let them flow in cease - less praise.
Take my lips and let them be filled with mes - sag - es from Thee.
Take my heart, it is Thine own, it shall be Thy ro - yal throne.
삶 의 모 - 든 순 - 간 - 이 - 찬 - 양 되 - 게 하 - 소 서 -
내 입 술 - 엔 주 - 말 - 씀 - 가 - 득 하 - 게 하 - 소 서 -
나 의 마 - 음 드 - 리 - 니 - 주 - 보 좌 - 삼 으 - 소 서 -

Take my hands and let them move at the im - pulse of Thy love.
Take my sil - ver and my gold, not a mite would I with - hold.
Take my love, my Lord, I pour as Your feet its treas - ure store.
내 손 은 - 주 님 - 사 - 랑 - 인 도 하 - 심 따 - 르 며 -
나 의 보 - 화 주 - 앞 - 에 - 아 낌 없 - 이 드 - 리 니 -
내 안 의 - 귀 한 - 사 - 랑 - 주 발 앞 - 에 흐 - 르 니 -

Take my feet and let them be swift and beau - ti - ful for Thee.
Take my in - tel - lect and use ev - 'ry pow - er as You choose.
Take my - self and I will be ev - er, on - ly, all for Thee.
나 의 발 - 은 주 - 위 해 - 민 - 첩 하 - 게 하 - 소 서
모 든 힘 - 과 지 - 혜 도 - 주 - 뜻 대 - 로 쓰 - 소 서
평 생 토 - 록 주 - 위 해 - 봉 - 사 하 - 게 합 - 소 서

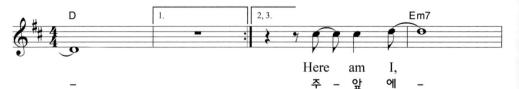

Here am I,
주 - 앞 에 -

Take My Life

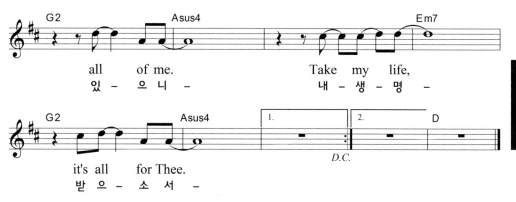

G2   Asus4   Em7

all   of me.   Take   my   life,

있 – 으니 –   내 – 생 – 명 –

G2   Asus4   1.   2.   D

it's all   for Thee.

받으 – 소 서 –

D.C.

O.T. : Take My Life / O.W. : Chris Tomlin, Louie Giglio
O.P. : Rising Springs Music, worshiptogether.com Songs, Vamos Publishing / S.P. : Universal Music Publishing Korea, CAIOS
Adm. : Capitol CMG Publishing / All rights reserved. Used by permission.

115

Teach Me To Dance
(주님의 춤추리)

Steve A. Thompson & Graham Kendrick

Teach me to dance   to the beat of Your heart.   Teach me to move
with Your heart of com - pas - sion. Teach me to trust

주 님 의 마   음 으 로 나 춤 추 – 리   성 령 의 능
음 으 로 사 랑 하 – 리   주 님 약 속

in the pow'r of Your Spi - rit.   Teach me to walk   in the light of Your pre-
in the word of Your pro - mise. Teach me to hope   in the day of Your co-

력 으 로 따 라 가 – 리   주 님 의 빛   가 운 데 걸 어 가
의 말 씀 신 뢰 하 – 리   다 시 오 실   주 님 나 바 라 보

- sence.Teach me to dance   to the beat of Your heart.   Teach me to love
- ming. Teach me to dance   to the beat of Your heart.   Teach me to love

– 리 주 님 의 마   음 으 로 춤 추 리 –   주 님 의 마
– 리 주 님 의 마   음 으 로 춤 추 리 –   주 님 의 마

You wrote the rhy - thm of life,
Let   all my move-ments ex-press

주 는 생 명 의 근 원
매 일 의 삶 속 에 서

cre - a - ted hea-ven and earth   in You is joy with-out mea - sure.
A heart that loves to say 'yes'   A will that leaps to obey you

하 늘 과 땅 의 주 인   주 안 에 넘 치 는 기 – 쁨
주 님 을 위 한 사 랑   순 종 으 로 주 께 드 – 려

Teach Me To Dance

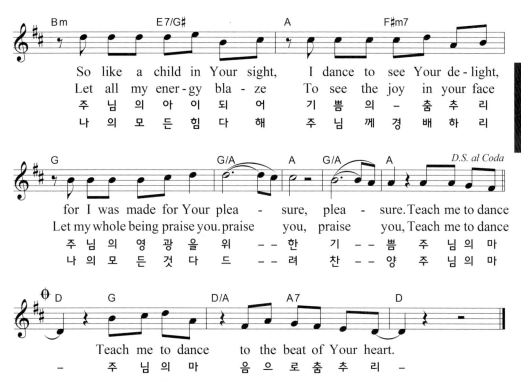

So like a child in Your sight,   I dance to see Your de - light,
Let all my ener - gy bla - ze   To see the joy in your face
주 님 의 아 이 되 어   기 쁨 의 – 춤 추 리
나 의 모 든 힘 다 해   주 님 께 경 배 하 리

for I was made for Your plea - sure, plea - sure. Teach me to dance
Let my whole being praise you. praise you, praise you, Teach me to dance
주 님 의 영 광 을 위 – –한 기 – –쁨 주 님 의 마
나 의 모 든 것 다 드 – –려 찬 – –양 주 님 의 마

Teach me to dance   to the beat of Your heart.
– 주 님 의 마 음 으 로 춤 추 리 –

116 The Greatest Thing In All My Life
(내 생에 가장 귀한 것)

Mark Pendergrass

The great-est thing   in   all my life   is   know-ing You
내 생에 — 가 장 귀 한것 주 앎 이 라 —
내 생에 — 가 장 귀 한것 주 사 랑 함 —
내 생에 — 가 장 귀 한것 주 찾 는 것 —
내 생에 — 가 장 귀 한것 섬 기 는 삶 —

The great-est thing   in   all my life   is   know-ing You
내 생에 — 가 장 귀 한것 주 앎 이 라 —
내 생에 — 가 장 귀 한것 주 사 랑 함 —
내 생에 — 가 장 귀 한것 주 찾 는 것 —
내 생에 — 가 장 귀 한것 섬 기 는 삶 —

I want to know You   more   I want to know You   more
주 님 을 알 기 를 간 절 히 원 하 네
주 사 랑 하 기 를 간 절 히 원 하 네
주 님 을 찾 기 를 간 절 히 원 하 네
주 님 을 섬 기 기 간 절 히 원 하 네

The great-est thing   in   all my life   is   know - ing   You
내 생에 — 가 장 귀 한것 주 앎 이 라
내 생에 — 가 장 귀 한것 주 사 랑 함
내 생에 — 가 장 귀 한것 주 찾 는 것
내 생에 — 가 장 귀 한것 섬 기 는 삶

The Lord Reigns

(주 다스리네)

Dan Stradwick

118 The Heart Of Worship

(마음의 예배)

Matt Redman

when the mu-sic fades, all is stripped a-way,
King of end-less worth, no one could ex-press
찬 양 의 열 기 – 모 두 끝 나 면
영 원 하 신 왕 – 표 현 치 못 할

and I simp-ly come; Long-ing just to bring
how much You de-serve. Though I'm weak and poor,
– 주 앞 에 나 와 – 더 욱 진 실 한
– 주 님 의 존 귀 – 가 난 할 때 도

some-thing that's of worth that will bless Your heart.
all I have is Yours, ev-'ry sin-gle breath.
– 예 배 드 리 네 – 주 님 을 향 한 –
– 연 약 할 때 도 – 주 내 모 든 것 –

I'll bring You more than a song for a song in it-self
노 래 이 상 의 노 래 – 내 맘 깊 은 곳 에

is not what You have re-quired
주 께 서 원 하 신 것 –

You search much deep-er with-in through the way things ap-pear.
화 려 한 음 악 보 다 – 뜻 없 는 열 정 보 다

The Heart Of Worship

You're look - ing in - to my heart. – –
중 심 을 원 하 시 죠 – –

I'm com - ing back to the heart of wor - ship and it's
주 님 께 드 릴 – 맘 – 의 예 – 배 주 –

all a - bout You, all a - bout You Je - sus.
님 을 위 한 – 주 님 을 향 한 노 래

I'm sor - ry, Lord, for the thing I've made it,
중 심 잃 은 예 배 내 – 려 놓 – 고

when it's all a - bout You, all a - bout You, Je - sus.
이 제 나 돌 아 와 – 주 님 만 예 배 해 요 –

O.T. : The Heart Of Worship (When The Music Fades) / O.W. : Matt Redman
O.P. : Thankyou Music Ltd / S.P. : Universal Music Publishing Korea, CAIOS
Adm. : Capitol CMG Publishing / All rights reserved. Used by permission.

D

119 There Is Power In The Name Of Jesus

(주 이름 큰 능력 있도다)

Noel Richards

There is power in the name of Je - sus
There is power in the name of Je - sus
주 이 름 – 큰 능 력 – 있 도 – 다
주 이 름 – 큰 능 력 – 있 도 – 다

We be - lieve in His name
Like a sword in our hands
난 믿 네 – 그 이 름 –
예 리 한 – 검 처 럼 –

We have called on the name of Je - sus
We de - clare in the name of Je - sus
예 수 의 – 그 이 름 – 부 를 – 때
예 수 의 – 그 이 름 – 외 치 – 며

We are saved We are saved
We shall stand We shall stand
새 생 명 – 얻 었 네 –
일 어 나 – 나 가 세 –

At His name the de - mons flee
At His name God's en - e - mies
마 귀 는 – 떠 나 – 가 고
원 수 는 – 주 발 – 앞 에

There Is Power In The Name Of Jesus

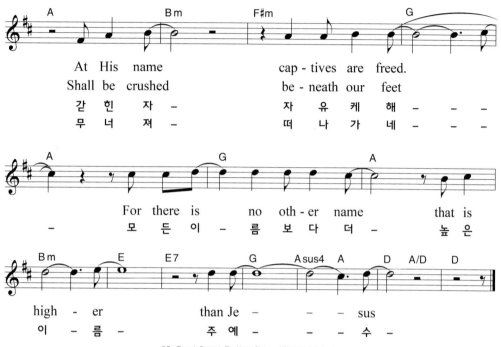

At His name cap - tives are freed.
Shall be crushed be - neath our feet
갇 힌 자 – 자 유 케 해 – – –
무 너 져 – 떠 나 가 네 – – –

For there is no oth - er name that is
– 모 든 이 – 름 보 다 더 – 높 은

high - er than Je – – – sus
이 – 름 – 주 예 – – – 수 –

O.T. : There Is Power In The Name Of Jesus / O.W. : Noel Richards
O.P. : Thankyou Music Ltd / S.P. : Universal Music Publishing Korea, CAIOS
Adm. : Capitol CMG Publishing / All rights reserved. Used by permission.

D

120 The Wonderful Cross
(놀라운 십자가)

J. D. Walt & Chris Tomlin, Jesse Reeves

When I sur - vey the won - drous cross
See from His head His hands His feet,
Were the whole realm of na - ture mine
주 달 려 죽 은 — 십 자 — 가
죽 으 신 구 주 — 밖 에 — 는
온 세 상 만 물 — 가 져 — 도

on which the Prince of Glo - ry died,
sor - row and love flow min - gled down;
that were an of - fering far too small.
우 리 가 생 각 — — 할 때 — 에
자 랑 을 말 게 — — 하 소 — 서
주 은 혜 못 다 — — 갚 겠 — 네

my rich - est gain I count but loss,
did e'er such love and sor - row meet,
Love so a - maz - ing, so di – vine,
세 상 에 속 한 — 욕 심 — 을
보 혈 의 공 로 — 입 어 — 서
놀 라 운 사 랑 — 받 은 — 나

and pour con - tempt on all my pride. O the
or thorns com - pose so rich a crown?
de - mands my soul, my life, my all.
헛 된 줄 알 고 버 리 – – 네 놀
교 만 한 맘 을 버 리 – – 네
몸 으 로 제 물 삼 겠 – – 네

The Wonderful Cross

won - der - ful cross, O the won - der - ful cross
라 운 십 - 자 가 - 놀 라 운 십 - 자 가

bids me come and die and find that I may tru-
all who gath - er here by grace draw near and bless
- 날 - 위 해 - 죽 으 - 신 주 - 인 해 - 생 명
- 모 - 두 나 - 와 주 - 의 은 - 혜 를 - 찬 양

1.
- ly live. O the
Your name
- 얻 네 - 놀 -
- 하 리 -

O.T. : Wonderful Cross / O.W. : Jesse Reeves, J.D. Walt, Chris Tomlin
O.P. : worshiptogether.com Songs, sixsteps Music, Vamos Publishing / S.P. : Universal Music Publishing Korea, CAIOS
Adm. : Capitol CMG Publishing / All rights reserved, Used by permission,

121 The Stead Fast Love Of The Lord

(주의 인자는 끝이 없고)

Edith McNeill

The stead - fast love of the Lord ne - ver cea - ses
주 의 인 자 는 – 끝 이 – 없 고
주 의 사 랑 은 – 끝 이 – 없 고
주 의 보 호 는 – 끝 이 – 없 고

His mer - cies ne - ver come to and end
그 의 자 비 는 – 무 궁 하 며 –
그 의 공 의 는 – 영 원 하 며 –
그 의 자 비 는 – 풍 성 하 며 –

They are new eve - ry mor - ning new eve - ry mor - ning
아 침 마 다 새 롭 고 늘 새 로 우 니

Great is Thy faith - ful - ness, O, Lord,
주 의 성 실 이 큼 이 라

Great is Thy faith - ful - ness
성 실 하 신 주 님 –

Think About His Love

(주의 사랑을 주의 선하심을)

122

Walt Harrah

Think a-bout His love   think a-bout His good-ness
주 의 사 랑 을 — 주 의 선 하 심 — 을 —

think a-bout His grace   that's brought us through   For as
주 의 은 혜 를   생 각 해 보 라 —   하 늘

high as the hea-ven's a-bove   so great is the mea-sure of our Fa-ther's
보 다 도 더 높 으 신 —   아 버 지 의 사 랑 크 고 놀 랍

love   Great is the mea-sure of our Fa-ther's love
네 — — — —   아 버 지 사 랑 크 고 놀 랍 네 —

Fine

How could I   for-get   his   love?
Ev-en when I've strayed   a-way
내 어 찌 — 그 사 랑 —   잊 으 리 —
나 길 을 — 잃 고 —   헤 맬 때 —

How   could I   for-get   His mer-cy?
his   love   has sought   me out   and found   me
내 어 찌 주 의 — 긍 휼 —   잊 으 리 —
그 사 — 랑 날 — 찾 아 —   내 셨 네 —

He   sat-is-fies   He   sat-is-fies
내 영 혼 의 — —   모 든 소 원 — —

He   sat-is-fies   my   de-sires
만 족 시 킨 — —   하 나 님 — —

D.C.

123 This Kingdom
(예수 하나님의 공의)

Geoff Bullock

Je - - - sus, God's right-eous-ness re - vealed,
Je - - - sus, the expres-sion of God's love,
예 – 수 – 하 나 님 의 공 의
예 – 수 – 하 나 님 의 사 랑

the Son of Man, the Son of God, His king-dom comes;
the grace of God, the Word of God, re-vealed to us;
주 독 생 자 그 의 나 라 임 하 시 – 네 –
주 은 혜 와 말 씀 으 로 나 타 났 – 네 –

Je - sus, re - demp-tion's sac - ri - fice,
Je - sus, God's hol - i - ness dis-played,
– 예 – 수 – 제 물 이 되 신 주
– 예 – 수 – 거 룩 한 하 나 님

now glo - ri - fied, now jus - ti - fied, His king-dom
– 영 광 중 에 그 의 나 라 임 하 시

comes. And this king-dom will know no end,
– 네 – – 주 의 나 라 영 원 하 며

and its glo-ry shall know no bounds, for the
– – 그 의 영 광 무 궁 하 리 – – 왕 의

This Kingdom

D

ma‑jes‑ty   and pow‑er   of this king‑dom's King   has come;
위 엄 과 – 능 력 – 이 – 이 제 임 하 였 – 으 니

And this king‑dom's reign,   and this king‑dom's rule,   and this
– 주 의 주 권 과 – 주 의 통 치 와 – 주 의

king‑dom's pow‑er and au‑tho‑ri‑ty   Je ‑
나 라 힘 – 과 권 세 임 하 네 – 예 –

sus,   God's right‑eous‑ness   re‑vealed.
수 하 나 님 의 – 공 의 –

124 Unending Love
(변함없는 사랑)

Jill Mccloghry & Sam Knock

There's no sil - ver or gold, and no trea - sure un-toid that could draw
of my pride I lay down my de-sires just to wor-
부 귀 와 -영 화 도 그 어 떤 -비 밀 도 주 와 날
-버 리 고 욕 심 도 -버 리 고 영 과 진

me a-way fromYour heart. Nei-ther love of my-self or of a-
- ship in Spi - rit and truth. More than all of my dreams, more than fame,
-멀 게 하 -진 못 해 -세 상 그 -누 구 도 주 와 날
-리 로 경 -배 하 리 -꿈 과 명 -성 보 다 더 값 진

- - ny - one else will do.
I will seek You, Lord
-끊 지 못 -하 네 -
-주 님 찾 -으 리 -

Je - sus no-thing com-pares to thisgrace that res-cues me.
예 수 -날 구 하 신 -은 혜 비 -할 데 -없 네 -

Sa - viour, now and for - ev - er Your face is all I seek.
구 주 -영 원 히 주 -님 만 을 -나 찾 -으 리 -

Now all I am, I lay at Your feet.
나 의 전 부 주 께 드 리 리

I'm hum-bled by the won-der of Your maj - es-ty One thing I know
- 나 겸 손 히 주 위 엄 앞 에 경 -배 해 나 는 아 네

Unending Love

Words and Music by Jill Mccloghry, Sam Knock
© 2011 Hillsong Music Publishing Australia (admin in Korea by Universal Music Publishing/ CAIOS)

125 We Bring The Sacrifice Of Praise
(찬양의 제사 드리며)

Kirk Carroll Dearman

We Bring The Sacrifice Of Praise

of - fer up to You   the sac - ri - fic - es of thanks - giv - ing and we
모 두 주 님 께 — 감 사 의 제 사 를 드 리 세 우 리

of - fer up to You   the sac - ri - fic - es of joy
모 두 주 님 께 — 기 쁨 의 제 사 드 리 네

O.T. : We Bring The Sacrifice Of Praise / O.W. : Kirk Carroll Dearman
O.P. : Universal Music – Brentwood Benson Publ, / S.P. : Universal Music Publishing Korea, CAIOS
Adm. : Capitol CMG Publishing / All rights reserved, Used by permission,

126 With All I Am

(전심으로)

Reuben Morgan

In - to Your hands　　I com-mit a-gain　　all I am
I'll walk with You　　wher-e - ver You　　go through tears and joy,
주 님 손 에 - - 맡 겨 드 - 리 리 - 나 의 - 삶
주 와 함 께 - - 걸 어 가 리 라 - - 모 든 길 을

for You, Lord.　　You hold my world　　in the palm of Your hand.
I'll trust in You.　　And I will live　　in all of Your ways.
- 주 님 께 - - 주 님 손 이 - - 나 의 삶 붙 드 네
- 주 신 리 해 주 뜻 안 에 - - 나 살 아 가 리

And I am Yours　　for - e - ver.
And Your Pro - mi - ses　　for - e - ver.
- 나 주 의 - 것 - 영 원 히 - -
- 주 의 약 속 - 은 - 영 원 해 - -

Je-sus, I be-lieve　　in you Je-sus, I be-long　　to you
내 가 믿 - 는 분 - 예 수 - 내 가 속 - 한 분 - 예 수

you're the rea-son that I live,　　the rea-son that I sing　　with all I
- 삶 의 이 유 되 - 시 네 - - 내 노 래 되 - 시 네 - - 전 심 - 으 -

am.　　Je-sus, I be-lieve　　with all I
로 - - 내 가 믿 - 는 분 - - 전 심 - 으 -

With All I Am

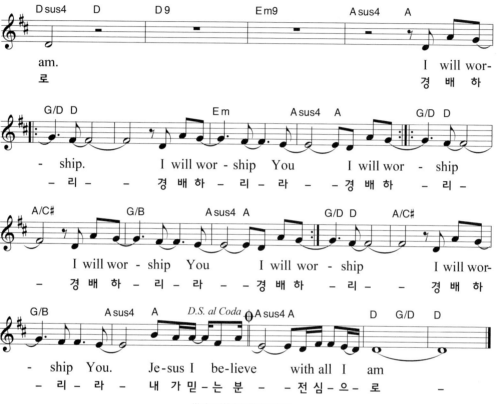

D sus4   D   D 9   E m9   A sus4   A

am.   I will wor-
로   경 배 하

G/D D   E m   A sus4 A   G/D D

- ship.   I will wor - ship You   I will wor - ship
– 리 –   경 배 하 – 리 라 –   경 배 하 – 리 –

A/C#   G/B   A sus4 A   G/D D   A/C#

I will wor - ship You   I will wor - ship   I will wor-
– 경 배 하 – 리 – 라 –   경 배 하 – 리 –   경 배 하

G/B   A sus4 A   *D.S. al Coda* A sus4 A   D G/D D

- ship You.   Je-sus I be-lieve   with all I am
– 리 – 라 –   내 가 믿 – 는 분 –   – 전 심 – 으 – 로   –

Words and Music by Reuben Morgan
© 2003 Hillsong Music Publishing Australia (admin in Korea by Universal Music Publishing/ CAIOS)

D

127 Again I Say Rejoice

(주님 안에서 기뻐하라)

Aaron Lindsey & Israel Houghton

Come bless the Lord, come bless the Lord, draw near to wor-
다 나 와 서 주 송 축 해 주 께 나 아

-ship Christ - - - the Lord and bless His name, His ho - ly name,
와 경 - - - 배 해 거 룩 하 신 주 의 이 름

de - clar - ing He is good. - - - is good. - - -
선 하 심 선 포 해 - - - 포 해 - - -

O that men would praise Him, O that men would praise
주 님 찬 양 하 리 - 주 님 찬 양 하

Him. Re - joice in the Lord - - al - ways, and a - gain
리 항 상 기 뻐 하 - 여 - 라 주 님 안

I say, and again I say, Re - joice in the Lord - - al-
에 서 - 기 뻐 하 라 - 항 상 기 뻐 하 - 여

- - - ways, and a - gain I say, and again I say, Re - joice
라 주 님 안 에 서 항 상 기 뻐 하 라

O that men would praise His - name, praise His - name to the ends
찬 양 하 리 주 이 름 땅 끝 까 지 주 이

Again I Say Rejoice

E

128 At The Cross

(십자가 보혈 앞에)

Reuben Morgan & Darlene Zschech

O Lord, You've searched me, You know my way.
You ho-ly pres-ence sur-round-ing me
You go be-fore me, You shield my way.
And when the earth fades, falls from my eyes,

날 찾 – 으 신 – 주 – 날 인 – 도 해 –
주 님 – 의 임 – 재 – 날 감 – 싸 며 –
주 앞 – 서 가 – 며 – 지 키 – 시 네 –
세 상 – 모 든 – 것 – 사 라 – 질 때 –

E-ven when I fail You, I know You love me.
in ev-'ry sea - son, I know You love me.
Your hand up-holds me I know You love me.
and You stand be-fore me, I know You love me.

내 연 약 – 함 까 – 지 – 사 랑 – 하 시 네 –
늘 한 – 결 같 – 이 – 사 랑 – 하 시 네 –
날 붙 – 드 신 – 주 – 사 랑 – 하 시 네 –
주 내 앞 – 에 계 – 셔 – 사 랑 – 하 시 네 –

I know You love me. At the cross I bow my

사 랑 – 하 시 네 – 십 자 가 보 혈 앞

knee, where Your blood was shed for me. There's no great-er love than

에 무 릎 꿇 어 경 배 해 더 큰 사 랑 은 없

this. You have o-ver-come the grave,

– 네 – 무 덤 이 기 신 주 님

At The Cross

Your glo - ry fills the high - est place. What can sep - a - rate me
주 영 광 하늘 가 득 해 끊 을 수 없 는 사

now? You tore the veil, You made a way
- 랑 휘 장 찢 고 - 길 되 셨 네

when You said that, "It is done." You tore the veil,
- 다 이 뤘 - 다 하 - 실 때 - 휘 장 찢 고

You made a way when You said that, "It is done."
- 길 되 셨 네 - 다 이 뤘 - 다 하 - 실 때

You tore the veil You made a way when You said
- 휘 장 찢 고 - 길 되 셨 네 - 다 이 뤘

that, "It is done."
- 다 하 - 실 때 -

Words and Music by Darlene Zschech, Reuben Morgan
© 2006 Hillsong Music Publishing Australia (admin in Korea by Universal Music Publishing/ CAIOS)

129 Awesome In This Place

(주의 위엄 이곳에)

David Billington

As I come in-to your pres - ence,
주 님 계 신 곳 – 에 나 – 가 – 리

past the gates of praise in-to your sanc - tu - ar-
찬 양 드 – 리 며 – 그 성 소 에 – 들 어

- y till we're stand-ing face to face; I
– 가 – – – 주 의 얼 굴 뵈 – 오 리 – 그

look up-on Your coun - tenance, I see the full-ness of Your grace,
얼 굴 을 뵈 올 – 때 주 님 의 은 혜 넘 – 치 네

and I can on - ly bow down and say.
– – – 엎 드 려 고 백 하 네 – – – – 주 께 –

You are awe - some in this place, might - y
주 의 위 엄 이 – 곳 에 – 가 득

God, You are awe - some in this place, Ab - ba
해 – 전 능 하 신 하 – 나 님 – 아 바

Awesome In This Place

Fa - ther, You are wor - thy of all praise,
아 버 - - 지 - 찬 양 받 기 합 - 당 한

to You our lives we raise, You are
- 존 귀 하 신 - 주 님 - 주 의

awe - some in this place, might - y God.
위 엄 이 - 곳 에 - 가 득 - 해 -

E

130 Better Is One Day

(주 장막이 어찌 그리 사랑스러운지)

Matt Redman

How love-ly is Your dwell-ing place, O Lord Al-migh-
주 장 막 이 어 찌 그 리 사 랑 스 러

-ty. — For My soul longs and e-ven faints for You
－운 지 내 영 혼 이 주 갈 망 합 니 다

For here my heart is sat-is-fied With-in — Your pre-
내 주 계 신 이 곳 에 서 내 영 － 만 족

-sence — I sing be-neath the sha-dow of Your
－해 － 주 날 개 밑 나 노 래 하 리

wings — — Bet-ter is one day in Your courts, bet-ter is
라 － － － 주 의 전(의) 하 루 가 내 겐 주 의 집(의)

one day in Your house, Bet-ter is one day in Your courts than thou-sands
하 루 가 내 겐 다 른 곳(의) 천 날 보 다 더 나 음

1. E/B   B   E/G#   2. Bsus4   B   E

else-where Bet-ter is else-where — One thing I ask and
이 라 － 주 의 전(의) 이 라 － 나 바 라 고 구

I would seek; to see Your beau-ty; — to
하 는 것 주 를 보 는 －것 － 주

Better Is One Day

find You in the place Your glo - ry dwells　Bet-ter is
영 광 이 가 득 하 신 이 곳　주 의전(의)

one day in Your courts, bet - ter is one day in Your house, bet-ter is
하 루 가 내 겐 주 의집(의) 하 루 가 내 겐 다 른 곳

one day in Your courts than thou - sands else-where　Bet - ter is
천 날 보 다 더 나 음 이 라　주 의 전(의)

else-where　–　else-where　–　–
이 라 –　이 라 –　–

Fine

My heart and flesh cry out　for You, the liv - ing God –
내 맘 이 외 치 네　살 아 계 신 주 께 –

Your Spi - rits wa - ter to my soul　I've tas - ted and I've seen,
주 성 령부 어 주 시 네　나 주 를 느 끼 네

come once a - gain to me –　I will draw near to You
주 다 시 오 소 서 –　주 께 더 가 까 이

I will draw near to You –　Bet - er is
주 께 더 가 까 이 –　주 의전(의)

D.S. al Coda

O.T. : Better Is One Day / O.W. : Matt Redman
O.P. : Thankyou Music Ltd / S.P. : Universal Music Publishing Korea, CAIOS
Adm. : Capitol CMG Publishing / All rights reserved. Used by permission.

131 Come Bless The Lord
(찬송하라 여호와의 종들아)

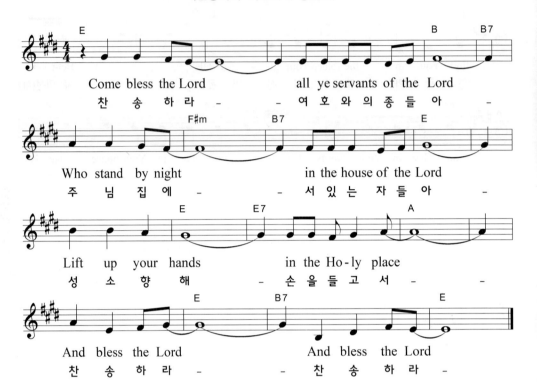

Come bless the Lord   all ye servants of the Lord
찬 송 하 라 -   - 여 호 와 의 종 들 아 -

Who stand by night   in the house of the Lord
주 님 집 에 -   - 서 있 는 자 들 아 -

Lift up your hands   in the Ho-ly place
성 소 향 해   - 손 을 들 고 서 - -

And bless the Lord   And bless the Lord
찬 송 하 라 -   - 찬 송 하 라 -

132 God Is Good
(좋으신 하나님)

Graham Kendrick

God is so good   God is so good
좋 으 신 하 나 님   좋 으 신 하 나 님
우 리 의 기 도 를   응 답 해 주 시 는
한 없 는 축 복 을   우 리 게 주 시 는

God is so good He's so good to me.
참 좋 으 신 나 의 하 나 님

Deep Down

(Deep Down 딥다운)

Deep Deep Woo Deep down down Deep down in my heart   I love my Je - sus

Deep Deep Woo   Deep down down   Deep down in my heart

Do you love your   Je - sus   Deep down in your   heart

Yes, I   love my   Je - sus   deep down in my   heart

E

134 Day By Day
(날마다 숨쉬는 순간마다)

Carolina Sandell &
Oscar Ahnfelt (Arr. Brentwood Benson Music Publications)

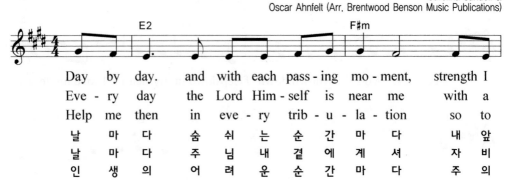

Day by day. and with each pass-ing mo-ment, strength I
Eve-ry day the Lord Him-self is near me with a
Help me then in eve-ry trib-u-la-tion so to

날 마 다 숨 쉬 는 순 간 마 다 내 앞
날 마 다 주 님 내 곁 에 계 셔 자 비
인 생 의 어 려 운 순 간 마 다 주 의

find to meet my tri-als here; Trust-ing in my Fa-ther's wise be-
spe-cial mer-cy for each hour. All my cares He fain would bear, and
trust Thy prom-is-es. O Lord, that I lose not faith's sweet con-so-

에 어 려 운 일 보 네 주 님 앞 에 이 몸 을 맡
로 날 감 싸 주 시 네 주 님 앞 에 이 몸 을 맡
약 속 생 각 해 보 네 내 맘 속 에 믿 음 잃 지

stow-ment, I've no cause, for wor-ry or for fear. He whose
cheer me. He whose name is Coun-sel-lor and power The pro-
la-tion. of-fered me with-in Thy ho-ly word. Help me,

길 때 슬 픔 없 네 두 려 움 없 네 주 님
길 때 힘 주 시 네 위 로 함 주 네 어 린
않 고 말 씀 속 에 위 로 를 얻 네 주 님

heart is kind be-yond all mea-sure Gives un-to each day what He deems
te-ction of His child and trea-sure is a charge that on Him-self He
Lord, when toil and trou-ble meet-ing. E'er to take as from a fa-ther's

의 그 자 비 로 운 손 길 항 상 좋 은 것 주 시 도
나 를 품 에 안 으 시 사 항 상 평 안 함 주 시 도
의 도 우 심 바 라 보 며 모 든 어 려 움 이 기 도

Day By Day

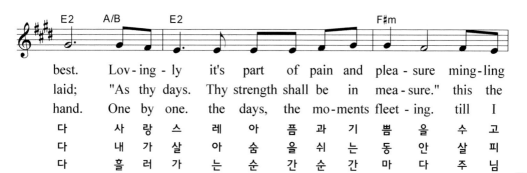

best.	Lov - ing - ly	it's	part	of	pain	and	plea - sure	ming - ling
laid;	"As thy days.	Thy	strength	shall	be	in	mea - sure."	this the
hand.	One by one.	the	days,	the	mo - ments	fleet - ing.	till	I

다	사	랑	스	레	아	픔	과	기	쁨	을	수	고
다	내	가	살	아	숨	을	쉬	는	동	안	살	피
다	흘	러	가	는	순	간	순	간	마	다	주	님

toil	with	peace	and	rest.
pledge	to	me	He	made.
reach	the	prom - ised	land.

와	평	화	와	안	식	을
신	다	약	속	하	셨	네
약	속	새	겨	봅	니	다

E

O.T. : Day By Day / O.W. : Carolina Sandell, Oscar Ahnfelt (Arr. Brentwood Benson Music Publications)
O.P. : Integrity Pd Arrangement / S.P. : Universal Music Publishing Korea, CAIOS
Adm. : Capitol CMG Publishing / All rights reserved. Used by permission.

135 For The Lord Is Good

(주님께 감사드리라)

Billy Funk

En-ter his gates with thanks-giv-ing come in-to His courts with
주 님 – 께 감 사 – 드 리 라 – 주 께 찬 – 양 드 리

praise En-ter His pre-sence re-joi-cing Sing-ing
라 기 쁨 – 으 로 주 – 께 나 와 – 주 의

gre-at and migh-ty is His name Prai-se Him with the sound of the
이 름 – 을 – 찬 양 하 – 라 나 팔 불 – 며 주 찬 – 양

trum – pet prai – se Him with the tim-brel and harp;
하 라 – 북 소 리 – 로 찬 양 – 하 라

Let ev – 'ry crea-ture in heav-en and earth lift a sound of praise sing with
모 든 – 만 물 소 리 높 여 – 찬 양 마 음 다 하 – 여 – 주 를

all their heart For the Lord is good For the Lord is good For the
찬 양 – 해 – 선 하 신 주 님 – (선 하 신 주 – 님 –) 선 하

Lord is good For the Lord is good For the Lord is good and His
신 주 – 님 – (선 하 신 주 – 님 –) 선 하 신 주 – 님 – 그 의

For The Lord Is Good

136 Friend Of God

(나는 주의 친구)

Michael Gungor & Israel Houghton

Who am I that You are mind-ful of me
주 님 어 - 찌 날 - 생 각 - 하 시 는 - 지 -

That You hear me - - - when I call
들 - 으 시 는 - 지 - 내 - 기 도 - -

Is it true that You are think-ing of me
주 님 진 - 실 로 - 날 생 - 각 하 시 - 네 -

How You love me it's a-maz-ing
날 - 사 랑 하 - 네 - 놀 라 워 - 라 - -

it's a-maz-ing!
놀 라 워 - 라 - -

I am a frie-nd of God   I am a frie-nd of God
나 는 주 의 - 친 - 구 -   나 는 주 의 - 친 - 구 -

I am a frie-nd of God He calls me friend
주 님 날 친 - 구 - 로 - 부 르 - 셨 - 네 -

Friend Of God

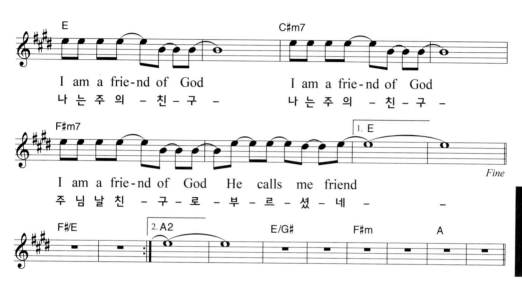

I am a frie-nd of God   I am a frie-nd of God
나 는 주 의 – 친 – 구 –   나 는 주 의 – 친 – 구 –

I am a frie-nd of God He calls me friend
주 님 날 친 – 구 – 로 – 부 – 르 – 셨 – 네 –   –

Fine

2. A2

God Al – migh – ty, Lord of Glo – ry You have
전   능   하   신   영   광   의   주   주   는

D.S. al Fine

called me friend
내   친   구 –   –   –   –

137 From The Dust Of The Earth My God Created Man

(흙으로 사람을)

Great And Mighty Is The Lord Our God   138

(위대하고 강하신 주님)

Mariene Bigley

Great and migh - ty is the Lord our God   Great and migh-ty is   He
위 대 하 – 고 강 하 신 주 님 –   우 리 주 하 나 님

Great and migh - ty is the Lord our God   Great and migh-ty is   He
위 대 하 – 고 강 하 신 주 님 –   우 리 주 하 나 님

Life up your ban-ner let the an-thems ring   prais - es to   our King
깃 발 을 높 이 들 고 흔 들 며 –   왕 께 찬 – 양 해

Great and migh - ty is the Lord our God Great and migh-ty is   He
위 대 하 – 고 강 하 신 주 님 –   우 리 주 하 나 님 – – –

Great and migh - ty is the Lord our God Great and migh - ty is   He
위 대 하 – 고 강 하 신 주 님 –   우 리 주 하 나 님

E

139

Great Is The Lord

(크신 주께 영광돌리세)

Robert Ewing

Great   is   the   Lord   great - ly   to   be   praised   In   the
크   신   주   께   영   광   돌   리   세   하   나

ci - ty   of   our   God   in   the   moun - tain   of   His   holi - ness
님   의   성   에   서   그   의   거룩   한   사   산   에   서

Beau - ti ful in el - e - va-tion   the   joy   of   the   whole earth
터   가   높고   아   름   다   와   온   세   상   의   기   쁨

is   mount   Zi - on   on   the   sides of the north the   city   of   the   great King
저   북   방   에   있   는   시   온   산   큰   왕   의   성   일   세

Sing   Hal - le - lu - jah   Sing   Hal - le - lu - jah
Sing   할   렐   루   야   Sing   할   렐   루   야

Sing   Hal - le - lu - jah   the   city   of   the great   King
Sing   할   렐   루   야   큰   왕   의   성   일   세

Healing Grace

(우리를 사랑하신)

140

John Chisum & Gary Sadler

Mer - ci - ful God and Fa - ther, lov - ing us like no oth - er,
우 리 를 사 랑 하 신 자 비 의 주 아 버 지

hear our prayer, the cry of our hearts as we come to you
주 께 로 – 나 아 갈 때 에 – 기 도 들 으 사

we ac - know - ledge our trans - gres - sions, we con - fess to you our sins,
우 리 죄 악 과 – 강 팍 – 함 – 주 님 께 고 백 – 하 니 –

show us mer - cy and com - pas - sion, touch our lives with your
우 릴 민 망 히 – 여 기 사 – 치 료 의 은 혜

heal - ing grace a - gain. Re - lease us from our past
허 락 하 소 서 주 얼 굴 구 – 할 때 –

As we seek Your face Wash us free at last
자 유 주 시 고 씻 어 주 소 서 –

We re - ceive Your love We re - ceive your heal - ing – grace
치 료 하 시 는 – 주 의 은 혜 임 – 하 – 네

We re - ceive Your love We re - ceive your heal - ing – grace.
치 료 하 시 는 – 주 의 은 혜 임 – 하 – 네 –

141 He Has Made Me Glad

(감사함으로 그 문에 들어가며)

Leona Von Brethorst

E / **A** / **E**

I will en - ter His gates with thanks - giv - ing in my heart, I will
감 사 함 으 로 그 문 에 들 어 가 – 며 그 의

E / **A** / **B7** / **E** / **A**

en - ter His courts with praise, – – I will say this is the day that the
궁 전 에 들 어 가 – – 주 께 감 사 드 리 며 그 –

E **G#/D#** **C#m** / **F#m** / **B7** / **E**

Lord has made, I will re - joice for He has made me glad.
이 름 – 을 송 축 – 할 – 지 – 어 – 다

E / **A** / **E**

He has made me glad, He has made me glad, I
주 님 의 기 쁨 내 게 임 하 네 나

A / **B7** / **E** **A** **E**

will re - joice for He has made me glad.
항 상 기 쁨 안 – 에 서 주 찬 양

E / **A** / **E** **G#/D#** / **C#m**

He has made me glad, He has made me glad I
주 님 의 기 쁨 내 게 임 하 네 나

F#m7 / **B7** / **E**

will re - joice for He has made me glad.
기 쁜 찬 송 주 께 드 리 네

He Is Our Peace

(주는 평화)

Kandela Groves

He is our peace who has bro-ken down ev-'ry wall.
주 는 평 화 막 힌 담 을 모 두 허 셨 네

He is our peace, He is our peace. peace.
주 는 평 화 우 리 의 평 화 화

Cast all Your cares on Him, For He cares for you.
염 려 다 맡 기 라 주 가 돌 보 시 니

He is our peace He is our peace. peace.
주 는 평 화 우 리 의 평 화 화 —

E

143 He Knows My Name

(내 이름 아시죠)

Tommy Walker

I have a Mak - - er,   He form - ed my heart.
I have a Fa - - ther,   He calls me His own.
나를 - 지으 신 주 님 -   내 안 - 에 계 셔 -
그 는 - 내 아 - 버 지 -   난 그 - 의 소 유 -

Be - fore e - ven time be - gan   my life was in   His hands.
He'll ne - ver leave me   no mat - ter where I go.
처 음 - 부 터 내 삶 은 -   그 의 손 에 - 있 었 죠 -
내 가 - 어 딜 가 든 지 -   날 떠 나 지 - - 않 죠 -

He knows my name.   He knows my ev - 'ry thought.
내 이 - 름 아 - 시 죠 -   내 모 - 든 생 - 각 도 -

He sees each tear that falls, and hears me when I call.
내 흐 - 르 는 - 눈 물 - 그 가 닦 아 - 주 셨 죠 -

Here am I

(나 여기 있으니)

144

Bob Kilpatrick

145 Here I Am Again

(내 마음을 가득 채운)

Tommy Walker

Here I Am Again

Lord I love You once a-gain re-ceive my praise
사 랑 해 요 찬 양 받 아 주 소 서 –

–

Help me find the words to say that
Thank You for a brand new day a
주 님 사 랑 다 시 고 백
주 님 사 랑 다 시 고 백

tell You in a brand new way I love – – You –
brand new chance to stand and say I love – – You –
하 는 새 날 주 심 감 사 해 – – 요 –
하 는 찬 양 주 심 감 사 해 – – 요 –

E

O.T. : Here I Am Again / O.W. : Tommy Walker
O.P. : Universal Music – Brentwood Benson Songs / S.P. : Universal Music Publishing Korea, CAIOS
Adm. : Capitol CMG Publishing / All rights reserved, Used by permission.

146 Here I Am To Worship
(빛 되신 주)

Tim Hughes

Light of the world, You stepped down in-to dark-ness, opened my eyes, let me see.
King of all days, oh so high-ly ex-alt - ed, glo-ri - ous in Hea'vn a - bove.
빛 되신 주 어둠 가운데 비추사 내 눈 보게 하소 서
만 유의 주 높임 을 받으소 서 영광 중에 계신 주

Beau - ty that made this heart a - dore You, hope of a life spent with You.
Hum - bly You came to the earth You crea - ted, all for love's sake be-came poor
예 배 하는 선한 마음 주시 고 산 소망 이 되시 네
겸 손 하게 이 땅 에 임하신 주 높여 찬 양 하리 라

(so) Here I am to wor-ship, here I am to bow down, here I am to
나 주를 경배 하리 엎 드려 절 하 며 고 백해 주

say that You're my God. And You're al-to-ge-ther love - ly al-to-ge-ther
나 의 하 나 님 오 사 랑 스 런 주 님 존 귀 한 예

Fine

wor - thy, al-to-ge-ther won-der-ful to me And I'll ne-
수 님 아름 답고 놀 라 우신 주 다 알 수

- ver know how much it cost to see my sin u-pon
- 없 네 - 주 의 - 은 혜 - 내 죄 - 위 한 - 주 십

1. A   2. A   *D.S. al Fine*

that cross. And I'll ne - that cross.   (so) Here I am to
- 자 가 - 다 알 수 - 자 가 -   나 주를 경배

Holy Ground
(거룩한 땅에)

Christopher Beatty

147

E

This is ho-ly ground We're stan-ding on ho-ly ground
These are ho-ly hands He's gi-ven us ho-ly hands
거 룩 한 땅 에 – 우 리 여 기 에 서 있 네 –
거 룩 한 손 을 – 우 리 에 게 주 셨 네 –

for the Lord is pre-sent And where He is ho - ly
He works through these hands And so these hands are ho - ly
주 님 계 신 이 곳 곧 거 룩 한 땅 이 – 라 –
우 리 손 으 로 – 주 의 일 이 루 시 – 네 –

This is ho-ly ground We're stan-ding on ho - ly ground
These are ho-ly hands He's gi-ven us ho - ly hands
거 룩 한 땅 에 – 우 리 여 기 에 서 있 네 –
거 룩 한 손 을 – 우 리 에 게 주 셨 네 –

For the Lord is pre-sent And where He is ho - ly
He works through these hands And so these hands are ho - ly
주 님 계 신 이 곳 곧 거 룩 한 땅 이 – 라 –
우 리 손 으 로 – 주 의 일 이 루 시 – 네 –

148 Hosanna

(호산나)

Brooke Ligertwood

1. I see the King of glo-ry, co-ming on the clouds with fire.
2. I see His love and mer-cy, wa-shing o-ver all our sin.
   난 보네 영광-의 -왕- 구름 타고 오 시 네
   난 보네 사랑의 -주- 우 리 죄 를 씻 기 네

The whole earth shakes, the whole earth shakes.
The peo-ple sing, the peo-ple sing.
- 주위 엄-에- 모두 떠네 - - - - - - -
- 노 래 하 고 - 찬 양 하 네

Ho-san - na, Ho-san - na, Ho-san-na in the high-est.
- 호산 - 나 호산 - - 나 - 호 산 나 높은 곳 에

Ho-san - na, Ho-san - na. Ho-san-na in the high - est.
호산 - 나 호산 - - - 나 호 산 나 높은 곳 에 -

3. I see a ge-ne-ra-tion, ri-sing up to take their place,
4. I see a near re-vi-val. Stir-ring as we pray and seek.
   난 보네 이 세-대-가- 주 위 해 일 어 나 -네
   난 보네 큰 부-흥-이- 기 도 로 일 어 나 -네

with self-less faith. with self-less faith. we're on our kness.
We're on our kness,
- 믿 음 으-로 - 믿음 으-로 - - - 무 릎 으 -로
- 무 릎 으 -로

Ho-san - na, Ho-san - na. Ho-sna-na in the high-est. Ho-san-
- 호산 - 나 호산 - - - 나- 호 산 나 높은 곳 에 호산

Hosanna

- na, Ho-san - na. Ho-san-na in the high-est.
– 나 호산 – – –나 호 산 나 높은 곳 에 –

Heal my heart and make it   clean.   O - pen up my eyes to the
Break my heart for what breaks Yours.   Ev - ery-thing I am, for Your
나 의 맘을 깨 끗 – 게 –   나 의 눈 열 어 보 게
주 의 아 픔 느 끼 – 며 –   주 나 라 위 해 모 두

things un - seen. Show me how to love like You   have loved me.
King-dom's cause. As I walk from earth in - to
하 소 – 서 –   주 사 랑 으 로 살 – 게 – 하 소 서 –
드 리 리 –   이 땅 에 서 영 원 – 한

e - ter-ni-ty.   Ho-san - na, Ho-san-
– 그 곳 까 지 –   호 산 – 나 호 산

- na.   Ho-san-na in the high-est.   Ho-san - na, Ho-san - na. Ho-
– – –나– 호 산 나 높은 곳 에   호 산 – 나 호 산 – – –나 호

san-na in the high - est.   Ho-san - san-na in the high - est.   Ho-
산 나 높은 곳 에 –   호 산 산 나 높은 곳 에 – 호

san-na in the high - est.
산 나 높은 곳 에 –

149 Holy Spirit Fire

(성령의 불로)

Scott Brenner

Humble King

(겸손의 왕)

150

Brenton Brown

Oh kneel me down a-gain here at Your feet
주 발 앞 에 무 릎 꿇 게 하 사

show me how much You love hu - mi - li - ty
주 님 의 겸 손 함 보 이 소 서

Oh spi - rit be the star that leads me to
성 령 이 여 나 를 이 - 끄 소 - 서

the hum-ble heart of love I see in You
겸 손 한 사 랑 - 의 마 음 으 로 -

You are the God of the bro - ken the friend of the weak
상 - 한 자 - 의 - 하 나 - 님 약 한 자 의 - 친 구 - -

You wash the feet of the wea - ry em-brace the ones in need
가 난 한 자 - 안 - 으 시 - 며 발 을 씻 기 - 시 네 - -

I want to be like You Je - sus to have this heart in me
주 님 나 를 - 빚 - 으 시 - 사 주 닮 게 하 - 소 서 - -

You are the God of the hum - ble You are the hum-ble king
겸 손 한 자 - 의 - 하 나 - - - - 님 주 는 - 겸 손 - 의 왕 -

You are the God of the hum - ble You are the hum-ble king
겸 손 한 자 - 의 - 하 나 - - - - 님 주 는 - 겸 손 - 의 왕 -

E

151 I Could Sing Of Your Love Forever

(나를 향한 주의 사랑)

Martin Smith

O - ver the moun - tains and the sea Your ri-ver runs with love for me.
나 를 향 한 – 주 의 – 사 랑 산 과 바 다 – 에 넘 – 치 니

and I will o - pen up my heart and let the Heal - er set me free
내 마 음 열 때 주 님 나 에 게 참 자 유 주 – 셨 네

I'm hap - py to be in the truth and I will dai - ly lift my hands,
늘 진 리 속 – 에 거 – 하 며 나 의 손 을 – 높 이 – 들 고

for I will al - ways sing of when Your love came down yeah
언 제 나 주 님 의 사 랑 을 노 래 하 리 –

3rd time to ⬤

I could sing of Your love for - e - ver I could sing of Your love
주 의 사 랑 노 래 – 하 – 리 – 라 – 영 원 토 록 노 래

for - e - ver I could sing of Your love for - e - ver
– 하 – 리 – 라 – 주 의 사 랑 노 래 – 하 – 리 – 라 –

1. A B sus4 B7 2. A
I could sing of Your love for - e - ver I could sing of Your love
영 원 토 록 노 래 – 하 – 리 라 – 영 원 토 록 노 래

for - e - ver Oh, I feel like danc-ing
– 하 – 리 – 라 – 내 가 춤 – 을 출 때

I Could Sing Of Your Love Forever

it's fool-ish-ness, I know but when the world has
다 비 웃 겠 - 지 - - 그 들 도 주 - 알

seen the light they will dance with joy like we're dan - cing now
게 되 면 함께 기 - 뻐 - 춤 - 을 추 게 - 되 리 -

D.S.

I could sing of Your love for - e - ver
영 원 토 록 노 래 - 하 - 리 라 - -

E

152

I Lift My Hands

(두 손 들고 찬양합니다)

Andre Kempen

I lift my hands to the com-ing King to the Great I Am to
두 손 들 고 찬 양 합 니 다 다 시 오 실 왕 여

You I sing for You are One who reigns wi-thin my heart
호 와 께 오 직 주 만 이 나 를 다 스 리 네

and I will serve no for-eign God or any-other trea-sure
나 주 님 만 을 섬 기 리 헛 된 마 음 버 리 고

You are my heart's de - sire Spi-rit with-out mea-sure
성 령 이 여 내 영 혼 충 만 하 게 하 소 서

Un - to Your name I will raise my sa-cri-fice
주 님 앞 에 내 생 명 드 리 리 라

I Love You Lord
(사랑해요)

Laurie B. Klein

153

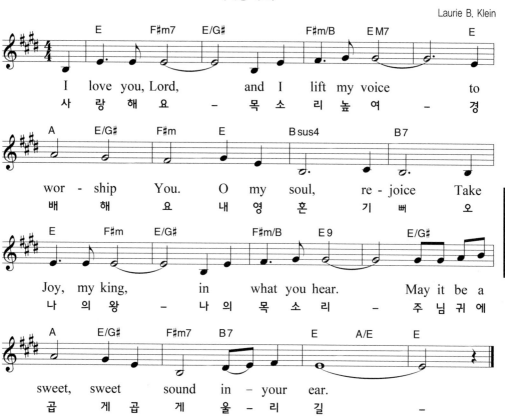

E   **F#m7**   **E/G#**   **F#m/B**   **E M7**   **E**

I love you, Lord,   and I lift my voice   to
사 랑 해 요   –   목 소 리 높 여   –   경

A   **E/G#**   **F#m**   **E**   **B sus4**   **B7**

wor - ship You. O my soul, re - joice Take
배 해 요 내 영 혼 기 뻐 오

E   **F#m**   **E/G#**   **F#m/B**   **E 9**   **E/G#**

Joy, my king,   in what you hear.   May it be a
나 의 왕   –   나 의 목 소 리   –   주 님 귀 에

A   **E/G#**   **F#m7**   **B7**   **E**   **A/E**   **E**

sweet, sweet sound in - your ear.
곱 게 곱 게 울 – 리 길   –

E

154 Is Anyone Thirsty?

(목마른 자들아)

Graham Kendrick

I Will Bow To You

(주 앞에 엎드려)

155

Pete Episcopo

Lord, I will bow to You, to on o - ther God but You a - lone;
주 앞에엎 – 드 려 경배합 – 니 다 – 오 직 – 주 께 –

Lord, I will wor-ship you, noth-ing hands have made, but You a - lone.
주 경배합 – 니다 – – 다 른신 – 아 닌 – 오 직 – –주께 –

I will lay down my i - dols, and thrones I have made,
나 의모 – 든 – 우 상 – 들 – 나 의 – 보 좌 –

all that has take - n my heart; Lord, I will bow to You,
모 두 다 내 – 려 – 놓고 – 주 앞 에엎 – 드 려

to no o - ther God but You a - lone.
경 배 합 – 니 다 – 오 직 – 주 께

156 I'm Accepted I'm Forgiven

(나는 용서받았네)

Rob Hayward

I'm ac-cep-ted, I'm for-gi-ven I am fa-thered by the true and liv-ing God.
나 는 용 - 서 받 - 았 - 네 살 아 계 신 아 버 지 - 사 랑 으 로

I'm ac-cep-ted no con-dem-na-tion, I am
- 용 납 되 - 고 정 죄 함 없 - 네 진 실

loved by the true and liv-ing God. There's no guilt of fear as
하 신 아 버 지 사 랑 으 로 온 세 상 구 주 창

I draw near to the Sa-viour and Cre-a-tor of the world. There is
조 주 께 나 아 갈 때 두 려 움 전 혀 없 네 주 께

joy and peace as I re-lease my wor-ship to You, O Lord.
예 배 드 릴 때 - 에 기 쁨 과 평 화 - 있 네

Just Let Me Say

(주를 향한 나의 사랑을)

157

L Geoff Bullock

E

Just let me say how much I love you let me speak of your mer-cy and grace
Just let me hear Your fine-st whis-per as You gent-ly call my name
Let me say how much I love You with all my heart I long for You

주 를 향 한 나 의 사 랑 을 주 께 고 백 하 게 하 소 서
부 드 러 운 주 의 속 삭 임 나 의 이 름 을 부 르 시 네
온 맘 으 로 주 를 바 라 며 나 의 사 랑 고 백 하 리 라

Just let me live in the sha-dow of Your beau-ty let me see You face to face
And let me sdd you-r pow-er and Your glo-ry let me feel Your spi-rit's flame
For I am caught in this pass-ion of know-ing, this endless love I've found in You.

아 름 다 운 주 의 그 늘 아 래 살 며 주 를 보 게 하 소 서
주 의 능 력 주 의 영 광 을 보 이 사 성 령 을 부 으 소 서
나 를 향 한 주 님 의 그 크 신 사 랑 간 절 히 알 기 원 해

And the earth will shake as Your word goes forth and the heavens can tremble and fall.
Let me find You in the des-ert til this end is ho-ly ground
And the depth of grace, the for-give-ness found to be called a child of God

주 님 의 말 씀 선 포 될 때 에 땅 과 하 늘 진 동 하 리 니
메 마 른 곳 거 룩 해 지 도 록 내 가 주 를 찾 게 하 소 서
주 의 은 혜 로 용 서 하 시 고 나 를 자 녀 삼 아 주 셨 네

But let me say how much I love You, O my Sa-vior, my Lord and friend.
And I am found com-pletely su-rren-dered, to You mu Lord and friend.
Just makes me say how much I love You, O my sa-viour my Lord and friend.

나 의 사 랑 고 백 하 리 라 나 의 구 주 나 의 친 구
내 모 든 것 주 께 드 리 리 나 의 구 주 나 의 친 구
나 의 사 랑 고 백 하 리 라 나 의 구 주 나 의 친 구

158 Knocking On The Door Of Heaven

(우린 쉬지 않으리)

Steve Cantellow & Matt Redman

We will give our-selves no rest   'til your king-dom comes on earth;
우린 쉬지 않-으리-   천국 임할 때-까지-

We've po-si-tioned watch men on the walls.
우리는 성 벽-의 파-수 꾼-

Now our prayers will flow   like tears,   for You've shared Your heart
주가 주신 맘-으로-   무릎 꿇고 엎

with us;   God of hea-ven, on   our knees we fall.
-드 려-   하 늘의 주-께-기 도-하 리-

Come down   in pow-er   re-veal Your heart a-gain;   come
주 의-   능 력-   곧 나 타 내 소-서   흐

hear-   our cries,-   the tears that plead for- rain.-   We're
르는   눈 물의   기 도 들 으 소-서-   우린

knock-ing,   knock-ing on the door — of hea - ven; we - 're
watch-ing,   watch-ing on the walls — to   see   you; we - 're
두 드   리 리 천 국 문-을 향 - 해 우 린
보 게   되 리 주 님 의-얼 굴-을 우 린

Knocking On The Door Of Heaven

C#m7

cry - ing,   cry - ing for this   ge - ne - ra - tion;   we're
look - ing,   look - ing for a   time — of break through; we're
간 구   하 리 이 세 대 — 를 위 — 해   주
기 다   리 리 주 님 오 — 실 그 — 날   주

F#m7   A2

pray - ing for Your name to be known   in all of the
pray - ing for Your word to bear fruit
님 의 이 — 름 선 — 포 되 — 리   온 세 계 — 위
님 의 말 — 씀 이 — 뤄 지 — 리

1. B   2. B   E

earth.—   We're earth,— in all of the earth.
에 —   우린 에 — 온 세 계 — 위 에

O.T. : Knocking On The Door Of Heaven / O.W. : Matt Redman, Steve Cantellow
O.P. : Thankyou Music Ltd / S.P. : Universal Music Publishing Korea, CAIOS
Adm. : Capitol CMG Publishing / All rights reserved, Used by permission,

E

159 Let Everything That Has Breath
(호흡 있는 모든 만물)

Matt Redman

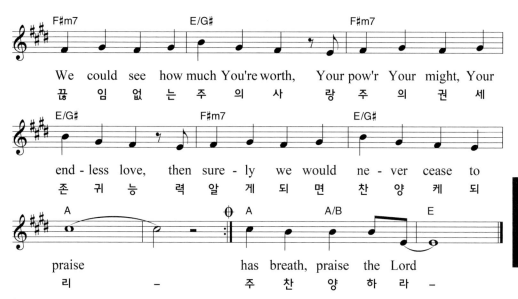

We could see how much You're worth, Your pow'r Your might, Your
끊 임 없 는 주 의 사 랑 주 의 권 세

end - less love, then sure - ly we would ne - ver cease to
존 귀 능 력 알 게 되 면 찬 양 케 되

praise has breath, praise the Lord
리 – 주 찬 양 하 라 –

E

Jesus Name Above All Names 160
(예수 귀하신 이름)

Naida Hearn

Je-sus name a-bove all names, beau-ti-ful Sav-ior, glo-ri-ous Lord
예 수 – 귀 하 신 이 름 – 아 름 다 운 – 영 광 의 주 – – –

Em-memu-el, God is with us, Bless-ed Re-deem-er, liv-ing Word.
임 마 누 엘 – 함 께 하 시 는 – 은 혜 의 구 주 – 말 씀 이 라 –

161 Let The Praises Ring

(주님 찬양해)

Lincoln Brewster

O Lord my God, in You I put my trust O Lord
my God, to You I give my hands O Lord
오 주 안 에 – 내 믿 음 이 – 있 네 – 오

my God, in You I put my hope O Lord
my God, to You I give my feet
주 안 에 – 내 소 망 이 – 있 네 – 오

In You, in You I find my peace In You,
주 안 – 에 평 – 화 찾 았 네 – 주 안

in You, I find my strength In You
– 에 내 – 힘 찾 았 네 – 주 안

I live and move and breathe Let
– 에 살 – 고 숨 쉬 네 – 내

ev-'ry-thing I say and do be found-ed by my faith in You I
모 든 말 – 과 행 – 동 이 주 님 의 뜻 – 을 따 – 르 니 내

lift up ho – ly hands and sing, let the prais-es ring.
거 룩 한 – 손 들 고 – 서 주 님 찬 양 – 해

Let The River Flow

(가난한 자 부요케 하소서)

Darrell Evans

162

Let the poor man say, 'I am rich in Him', let the lost man say, 'I am
가 난 한 자 부요케 하소서 - - 잃어버린 자 회복

found in Him.' let the ri-ver flow; Let the
하 소 서 - - 생 수 의 강 물 로 - - 눈 먼

blind man say, 'I can see a-gain,' let the dead man say, 'I am born a-gain.'
자 다 시 보 게 하 소 서 - - 죽 은 자 거 듭 나 게 하 소 서 - -

let the ri-ver flows, let the ri-ver flow
생 수 의 강 물 을 - - 넘 쳐 주 소 서 - -

Let the ri-ver flow, let the ri-ver flow
생 수 의 강 물 - - 넘 치 게 하 사 -

Ho - ly spi-rit come, move in pow-er.
성 령 의 능 력 - - 임 하 소 서 -

pow-er. Let the ri-ver flow, let the
소 서 - 생 수 의 강 물 - - - 생 수

ri-ver flow let the ri-ver flow
의 강 물 - - - 생 수 의 강 물 - -

163 Let Us Rejoice And Be Glad

(우리 함께 기뻐해)

Gerrit Hansen

Let us re-joice and be glad, giv-ing the glo-ry to
우리 함께 – 기 뻐 – 해   주 께 영 광 – 돌 리 –

Him;   For the mar-riage of the Lamb has come and His
세   어 린 양 의 혼 – 인 잔 – – 치 와 – 신 부

bride has made her-self ready   Hal-le-lu-jah, for the
가 준 비 – 되 었 네 – –   할 렐 루 야 전 능

Lord our God the Al-might-y reigns;   Ha-le-lu-jah, for the
하 신 주 – 가 다 스 리 네   할 렐 루 야 전 능

Lord our God, the Al-might-y reigns;
하 신 주 – 가 다 스 리 – 네

Mighty Warrior

(강한 용사 무장하신)

164

Debbye Graafsma

Might-y war-ri-or, dressed for bat - tle Ho-ly Lord of all is
강 한 용 - 사 무 장 하 신 거 룩 한 만 군 의

He. Com-man - der in chief bring us to at-ten - tion,
주 대 장 되 신 주 우 리 들 을 모 아

lead us in - to bat - tle to crush the en - e - my.
출 정 케 하 시 네 원 수 무 찌 - 르 려 -

Sa - tan has no au - thor - i - ty here in this place. He
Je - sus has all au - thor - i - ty here in this place. He
이 젠 원 수 는 힘 없 네 이 곳 에 서 아
이 젠 주 님 만 힘 있 네 이 곳 에 서 모

has no au - thor - i - ty here. For this hab - i - ta - tion was
has all au - thor - i - ty here. For this hab - i - ta - tion was
무 힘 과 권 세 없 네 여 긴 주 님 께 서 계
든 힘 과 권 세 있 네 여 긴 주 님 께 서 계

fash-ioned for the Lord's pres-ence. No au - thor - i - ty here!
fash-ioned for the Lord's pres-ence. All au - thor - i - ty here!
시 는 곳 이 니 이 젠 아 무 권 세 없 네
시 는 곳 이 니 이 젠 모 든 권 세 있 네

E

165 More Precious Than Silver

(은보다 더 귀하신 주)

Lynn DeShaz

Lord, You are more pre-cious than sil - ver
은 보 다 더 귀 하 신 주

Lord, You are more cost - ly than gold.
금 보 다 더 귀 하 신 주

Lord You are more beau - ti - ful than dia - monds
금 강 석 보 다 더 아 - 름 다 운

and noth-ing I de - sire com-pares with You.
내 주 님 같 은 분 더 없 도 다

My Redeemer Lives

(내 영혼 구하시고)

166

Reuben Morgan

E

I know he res-cued my soul   His blood has
My shame he's ta-ken a-way   My pain is
내 영혼 구하시고 -   보혈로
내 수 치 걷으시고 -   아픔을

co-vered my sin I be-lieve   I be-lieve
healed in his name
덮으셨네 난믿네 -   난믿네 -
고치셨네 난믿네 -   난믿네 -

I'll raise a ban-ner 'cause my Lord has con-quered the grave my Re-
난 깃발들 -리   죽음을 이기신주 - 나의

deem - er lives   my Re-deem - er lives   my Re-
구 세 주 -   살아계시네 -   나의

deem - er lives   my Re-deem - er lives
구 속 자 -   살아계시네 -

You lift my bur - dens   I'll rise with you   I
주 께서 내 -짐 -   벗기셨네 -   주

dan-cing on this moun-tain top   to see your king-dom come
님의 나라임 -했네   난 춤을 추 -리 라 -

My Re
나 의   -   -

Words and Music by Reuben Morgan © 1998 Hillsong Music Publishing Australia (admin in Korea by Universal Music Publishing / CAIOS)

167 Now That You're Near

(나 주 앞에 서서)

Marty Sampson

I stand be-fore You, Lord   And give. You all my praise
My life be-longs to You   You gave Your life for me
나 주 앞 에 서 서   찬 양 을 드 리 네
내 삶 주 께 있 네   주 생 명 주 셨 네

Your love is all I need   Je - sus, You're all I need
Your grace is all I need   Je - sus, You're all I need
내 가 필 요 한 것   예 - 수 - 주 의 - 사 랑
내 가 필 요 한 것   예 - 수 - 주 의 - 은 혜

Hold me in Your arms   Ne-ver let me go   I want to spend e -
주 님 품 - 안 에 -   - 품 어 주 - 시 니 -   주 님 과 함 께

ter-ni-ty with You   And now   that You're near   Ev-ery-thing is
영 원 히 - 살 리 -   이 제   주 게 시 니   모 든 것 - 다

diff - erent Ev-ery-thing's so   diff-erent, Lord   I know   I'm not the same
변 해 모 든 것 - 다   변 하 네   이 제   달 라 진 - 나

Last time to Coda 1. A

My life You've changed   I want to be with You   I want to be with You
- 바 뀐 내 - 삶 -   나 주 님 과 - 함 께 -   있 기 를 원 - 하 네

2.,4. A   E   3. A

I want to be with You   And now You're   I want to be with You.
- 있 기 를 원 - 하 네 -   주 께 서 -   있 기 를 원 - 하 네

Now That You're Near

And I will sing for You al - ways
나 항 상 주 - 만 찬 - 양 해 -

'Cause in your pre - sence God is where I want to stay
주 님 계 - 신 -곳 에 - 나 있 - 기 원 - 하 네

I want to be with You.
있 기 를 원 - 하 네 -

Words and Music by Marty Sampson
© 2002 Hillsong Music Publishing (admin in Korea by Universal Music Publishing/ CAIOS)

E

168 One Desire
(나의 한 소망)

Joel Houston

You gave it all for me, my soul de-sire, my ev - ery-thing.
How could I fail to see You are the love that res-cued me.
모 든 것 주 - 신 - 주 - 나 의 영 혼 - 갈 망 - 하 네
날 구 원 하 - 신 - 분 - 주 님 은 사 - 랑 이 - 시 - 니

And all I am is de-vo-ted to You.
- 내 모 든 - 것 - 주 께 드 립 - 니 - 다 -

And oh, how could I not be moved, Lord here
- 내 영 - 주 님 곁 에 - 항 - 상 - 거 하

with You, so have Your way in me. 'cause Lord there is just
- 리 - 니 - 주 뜻 이 루 - 소 - 서 - - 주 님 나 의 모

on thing, and that I will seek. This is my cry,
- 든 - 것 - 난 찾 으 - 리 - 라 - - 외 치 리 라

my one de-si - re, just to be where You are Lord, now and for-e-
- 나 의 한 소 - 망 영 원 토 록 주 님 - 과 - 함 께 하 는

- ver. it's more than a song, my one de-si - re is to be with You,
- 것 난 외 치 리 라 - 나 의 한 소 - 망 영 원 히 - 주 와

One Desire

is to be with You, Je - sus. The
- 함께 하 - 는 것 - 주 - - 님 - - 나

one thing, the one thing I ask is to be with You.
오 직 - 나 오 직 - 주 - 와 - 함께하 - 리 라

The one thing, the one thing I ask is to be with You.
- 나 오 직 - 나 오 직 - 주 - 와 - 함께하 - 리 라

The is to be with You.
- 나 - 함께하 - 리 라 -

Words and Music by Joel Houston
© 2002 Hillsong Music Publishing Australia (admin in Korea by Universal Music Publishing/ CAIOS)

E

169 Once Again

(다시 한 번)

Matt Redman

Je-sus Christ, I think up-on Your sac-ri-fice; You be-came no-thing,
Now You are ex-al-ted to the high-est place. King of the hea-vens where
예 수 님 그 의 희 생 기 억 할 때 자 기 몸 버 려
이 제 는 저 높 은 곳 에 앉 으 신 하 늘 과 땅 의

poured out to death. Ma-ny times I've won-dered at Your gift of life, and
one day I'll bow. But for now, I mar-vel at this sav-ing grace, and
죽 으 신 주 나 항 상 생 명 주 신 그 은 혜 를 마
왕 되 신 주 나 이 제 놀 라 운 구 원 의 은 혜

I'm in that place once a-gain. I'm in that place once a-gain
I'm full of praise once a-gain. I'm full of praise once a-gain
음 에 새 겨 봅 니 다 마 음 에 새 겨 봅 니 다
높 여 찬 양 하 리 라 높 여 찬 양 하 리 라

Once a-gain I look up-on the cross where You died. I'm
주 달 리 신 십 자 가 를 내 가 볼 때 주

hum-bled by Your mer-cy and I'm bro-ken in-side. Once a-gain I thank You,
님 의 자 비 내 마 음 을 겸 손 케 해 주 께 감 사 하 며

Once a-gain I pour out my life Thank You for the cross.
내 생 명 주 께 드 리 네 감 사 드 리 리

Thank You for the cross. Thank You for the cross, my Friend. Friend.
주 의 십 자 가 나 의 친 구 되 신 주 주

Open Our Eyes

(내 눈을 떠서)

Robert M, Cull

170

O-pen our eyes, Lord;   we want to see Je - sus

내 눈을 떠 서   주 보게 하 시 고

내 맘을 다 해   사 랑케 하 시 고

주 님의 약 속   나 알게 하 시 고

to reach out and touch Him   and say that we love Him.

주 사 랑 한 다 고   말 하 게 하 소 서

주 사 랑 하 심 을   전 하 게 하 소 서

그 귀 하 신 언 약   이 루 게 하 소 서

O-pen our ears, Lord,   and help us to lis - ten.

내 귀를 열 어   날 사랑 한 다 는

내 정성 다 해   섬 기게 하 시 고

나 의 마음 을   다 스 려 주 시 고

O-pen our eyes, Lord;   we want to see Je - sus

주 님의 음 성   나 듣게 하 소 서

주 함께 하 심   나 알게 하 소 서

주 께 가 까 이   나 가게 하 소 서

171 Open The Eyes Of My Heart

(내 맘의 눈을 여소서)

Paul Baloche

O-pen the eyes of my heart Lord o-pen the eyes of my heart
내 맘 의 눈-을 여 소 서 내 맘 의 눈-을 열 어

I want to see You I want to see You
- 주 보 게 하 소 서 주 보 게 하 소 서

To see You high and lift - ed up shin-
주 이 름 높 이 들 - 리 고 -

- ing in the light of Your glo - ry Pour out Your pow'r and love
영 광 의 빛 비 춰 주 시 - 며 권 능 넘 치 길 보

As we sing Ho - ly, ho - ly, ho - ly
기 원 하 네 거 룩 거 - 룩 거 - 룩 -

Ho - ly, Ho - ly, Ho - ly, Ho - ly, Ho - ly, Ho - ly
거 룩 거 - 룩 거 - 룩 - 거 룩 거 - 룩 거 - 룩 -

Ho - ly, Ho - ly, Ho - ly, I want to see You.
거 룩 거 - 룩 거 - 룩 - 주 보 게 하 소 서 -

Praise Him On The Trumpet

172

(손을 높이 들고)

John Kennett

O.T. : Praise Him On The Trumpet / O.W. : John Kennett
O.P. : Thankyou Music Ltd / S.P. : Universal Music Publishing Korea, CAIOS
Adm. : Capitol CMG Publishing / All rights reserved. Used by permission.

173 Refiner's Fire

(나의 마음을)

Brian Doerksen

Pu - ri - fy　　my heart　　Let me be as gold　　　and
나 의 마 - 음 을 -　　정 금 과 같 이　　　정 결

pre - cious sil - ver pu - ri - fy　　my heart　　Let me be as gold
케 하 소 서 나 의 마 - 음 을 -　　정 금 과 같 이

pure　gold　Re - fi - ner's fire　　My hear-t's one de - sire　　is to
하 소 서　내 영 혼 에 -　　한 소 망 있 으 니 -　　주 님

be　ho - ly　　set - a - part for you　Lord　　I choose to be
과　같 - 이　거 룩 하 게　하 소 - 서 -　나 의 삶 을

ho - ly　　set a - part for you - - my mas - ter　Rea - dy to do Your will
드 리 니　거 룩 하 게 - 하 소 서 - - 오 주 - 님　나 를 받 으 - 소 서

Rea - dy to do　Your will
- 나 를 받 으 - 소 서 -

Saviour Of My Soul

(내 영혼의 구세주)

Kathryn Kublman

E

175

Salvation
(구원이 온 땅에 솟네)

Charlie Hall

Sal - va - tion, spring up   from   the ground,   Lord, rend the
구 원 이 온 땅 - 에 - 솟 네   하 늘 가

heav-ens and come down,   seek the lost   and   heal   the lame
르 고 - 온 - 예 - 수   갇 힌 영 - 혼 - 살 - 리 고

Je-sus, bring glo-ry to Your name.   Let all the pro-di-gals run home,
아 버 지 영광 - 보 - 였네   모 든 영 혼들 - 달 - 려 - 와

all   of cre - a-tion waits and groans.   Lord, we've heard
애 통 하 며 주 - 바 - 라 - 리   주 의 위

of Your great fame   Fa - ther, cause all to   shout Your name.
- 엄 - 들 - 을 - 때   만 물 이 주 께 - 외 - 치 리

Fine

Stir up our hearts,   oh   God
우 리 맘 흔 - 들 - 어 -

O - pen our spir - its to awe   who You are.
내 영 주 경 - 외 하 게 - 하 소 서 -

Salvation

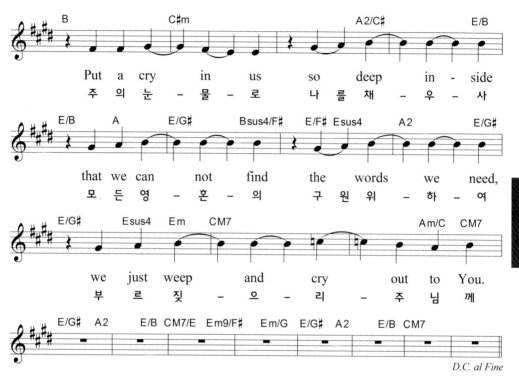

D.C. al Fine

O.T. : Salvation / O.W. : Charlie Hall
O.P. : worshiptogether.com Songs, sixsteps Music / S.P. : Universal Music Publishing Korea, CAIOS
Adm. : Capitol CMG Publishing / All rights reserved. Used by permission.

176 Sing Sing Sing
(모두 찬양해)

Chris Tomlin, Jesse Reeves, Matt Gilder &
Daniel Carson, Travis Nunn

What's not to love a - bout You? Heav - en and earth
You are the love that frees us. You are the light
사 랑 스 러 - 운 주 - 님 땅 과 하 늘
자 유 케 하 - 는 사 - 랑 타 오 르 는

a - dore You. Kings and king - doms bow down.
that leads us, like a fi - re burn - ing.
- 찬 양 - 해 열 - 방 이 - 경 배 - 해
- 불 처 - 럼 인 - 도 하 - 시 는 - 빛

Son of God, You are the One,
예 수 님 - 당 신 - 은 주 -

You are the One we're liv - ing for.
유 일 - 하 신 - 삶 의 - 이 유 -

You are the One
유 일 - - 하 신 -

we're liv - ing for. We will
삶 의 - 이 유 - - we will

sing, sing, sing, and make mus - ic with the heav - ens. We will
sing sing sing 천 국 에 - 울 리 - 는 노 - 래 we will

Sing Sing Sing

sing, sing, sing. Grate - ful that You hear us when we
sing sing sing 주 - 님 들 - 으 시 - 네 감 - 사

shout Your praise. Lift high the name of Je
드 리 며 - 예 수 이 름 - 높 이

- sus.
- 세 - -

O.T. : Sing Sing Sing / O.W. : Chris Tomlin, Daniel Carson, Jesse Reeves, Travis Nunn, Matt Gilder
O.P. : worshiptogether.com Songs, sixsteps Music, Vamos Publishing / S.P. : Universal Music Publishing Korea, CAIOS
Adm. : Capitol CMG Publishing / All rights reserved. Used by permission.

E

177 Still Standing

(일어서리)

Israel Houghton & Cindy Cruse-Ratcliff

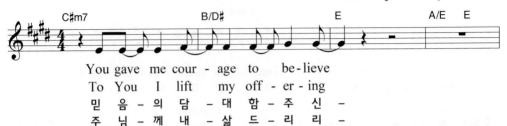

You gave me cour - age to be-lieve
To You I lift my off - er - ing
믿 음 - 의 담 - 대 함 - 주 신 -
주 님 - 께 내 - 삶 드 - 리 리 -

that all your good - ness I would see.
and set my heart on high - er things.
주 의 - 선 하 - 심 바 - 라 네
내 모 - 든 소 - 망 주 - 님 께

And if it had not been for You stand-ing on my side where would
언 제 - 나 곁 - 에 계 - 셔 서 - 나 - 를 인 - 도 하 - 여 주

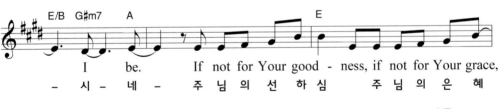

I be. If not for Your good - ness, if not for Your grace,
- 시 - 네 - 주 님 의 선 하 심 주 님 의 은 혜

I don't know where I would be to - day. If not for Your kind-
- 지 금 까 - 지 - 날 - 인 도 하 신 주 님 의 자 비

- ness, I nev - er could say I'm still stand - ing.
로 나 고 백 하 며 일 - 어 서 - - - 리 -

Still Standing

If not for Your mer - cy, if not for Your love, I most like-
주 님 의 은 혜 와 주 님 의 사 랑 – 나 는 포

- ly would have giv - en up. If not for Your fav - or I nev-er could say
– 기 – 하 – 지 않 으 리 주 님 의 자 비 로 나 고백하 며

I'm still stand - ing, but by the grace of God.
– 일 – 어 서 – – – 리 – 주 님 의 은 – 혜 – 로

E

178 The Father's Song
(아버지의 노래)

Matt Redman

I have heard so man-y songs,
수많은 노래들 중

lis-tened to a
가 장 뛰 어

thou-sand tongues but there is one
난 노 래 나 를 향 한

that sounds a-bove them all;
아 버 지 의 노 래

The Fa-ther's song, the Fa-ther's love,
아 버 지 의 사 랑 으 로

You sung it o-ver me, and for e-ter-ni-ty it's
영 원 히 내 맘 속 에 새 겨 져 있 는 — 아

writ-ten on my — heart.
버 지 의 노 — 래

Heav-en's per-fect mel-o-dy,
천 상 의 그 — 멜 로 디 —

The Cre-a-tor's sym-pho-ny;
창 조 주 — 의 — 심 포 니 —

You are sing-ing o-ver me
주 당 신 이 부 르 시 네 —

the Fa-ther's song.
나 를 향 — 해 —

Hea-ven's per-fect myst-e-ry;
사 랑 의 왕 — 을 주 신 —

the king of love has sent for me.
하 늘 의 그 — 신 비 를 —

And now You're sing-ing
주 당 신 이 부

o-ver me
르 시 네 —

the Fa-ther's song.
나 를 향 해

There's No One Like You

(내 주 같은 분 없네)

Eddie Espinosa

179

There's no one like You my Lord — No one could take Your place
내 주 같 - 은 분 없 - 네 - 그 어 - 느 누 구 - 도 -

My heart beats to wor-ship You — I live just to seek Your face
I long for Your pre-sence Lord — to ser-ve you my re - ward
- 내 생 명 - 다 하 도 - 록 - 주 얼 굴 - 만 구 하 리 -

There's no one like You, my Lord — No one could take Your place
- 내 주 같 - 은 분 없 - 네 - 그 어 - 느 누 구 - 도 -

There's no one like You, my Lord — No one like You
- 내 주 같 - 은 분 없 - 네 - 이 땅 - 위 - 에 -

You are my God — You're ev - 'ry - thing to me
오 하 - 나 님 - 주 나 의 모 - 든 - 것 - -

There's no one like You, my Lord — No one like You
- 내 주 같 - 은 분 없 - 네 - 이 땅 - 위 - 에 - - - - -

You are my God — You're e-very-thing to me
- 오 하 - 나 - 님 - - - 주 나 의 모 - 든 - 것 -

There's no one like You, my Lord — No one like You
- 내 주 같 - 은 분 없 - 네 - 이 땅 - 위 - 에 - -

180 The Sweetest Name Of All

(예수 가장 귀한 그 이름)

Tommy Coomes

Je - sus, You're the sweet-est name of all.
Je - sus, how I love to praise your name.
Je - sus, You're the soon and com - ing King.
예 수 가 장 귀 한 그 – 이 름
예 수 찬 양 하 기 원 – 하 네
예 수 왕 의 왕 이 되 – 신 주

Je - sus, You al - ways hear me when I call
Je - sus, You're still the first, the last the same.
Je - sus, we need the love that You can bring.
예 수 언 제 나 기 도 들 – 으 사
예 수 처 음 과 나 중 되 – 시 는
예 수 당 신 의 끝 없 는 – 사 랑

Oh, Je - sus, You pick me up each time I fall,
Oh, Je - sus, You died and took a - way my shame,
Oh, Je - sus, we lift our voic - es up and sing,
오 예 수 나 의 손 잡 아 주 시 는
오 예 수 날 위 해 고 통 당 하 신
오 예 수 목 소 리 높 여 찬 양 해

You're the sweet-est, the sweet-est name of all.
가 장 귀 한 – 귀 한 그 – 이 름

This Is My Destiny

(나의 부르심)

181

Scott Brenner

This is my des - ti - ny This is my hope e - ter - nal
나 - 의 부르심 - 나의 영원 - 한 소 - 망

To be con - formed in to the i - mage of love
예 수 님 의 - 형 상 - 을 닮 - - 는 것 - -

This is my pur - pose This is my high - est call - ing
나 - 의 목 적 - 나 의 높 은 - 부 르 - 심

To leave the world be - hind and live my life for You
세 상 을 뒤 로 - 하 고 - 주 위 - 해 사 - 는 것 - -

Ca - rry me hide me in the shel - ter of Your pure
덮 으 - 소 서 - 주 - 거 - 룩 한 - 품 에 - 품 으

em - brace The place where I be - long O Je - sus
- - 소 서 - - 이 곳 이 나 속 - 한 곳 - 오 예 - 수

co - ver me I come to You for shel - ter, to the
이 끄 - 소 서 - - 주 얼 굴 보 - 기 위 - 해 은 - 밀 한

se - cret place Where I live to see your face
- 곳 으 로 - - 내 가 나 아 갑 - 니 다 -

E

182 This Is Our God

(주 하나님)

Reuben Morgan

Your grace is e-nough more than I need At Your word,
Your pre-sence in me Je-sus light the way by the po
내 필요보다 크 - 신은 - 혜 - 주 말씀
내 안에 있는 예 수 나 - 의 빛 - 나 의 길

I will be - lieve I wait for You draw near a - gain
- wer of Your word I am re - stored I am re - deemed
- 나는 - 믿 - 네 주 를 더욱 - 기 다 리 니
- 비 추 시 - 네 주 님 나 를 - 구 하 셨 네

Let Your Spi - rit make me new And I will fall
By Your Spi - rit I am free
- 날 새 롭 - 게 하 소 서 - 나 주 께 엎
- 주 안 에 - 난 자 유 해 -

at Your feet I will fall at Your feet
- 드 - 리 - 어 - 주 를 - 경 - 배 - 하 리

And I will wor - ship Your here
- 나 주 를 경 - 배 - 하 - 리 -

Free-ly You gave it all for us Sur-ren-dered Your life u-pon that cross
우 릴 위 해 - 모 든 - 것 을 - 값 없 이 주 신 - 그 큰 - 사 - 랑

This Is Our God

Great is the love   poured out for all   This is our God
자 기 몸 을 -   내 어 주 신 -   주 하 나 - 님 -

Lif-ted on high   from death to   life   for - e - ver our God
부 활 하 신 -   영 광 - 의 - 주 -   영 원 히 높 임

is glo - ri - fied   Ser-vant and King   res-cued the world
- 받 으 - 소 - 서 -   온 세 상 을 -   구 원 하 신

This   is   our   God
- 주 하 나 - 님 -   -

Words and Music by Reuben Morgan
© 2008 Hillsong Music Publishing Australia (admin in Korea by Universal Music Publishing/ CAIOS)

E

183 Til I See You
(주의 얼굴 볼 때까지)

Jadwin Gillies & Joel Houston

The grea-test love that a-ny-one could e-ver know
날 구 원 하 - 신 주 의 십 - 자 가 - 사 랑

that o-ver-came the cross and grave to find my soul
- 누 구 도 알 - 수 없 - 는 위 - 대 한 - 사 랑

and 'til I see You face to face and grace a-ma
- - 놀 라 운 주 - 의 은 - 혜 로 - 주 의 얼 굴

-zing takes me home I'll trust in You
- 볼 때 - 까 지 주 의 지 - - 해 -

With all I am
전 심 으 로

I'll live to see Your King-dom come And in my heart
that called the u-ni-verse to be You are the whis
- 그 나 라 보 - 기 원 - 하 네 - - 주 뜻 이 뤄
- 조 하 - 신 주 - 님 은 - 말 씀 - - 내 안 에 속

I Pray You'd let Your will be done And 'til I see
- per in my heart that speaks to me
- 지 도 - 록 나 - 기 도 - 하 네 - 놀 라 운 주
- 삭 이 - 는 주 - 님 의 - 음 성 -

You face to face and grace a-ma - zing takes me home I'll trust in
- 의 은 - 혜 로 - 주 의 얼 굴 - 볼 때 - 까 지 - 주 의 지

Til I See You

Words and Music by Jadwin Gillies, Joel Houston
© 2010 Hillsong Music Publishing Australia (admin in Korea by Universal Music Publishing/ CAIOS)

184 This Is The Day

(이 날은 주가 지으신 날)

Rick Shelton

Undignified

(춤추며 찬양해)

185

Matt Redman

I will dance I will sing to be mad for my King
춤 추 며 찬 양 해 나 의 왕 주 님 께

No-thing Lord is hin-der-ing the pas-sion in my soul And
그 누 구 도 내 열 정 - - 빼 앗 을 수 없 네 나

I'll be-come e-ven more un-dig-ni-fied than this
춤 추 리 자 존 심 다 버 리 고 기 뻐 해

Some would say it's fool-ish-ness but I'll be-come
누 군 가 날 비 웃 어 도 춤 추 리

e-ven more un-dig-ni-fied than this
자 존 심 다 버 리 고 뛰 놀 며

Fine

Na na na na na Hey! Na na na na na Hey!
나 나 - 나 나 나 Hey! 나 나 - 나 나 나 Hey!

na na na na na Hey! na na na na na Hey!
나 나 - 나 나 나 Hey! 나 나 - 나 나 나 Hey!

D.C. al Fine

186

We Fall Down
(주 앞에 다 엎드려)

Chris Tomlin

We fall down, we lay our crowns at the feet of Je - sus the
주 앞 - 에 - 다 엎 드 - - 려 면 류 관 - - - 드 리 - 네

great-ness of mercy and love at the feet of Je - sus And we cry
사 랑 - 과 - 자 비 하 - 심 - 크 신 주 - - - 예 수 님 - 께 외 치 세

ho - ly ho - ly, ho - ly and We cry ho - ly, ho - ly, ho - ly. and we cry
거 - 룩 거 - 룩 거 - 룩 주 는 거 - 룩 거 - 룩 거 - 룩 외 치 세

ho - ly, ho - ly, ho - ly, is the Lamb.
거 - 룩 거 - 룩 하 - 신 어 - 린 양 - -

Worthy Is The Lord

(존귀 오 존귀하신 주)

Mark Kinzer

187

Worthy O wor-thy are you Lord. Worthy to be
존 귀 오 존 - 귀 하 - 신 주 - 감 사 찬 양

thank-ed and prais-ed and worsh-iped and a - dored.
과 - 경 배 - 다 받 으 실 주 님 - - - - -

Wor-thy O wor-thy are you Lord. wor-thy to be
존 귀 오 존 - 귀 하 - 신 주 - 감 사 찬 양

thank-ed and prais-ed and worsh-iped and a - dored. Sing-ing
과 - 경 배 - 다 받 으 실 주 님 - 찬 양

Hal - le - lu - jah! Lamb up-on the throne, We
할 렐 루 - 야 - 보 좌 위 어 린 양 께 - 우

worship and a - dore you. make your glo-ry known
리 경 배 하 - 며 - 영 광 돌 리 네 -

Ha - le - lu - jah! Glo-ry to the king You are
할 렐 루 - 야 - 우 리 왕 께 영 - 광 - 주 는

more than a con-quer-or you're Lord of ev - ry thing.
승 리 의 용 - 사 - 또 만 유 의 주 님 -

188 Way Maker

(길을 만드시는 분)

Osinachi Kalu Okoro

You are here mov-ing in our midst I wor-ship You I wor-ship You
You are here touch-ing e - very heart I wor-ship You I wor-ship You
You are here turn-ing lives a - round I wor-ship You I wor-ship You

주 여기 - 운행하 - 시 네 주 경 - 배해 - 주 경 - 배해 -
주 우리 - 마음만 - 지 네 주 경 - 배해 - 주 경 - 배해 -
주 우리 - 새롭게 - 하 네 주 경 - 배해 - 주 경 - 배해 -

You are here work-ing in this place I wor-ship You I wor-ship You
You are here hea-ling e - very heart I wor-ship You I wor-ship You
You are here mend-ing e - very heart I wor-ship You I wor-ship You

주 여기 - 역사하 - 시 네 주 경 - 배해 - 주 경 - 배해 -
주 우리 - 치유하 - 시 네 주 경 - 배해 - 주 경 - 배해 -
주 우리 - 회복시 - 키 네 주 경 - 배해 - 주 경 - 배해 -

Way Ma - ker mi - ra-cle wor-ker pro-mise keep-er light in the dark-ness
새 길을 만드시는 분 큰 기적을 행하시는 분

my God that is who you are   Way ma-ker mi-ra-cle wor-ker
그는 우리하나님   약속을 지키시는 분

pro-mise keep-er light in the dark-ness my God that is who you are
어둠속을 밝히시는 빛 그는 우리하나 님

are that is who you are   that is who you are   that is who you
님 그는 하나님   그는 하나 님   그는 하나

Way Maker

are   that is who you are   that is who you are   that is who you
님   그 는 하 나 님   그 는 하 나 님   그 는 하 나

are   that is who you are   that is who you are
님   그 는 하 나 님   그 는 하 나 님

e-ven when I don't see it, you're work-ing e-ven when I don't feel it, you're work-ing
주 의 일 하 심 볼 수 없 어 도   주 의 일 하 심 알 수 없 어 도

you nev-er stop you nev-er stop work-ing you nev-er stop you ne-ver stop work-ing
주 는 결 코 멈 추 지 않 네   주 는 결 코 멈 추 지 않 네

E

189 We Have Overcome

(우린 이겼네)

Meleasa Houghton & Israel Houghton

We Have Overcome

190

We Will Rejoice
(기뻐하며 승리의 노래 부르리)

David Fellingham

We will re-joice and sing our song of vic-tory
기 뻐하며 승리의노래부르리

God is res-tor - ing His peo - - - ple;
그 백성주가회복시 키시네

Ga - ther - ing in love the op-press'd, the poor and
그 사랑으로 억눌렸던자모

lame, giv-ing them praise and re-known in the earth.
아 칭찬과명 성얻게하시네

We will re-joice with all our
전심으로 기뻐하

We will re-joice with all our heart, al-migh-ty
전심으로기 뻐하리 전능의

heart, al-migh-ty King
리 전능의왕

King is in our midst, al-migh-ty Warr-i - or who saves
왕우리함께 우리의강하신용사

We Will Rejoice

O.T. : We Will Rejoice And Sing Our Song Of Victory / O.W. : David Fellingham
O.P. : Thankyou Music Ltd / S.P. : Universal Music Publishing Korea, CAIOS
Adm. : Capitol CMG Publishing / All rights reserved, Used by permission.

191 You Are Good
(좋으신 하나님)

Israel Houghton

Lord, You are good and Your mer-cy en-du-reth for-
좋 으 - 신 하 나 - 님 인 자 - 와 자 비 - 영

e - ver. Peo-ple from e-ve - ry na-tion and tongue
원 - 히 - - 각 나 - 라 족 속 - 과 백 성 - 방 언

from ge - ne - ra-tion to ge-ne - ta-tion. We wor - ship You,
세 상 - 모 든 세 - 대 영 원 - 토 록 주 경 배 - 해

Hal - le-lu - jah, Hal - le-lu - jah, We wor-ship You
- 할 렐 루 - - 야 할 - 렐 루 - - 야 주 경 배 - 해

for who You are We You are good
- 주 하 나 - 님 - 주

Fine

You are good All the time All the time You are good
주 하 나 님 -

D.C.

You Are Holy

(주는 거룩)

192

Reuben Morgan

You are ho - ly,   ho - ly,   Lord, there is none like You.
주 는 거 - - 룩 -   거 - 룩 -   오 직 주 님 - 만 - 이 -

You are ho - ly,   ho - ly,   glo - ry to You   a - lone.
주 는 거 - - 룩 -   거 - 룩 -   영 광 받 으 - 소 - 서 -

I'll sing Your prai - ses for e   - - - ver,   deep-er in love   with You.
영 원 히 찬 - 양 합 니 - - - 다 -   더 욱 사 랑 - 해 요 -

Here in Your courts where I'm close to Your throne, I've found where I   be-long.
주 보 좌 앞 - 영 원 히 - 거 하 리 -   주 께 더 가 - 까 이 -

E

193 You Are My King
(주 나의 왕)

Billy James Foote

I'm for-giv - en be-cause you were for-sak - en I'm ac-cept-ed;
주님 날위 - 해 - 버 림받으 - 심으 - 로 나용서받고

you were con-demned I'm a-live andwell Yourspir-it is with-in me be-
용 납 - 됐네 - 죽으시고 - 부활 - 하 신주로 - 인하 - 여 성

cause you died and rose a-gain A-maz-ing love how
령 내안 - 에 계 - 시 네 - 오 놀라운 - 주

can it be that You, my King would die for me
- 의 사 랑 - - 왜 날위 - 해 - 죽으 - 셨나 -

A-maz-ing love I know it's true it's my joy to hon-or You.
주님 사랑 - 깨 - 달 았네 - - 기쁨으 - 로 - 영광 - 돌려

1. Bsus   2. Bsus

In all I do I hon-or You
- - 온 맘 - 다 - 해 - 경 배 하 리 -

Fine

You are my King You are my King Je-sus
주 나 - 의 - 왕 주 나 - 의 - 왕 예수

You are my king Je-sus You are my King
님 나 - 의 - 왕 예 수 님 나 - 의 - 왕

D.S.

In Christ Alone

(예수 안에 소망있네)

194

Keith Getty & Stuart Townend

E

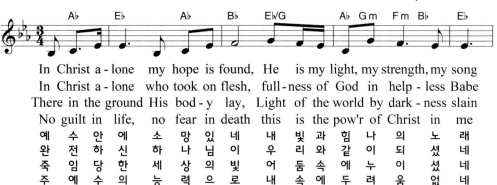

In Christ a-lone my hope is found, He is my light, my strength, my song
In Christ a-lone who took on flesh, full-ness of God in help-less Babe
There in the ground His bod-y lay, Light of the world by dark-ness slain
No guilt in life, no fear in death this is the pow'r of Christ in me

예　수　안　에　소　망　있　네　내　빛　과　힘　나　의　노　래
완　전　하　신　하　나　님　이　우　리　와　같　이　되　셨　네
죽　임　당　한　세　상　의　빛　어　둠　속　에　누　이　셨　네
주　예　수　의　능　력　으　로　내　속　에　두　려　움　없　네

this cor-ner-stone, this sol-id ground firm through the fierc-est drought and storm.
This gift of love and right-eous-ness, scorned by the ones He came to save.
then, burst-ing forth in glo-rious day, up from the grave he rose a-gain!
from life's first cry to fi-nal breath, Je-sus com-mands my des-ti-ny.

환　란　중　에　도　우　시　는　주　나　의　견　고　한　반　석
주　사　랑　과　그　공　의　로　세　상　을　구　원　하　셨　네
영　광　스　런　그　의　날　에　무　덤　에　서　부　활　했　네
나　의　사　는　모　든　순　간　주　께　서　다　스　리　시　네

what heights of love what depths of peace, when fears are stilled, when striv-ings cease.
'tll on the cross as Je-sus died, the wrath of God was sat-is-fied.
And as He stands in vic-to-ry, sin's curse has lost its grip on hand
No pow'r of hell, no scheme of man, can ev-er pluck me from His hand

크　신　사　랑　크　신　평　화　두　렴　에　서　날　건　지　네
십　자　가　에　주　달　리　사　그　진　노　를　거　두　셨　네
승　리　하　신　우　리　주　님　원　수　들　을　물　리　폈　네
어　느　것　도　주　손　에　서　날　빼　앗　지　못　하　리　라

My com-fort-er, my all in all, here in the love of Christ I stand.
For ev-'ry sin on Him was laid here in the death of Christ I live.
for I am His and He is mine, bought with the pre-cious blood of Christ.
'til He re-turns or calls me home, here in the pow'r of Christ I'll stand.

내　위　로　자　내　모　든　것　주　사　랑　안　에　서　리　라
내　모　든　죄　담　당　하　신　주　은　혜　안　에　살　리　라
나　주　의　것　주　나　의　것　주　보　혈　안　에　살　리　라
주　오　실　날　기　다　리　며　주　능　력　안　에　서　리　라

195

As David Did
(주 앞에 다윗 왕처럼)

Martin Nystrom

As Da - vid did in Jeho-vah's sight I will dance with
As Ju - dah did on the bat - tle ground We will make a

주 앞 에 다 윗 — 왕 처 럼 온 힘 다 해 —
전 쟁 터 의 유 — 다 처 럼 기 쁜 소 리 —

all my might Be - fore the King of kings
joy - ful sound Be - fore the King of kings

춤 추 리 왕 의 왕 주 앞 — — 에 —
외 치 리 왕 의 왕 주 앞 — — 에 —

As Mi - ri - am did with the tam-bou-rine I will clap my
As Jo-sh-ua did at Je - ti - cho We will shout to

그 탬 버 린 든 미 리 암 처 럼 손 뼉 치 며 찬
여 리 고 의 여 호 수 아 처 럼 적 을 부 수 며

hands and sing Be - fore the King of kings
defeat the foe Be - fore the King of kings

양 하 리 왕 의 왕 주 앞 — — — 에
외 치 리 왕 의 왕 주 앞 — — — 에

We can come be - fore Him And wor-ship Him to - day
주 님 우 리 위 — 해 길 예 비 하 셨 네 —

We can now ado - re Him Je - sus made a way
사 랑 의 주 예 — 수 경 배 드 리 네 —

Come And See

(다 와서 주 영광을 보며)

Lenny LeBlanc

196

come and see the glo-ry of the Lord, come be-hold the Lamb
come and give thanks un-to the Lord, come be-hold the Lamb
다 와 서 주 영광을 – 보며 어린양 보 – 라
다 와 서 감 사 를 드 – 리며 어린양 보 – 라

come and know the mer-cy of the King, bow-ing down be-fore Him
come and sing the prais-es of the King,
다 와 서 주 의 궁휼 – 보며 – 엎 드려 – 경 배 – – 하 – 라
다 와 서 찬 양을 드 – 리며 –

Him For He is Lord abo-ve the hea-ven Lord in all the earth
라 그 분은 하 늘과 – 땅 위의 만 유의 – 주님

Lord of all the an-gels wor-thy to be served A –lle - lu – – ia
천 사들 – 도 모 두 주만섬 – 기 네 할 – – 렐 루 – – – 야

A –lle - lu – – ia
할 – – 렐 루 – – – 야

D.C. al Fine　　　　　*Fine*

O.T. : Come And See / O.W. : Lenny Leblanc
O.P. : Universal Music – Brentwood Benson Songs / S.P. : Universal Music Publishing Korea, CAIOS
Adm. : Capitol CMG Publishing / All rights reserved, Used by permission,

197

Dwelling Places

(주의 아름다운 처소)

Miriam Webster

Love-ly are your dwell-ing place - es thirst-y
주 의 - 아 름 다 운 처 소 - - 간 절 히

I came af - ter you Je - sus my joy my re-ward
따 라 갑 - 니 다 - - 주 내 - 기 - 쁨 - 내 상 급

Your love's re - stor - ing my soul Now I'm
- - 주 사 - 랑 - 날 - 새 롭 - 게 - 해 - - 나 는

Your sand you are mine and from my heart and song will rise
주 께 속 - 했 - 네 - - - 내 마 음 다 - 해 - 찬 - 양 해 -

I love you I love you, I love you, I love you I love you,
I love you I love you, I love you, I love you I love you,

I love you, I love you I love you I love you
I love you, I love you I love you I love you

and my heart will fol - low wholl - y af - ter you
내 모 - 든 - 것 다 - 해 - 주 - 만 따 - 르 리 -

Father I Want You To Hold Me

(아버지 날 붙들어 주소서)

198

Brian Doerksen

199 Father Lift Me Up
(잡아 주시네)

Nancy Honeytree

Like a li-ttle child　Je-sus told　me to　come　and the
어 린 아 이 처 럼　그 저 오 라 하 시 네　나 를

Fa-ther lifts me　up　up to Hea-ven　up to home　Fa-ther, life me
잡 아 주 시 네　주 의 강 한 손 으 로　잡 아 주 시

up, al - le-lu - ia　ho - ly　is Your name　Fa-ther, life me
네 할 렐 루 – 야　거 룩 한 주 님　잡 아 주 시

up, al - le-lu - ia　ho - ly is Your name　If
네 할 렐 루 – 야　거 룩 한 주 님 –　나

I　be lifed up　higt　from the earth,　Je - sus　said
High　up　a-bove　all　po-wers and all　kings
가 난 한 맘 으 –로 –　주 께 가 기 만 하 면
하 늘 보 좌 위 –에 –　앉 아 계 신 예 수 님

I　will　draw　ev-ery per-son un - to　me
there　is　a throne　where　the fai - th ful sing
도 우 리 라　주 가 말 씀 하 셨 네
천 사 들 도　모 두 모 여 경 배 해

If　I die to　self　Je-sus told me　I will　live
Ho - ly, ho - ly,　holy　Is the Lamb　that was slain
내 가 죽 어 야 –만 –　많 은 열 매 맺 히 리
거 룩 하 신 이 –여 –　흠 이 없 는 구 주 여

Father Lift Me Up

Cru - ci - fied with Je - sus I with to be Fa - ther, lift me
through the Ho - ly Spi - rit I call up - on His name
주 와 함 께 못 - 박 - 혀 나 다 시 살 리 라 다 시 살 리
찬 양 받 으 소 - - - 서 나 소 리 높 여 서 찬 양 하 리

up Al - le - lu - ia ho - ly is Your name. Fa - ther, lift me
라 할 렐 루 - 야 거 룩 한 주 님 다 시 살 리
라 할 렐 루 - 야 거 룩 한 주 님 찬 양 하 리

up Al - le - lu - ia ho - ly is Your name
라 할 렐 루 - 야 거 룩 한 주 님
라 할 렐 루 - 야

200 Firm Foundation

(예수 나의 견고한 반석)

Nancy Gordon & Jamie Harvill

Je - sus You're my firm foun - da - tion　I know I can stand se - cure
예 - 수 나의 견 고한반석 -　나 주안에서 - 있네 -

Je - sus You're my firm foun - da - tion　I put my hope in Your ho
예 - 수 나의 견 고한반석 -　내 소 망 주 말 씀 에

- ly word　I put my hope in your ho - ly word
- 있 네 - - - -　내 소 망 주 말 씀 에 - 있 네 -

I have a li-ving hope I have a li-ving hope I have a fu - ture
Your word is faith - ful Your word is faith - ful Migh-ty with pow - er
내 겐 - 소 망 있 네　내 겐 - 소 망 있 네 내 겐 - 미 래 있 네
신 실 - 한 주 말 씀　신 실 - 한 주 말 씀 능 력 - 의 주 말 씀

I have a fu - ture God has a palne for me God has a plane for me of
Migh-ty with pow - er God will de-liv-er me God will de-liv-er me of
내 겐 - 미 래 있 네　주 계 - 획 하 시 네 주 계 - 획 하 시 네 내
능 력 - 의 주 말 씀　날 구 - 원 하 시 네 날 구 - 원 하 시 네 나

this I'm sure of this I'm sure　I put my hope in Your ho - ly word
this I'm sure of this I'm sure
미 래 를 - - 내 소 망 을 - - - -　내 소 망 주 말 씀 에 - 있 네 - -
는 믿 네 - - 확 신 하 네 - - - -

Give Thanks

(거룩하신 하나님)

Henry Smith

201

F

Give thaks with a great-ful heart Give thanks to the
거 룩 하 신 하 나 님 — 주 께 감 사
의 맘 과 뜻 다 해 — 주 를 사 랑

Ho-ly One. Give thanks be-cause He's giv-en Je-sus Christ,   His
드 리 세 — 날 위 해 이 땅 에 오 신 독 생 자   예
합 니 다 — 날 위 해 이 땅 에 오 신 독 생 자   예

Son.   Give Son.   And   now   Let the weak say, "I am
수   나   수   내   가   약 할 때 강 함 주

strong," let the poor say, "I am rich," be-cause of What the Lord has
고 가 난 할 때 우 리 를 부 요 케 하 신 나 의

done   for   us.   And   us.   Give thanks.
주   감 — 사   내   사   감 사   —

202 He Binds The Broken-Hearted

(마음이 상한 자를)

Stacy Swalley

You bind the bro – ken heart– ed　You heal the wound– ed soul
Fill me with Your Spi – rit　I want to see Your face
마음 이 상 - 한 자 - 를　고 치 시 는 - 주 님 -
성 령 으 로 - 채 우 사　주 보 게 하 - 소 서 -

Fa – ther of　all heav – en　I give You full　con – trol　come
To live in　Your pre – sence know Your glo – ry and Your grace　It's
하 늘 의 - 아 버 지　날 주 관 하 - 소 서 - - 주
주 의 임 - 재 속 에　은 혜 알 게 하 - 소 서 - - 주

have Your way　in us,　O Lord come set our spir – its free
not my will　but Yours　I choose to　foll – ow to　the end
의 길 로 - 인 도 -　하 사 자 유 케 하 - 소 서 -
뜻 대 로 - 살 아 -　가 리 세 상 끝 날 - 까 지 -

Fa – ther send re – viv – al　and start the work　in me
so mold me yes and make me　Let a　new　day　be-gin
새 일 을 행 하 - 사　부 흥 케 - 하 - 소 서 -
나 를 빚 으 시 - 고　새 날 열 어 주 - 소 서 -

Lord, I hun – ger, thirst　for your right – eous – ness
의 에 주 리 고 -　목 이 마 르 니 -

Fa-ther come and fill　me one a – gain　Lord, I hun-ger, thirst　for your
성 령 의 - 기 름 - 부 으 - 소 서　의 에 주 리 고 - 목 이

right-eous – ness　Fill me with　Your oil　and Your wine.
마 르 니 -　내 잔 을 - 채 워 - 주 소 서

He Is Exalted

(왕이신 하나님 높임을 받으소서)

203

Twila Paris

He is ex-alt-ed the King is ex-alt-ed on high   I will pra-ise Him
왕 이 신 하 나 님 높 임 을 받 으 소 서   찬 양 하 리 라

He is ex-alt-ed for-ev-er ex-alt-ed and I   will   praise His
영 원 히 높 임 을 받 으 실 그 이 름 찬   양   하 리

name   He is the Lord   For-ev-er His truth   shall
라 –   그 리 스 도   진 리 로 다 스 리

reign   Heav-en and earth   Re-joice in His ho - ly
네 –   기 뻐 하 라   온 땅 이 여 찬 양 하

name   He is ex-alt-ed the King is ex-alt-ed on high
라 – 거 –룩 하 –신 그 이 름 높 이 리 라   –

F

204 Holy Spirit Rain Down

(성령이여 임하소서)

Russell Fragar

Ho-ly Spi-rit rain down rain down O
성령이여 비 를 내 려 오

Com-for-ter and Friend how we need Your touch a-gain Ho-ly Spi-rit
위로의 친구 우릴 만져 주 소서 성령이여

rain down rain down Let Your pow-er fall let Your
비 를 내 려 주의 능력과 그의

voice be heard Come and change our hearts as we stand on Your word Ho-ly
음성을 들려 주 셔서 변화 시 키 소서 성령

Spi - rit rain down Ho-ly Spi-rit down
이 여 비 를 성령이여 를

No eye has seen no ear has heard no mind can know what
눈 과 귀 와 맘 으 로 도 알 수 없 네 그

God has on store so o-pen up hea-ven o-pen it wide
비밀한 것 하늘의 문을 활짝 열어

o-ver Your church and o-ver our lives o-ver our lives Ho-ly Spi-rit
교회들을 변화 시키소서 시키소서 성령이여

Holy Spirit Rain Down

down   Let Your pow-er fall   let Your voice be heard come and
-를- - - - - 주 의   능 력 과 - 그 의 음 성 을 - 들 려

change our hearts as we stand on Your word   Ho-ly Spir - it   rain
주 셔 서 - 변 화 시 키 소 서 -   성 령 이   여 - 비

down   Let Your   down
-를- - - - 주 의 -를- - -

F

205 Holiness Unto The Lord

(거룩하신 하나님)

Sheila Uselton

Ho - li-ness un-to the Lord. ho - li-ness un-to the Lord
거 룩 하 신 하 나 님 거 룩 하 신 하 나 님 - - - -

Ho - li-ness un-to the Lord ho - li-ness un-to the Lord, our God.
거 룩 하 신 하 나 님 거 룩 하 신 나 의 하 나 님

He is right-eous, He is faith-ful, He is sov-'reign o-ver all;
의 로 우 - 신 주 하 나 - 님 신 실 하 - 신 아 버 지

He is right-eous, He is faith-ful, He is sov-'reign o-ver all.
모 든 만 물 을 다 스 리 시 는 거 룩 하 - 신 - 하 나 님

I Am The God That Healeth Thee
(주 여호와 능력의 주)

Don Moen

207 I Bow My Knee
(보좌 앞에 무릎 꿇고)

Bonnie Deuschle

I Just Want To Praise You

(주를 찬양하며)

208

Arthur Tannous

I just want to prai - se You lift my hands and say; I love You
주 – 를 찬양 하 – 며 나 – 이 제 고 백 하 는 말
손 – 을 높이 들 – 고 나 – 이 제 고 백 하 는 말

You are ev-'ry-thing to me and I e-xalt Your ho - ly name on high
주 – 를 사랑 합니다 나의 – 모든 것 되 신 주 님 께 –
주 – 를 사랑 합니다 오 거 – 룩 하 신

ho - ly na - me I e - xalt Your ho - ly na - me
주 의 이 름 거 – 룩 하 신 주 의 이 름

I e - xalt Your ho - ly name on high
주 – 의 이 름 높 이 올 리 세 –

O.T. : I Just Want To Praise You / O.W. : Arthur Tannous
O.P. : Thankyou Music Ltd / S.P. : Universal Music Publishing Korea, CAIOS
Adm. : Capitol CMG Publishing / All rights reserved. Used by permission.

209

I Offer My Life

(나의 모습 나의 소유)

Claire Cloninger & Don Moen

I Offer My Life

Lord I off-er You my life   life
나 를 받 아 주 소 서   – 서

What can we give that You have not gi-ven and
우 리 가 진 – 이 모 든 것 들 – 을 다

What do we have that is not al-rea-dy yours
주 께 서 우 – 리 에 게 주 시 었 네 –

All we pro-ssess are these lives We're liv-ing and
몸 밖 에 드 – 릴 것 이 – 없 으 – 니 내

that's what we give to You Lord
삶 을 받 아 – 주 소 서

210 It Is You
(주님만 사랑하리)

Pete Sanchez

It is You, it is You, it is You that I love.
주 님 만 주 님 만 주 님 만 사 랑 하 리

It is You, my Lord and King, I ap-pre hend to know and be known You
나 의 왕 나 의 주 님 주 님 을 더 욱 알 기 원 해 나

it is You, it is You that I wor - ship.
주 님 께 오 직 주 께 경 배 하 네

Ho - ly ho - ly wor - thy, yes, You're wor - thy
거 룩 거 룩 존 귀 존 귀 하 신 주

How I love You, Lord.
사 랑 합 니 다 —

I Will Worship You

(예배합니다)

Rose Lee

211

Per-fect you are my God   Right-eous and holy in all
완 전 - 하 신 나 의 주   의 의 - 길 로 날 - 인

of Your ways We will-ing your glory in all that You do
도 하 소 - 서 - 행 하 신 - 모 든 일 주 님 의 영 광 -

All men will wor - ship You   I will wor - ship You
다 경 배 합 - 니 다 -   예 배 합 - 니 다

I will prai-se Your Name   For You are   the on-ly Lord and King
- 찬 양 합 - 니 다 -   주 님 만 - 날 다 스 리 소 서

I will wor - ship You   I will prai-se Your Name
- 예 배 합 - 니 다 -   찬 양 합 - 니 다

My de - sire   is to ho-nor You Lord
- 주 님 홀 - 로 높 임 받 으 소 서 -

212 Jesus Draw Me Close

(주께 가까이 날 이끄소서)

Rick Doyle Founds

Je - sus draw me close clo - ser Lord to you
주 께 가 - 까 이 - 날 이 끄 - 소 서 -

Let the world a - round me fade a - way
세 상 즐 - 거 움 - 다 버 리 리 -

Je - sus draw me close clo - ser Lord to you
주 께 가 - 까 이 - 날 이 끄 - 소 서 -

for I de - sire to wor - ship and o - bey
순 전 한 예 - 배 주 - 께 드 리 리 - -

Let The Peace Of God Reign

(아버지여 이끄소서)

Darlene Zschech

213

214 Let There Be Loved Shared Among Us

(우리 안에 사랑을)

Dave Bulbrough

Let there be love shared a-mong us Let there be love in our
우 리 안 에 사 　 랑 을 우 리 눈 에 사 랑

eyes May now Your love sweep this na-tion 'cause us oh Lord to a-
을 이 나 라 휩 쓸 　 도 록 채 우 소 서 　 오 주

rise Give us a fresh un-der-stand-ing of bro-ther-ly love that is
님 진 실 한 형 제 의 사 랑 새 롭 게 알 게 하 소

real Let there be love shared a-mong us Let there be love
서 우 리 안 에 사 　 랑 을 사 　 랑 을

No Condemnation

215

(이제는 내게)

Charles F. Monroe

There is there-fore now no con-dem-na-tion for those who are in
이 제 는 내 - 게 더 정 죄 함 없 - 네 나 를 구 원 하 신

1. F (C)
2. F Bbm7 F F/A F/C Am7 Dm7

Christ Je - sus
예 수 그 리 스 도 -

Fine

Je - sus
그 리 스 도 -

For the law of the spi - rit
주 의 성 령 의 법 - 이

Am7 Dm7 F Am C Dm C/D Dm Bbm7/C

of life in Christ Je-sus will set you free From the law of sin and death
예 수 안 에 있 는 나 를 자 유 케 했 네 죄 와 사 - 망 에 서 -

D.C. al Fine

Worthy You Are Worthy

216

(존귀 주는 존귀)

Don Moen

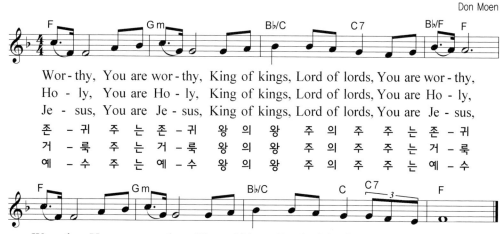

Wor - thy, You are wor - thy, King of kings, Lord of lords, You are wor - thy,
Ho - ly, You are Ho - ly, King of kings, Lord of lords, You are Ho - ly,
Je - sus, You are Je - sus, King of kings, Lord of lords, You are Je - sus,
존 - 귀 주 는 존 - 귀 왕 의 왕 주 의 주 주 는 존 - 귀
거 - 룩 주 는 거 - 룩 왕 의 왕 주 의 주 주 는 거 - 룩
예 - 수 주 는 예 - 수 왕 의 왕 주 의 주 주 는 예 - 수

Wor - thy, You are wor - thy, King of kings Lord of lords, I wor-ship You.
Ho - ly, You are Ho - ly, King of kings Lord of lords, I wor-ship You.
Je - sus, You are Je - sus, King of kings Lord of lords, I wor-ship You.
존 - 귀 주 는 존 - 귀 왕 의 왕 주 의 주 경 배 하 리
거 - 룩 주 는 거 - 룩 왕 의 왕 주 의 주 경 배 하 리
예 - 수 주 는 예 - 수 왕 의 왕 주 의 주 경 배 하 리

F

217 Offering

(왕 되신 주 앞에 나 나아갑니다)

Paul Baloche

The sun can-not com-pare to the glo - ry of Your love.
햇 살 - 보 다 - 밝 게 - 빛 나 는 주 의 - 영 광 -

There is no sha - dow in Your pres - ence.
모 든 - 어 두 - 움 물 - 리 치 - 네 -

No mor - tal man would dare to stand be-fore Your throne,
누 구 - 도 주 - 앞 에 - 다 가 - 설 수 - 없 네 -

be-fore the Ho - ly One of hea - ven. It's
주 의 - 거 룩 - 한 보 - 좌 앞 - 에 - 오

on-ly by Your blood, and it's on-ly through Your mer - cy, Lord, I come.
직 주 의 - 보 혈 - 주 의 긍 휼 의 - 지 하 - 여 나 아 가 리

I bring an of — fer-ing of wor - ship to my king
- 왕 되 신 주 - 앞 에 - 나 경 - 배 합 - 니 다

No one on earth de-serves the prai - ses that I sing.
- 주 님 만 찬 - 양 받 - 기 합 - 당 하 - 시 니

Je - sus, may You re-ceive the hon - or that You're due;
- 큰 존 귀 와 - 영 광 홀 로 - 받 으 - 소 서

Offering

O Lord,   I bring an of – fer-ing   to You   I bring an of
오 주 – 앞에 – 나 나 – 아 갑 – 니 다 –   왕 되 신 주

I bring an of - fer-ing to You   O Lord, I bring an of – fer-ing to You
– 앞에 – 나 나 – 아 갑 – 니 다 –   오 주 – 님 내 – 가 나 – 아 갑 – 니 다

O Lord,   I bring an of – fer – ing to You
오 주 – 님 내 – 가 나 – 아 갑 – 니 다 –

F

218

One Voice

(아버지여 구하오니)

Robert Gay

Fa-ther, we ask of You this day come and heal our
Now is the time for you and I to join our hearts in
아 버 지 여 구 하 오 니 – 이 제 이 땅 고 쳐 주 – 소
함 께 주 를 찬 양 하 며 – 이 제 우 리 마 음 합 – 치

land; Knit our hearts to-geth-er that Your glo-ry might be seen in us,
praise, that the name of Je-sus will be lift-ed hight. a – bove the earth;
서 우 리 맘 엮 으 사 주 의 영 광 나 타 – 내 소 서 –
세 주 예 수 그 이 름 온 땅 위 에 높 – 이 들 리 라 –

Then the world will know that Je - sus Christ is Lord. Let us be
만 유 의 – 주 님 온 세 상 알 도 록 목 소 리
만 유 의 – 주 님 온 세 상 보 도 록

one voice that glo - ri - fies Your names, Let us be
합 쳐 – 주 께 영 광 돌 – 리 며 – 주 님 의

one voice de - clar-ing that You reign Let us be one voice in
통 치 – 선 포 하 게 하 – 소 서 – 목 소 리 합 쳐 주

love and har- mon- y and we pray, O God, grant us u - ni - ty
님 을 찬 – 양 하 며 이 제 하 나 가 되 게 하 소 서

Praise To The Lord

(전쟁 중에도 주는 평화)

Bob Fitts

219

In the bat-tles, Lord, You are my peace, when I'm
전쟁 중에 도 - - 주는 - 평 화 - - - - 약 할

bro-ken, Lord, You are my strength, You're my strength; You're my love,
때 에 - 도 - - 주 나 의 힘 나 의 힘 - 내 사 랑

You're my life You're my joy, my song in the night how I
- 내 생 명 - 내 기 쁨 - 또 내 - 노 - 래 - - - 놀 라

mar-vel at Your mer - cy and I sing. I sing
우 신 주 의 긍 - 휼 찬 양 해 - 주 님

Praise, praise to the Lord, praise praise to the
을 - 찬 양 - 하 리 - 주 - 찬 양 - 하

Lord For He is good and mer-ci-ful; His
리 - 선 하 시 - 고 - 인 자 하 신 - 크

love is great, He's so won-der-ful, my Lord
신 사 랑 - 위 대 하 신 주 나 의 주 -

220

Psalm 145

(왕이신 나의 하나님)

Stephen Hah

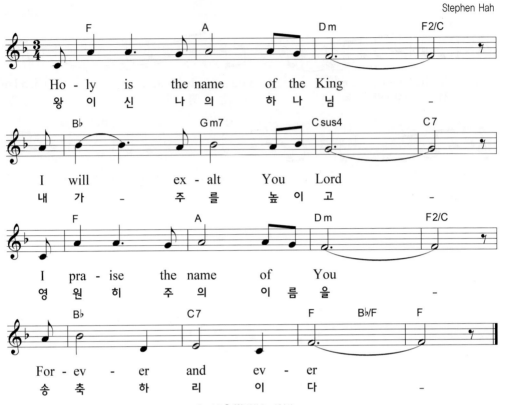

Ho - ly   is   the name   of   the King
왕   이   신   나   의   하   나   님   -

I   will   ex - alt   You   Lord
내   가 -   주   를   높   이   고   -

I   pra - ise   the name   of   You
영   원   히   주   의   이   름   을   -

For - ev - er   and   ev - er
송   축   하   리   이   다   -

Show Your Power

(주의 능력 보이소서)

Kevin Prosch

222

Spirit Come
(오소서 성령이여)

Jamie Burgess

We make the stand　we a-rise　to see this land　in re-
우 리 - 함 께 - 　일 어 나 - 　부 흥 - 위 해 - 　기 도

vi - val We pray down walls　of sa - tan's reign　Spi - rit rise
하 네 분 열 - 의 담 - 　다 허 - 물 고 - 　성 - 령

1. in us a - gain　We make the stand　2. Lord we
일 　어 나 - 도 록 - 　우 리 - 함 께 - 　성 령

call out to Your Spi - rit Lord we call out to Your Spi - rit　and we
이 여 임 하 소 서 우 리 에 게 임 하 소 - 서 주 를

cry out for this na - tion We ask come s - pi - rit come　We de-sire to see Ko-
떠 난 우 리 에 게 오 소 서 - 성 령 이 - 여 주 가 다 시 세 운

re - a　as a na - tion liv - ing for You Lord, we cry out for re -
나 - 라 　주 만 위 해 사 는 나 - 라 부 흥 의 불 타 는

vi - val　We ask come,　Spi - rit　come　We ask come,　Spi - rit
나 라 　오 소 서 　성 령 - 님 　오 소 서 　성 령 -

come　We ask come　Spi - rit　come　Spi - rit come
님 　오 소 서 　성 령 - 님 　오 소 서 　-

Thank You Lord

(감사해)

223

Don Moen & Paul Baloche

1. I come be-fore You to-day   And there's just one thing That I want to say
    For all You've giv-en to me   For all the bless-ings That I can-not see
2. For all You've done in my life   You took my dark-ness And gave me Your light
    You took my sin and my shame   You took my sick-ness And healed all my pain

1. 지 금 주 앞 에 나 와 –   나 오 직 드 리 고 싶 –은 말 은 –
    내 게 주 신 모 든 것 –   다 깨 닫 지 못 했 던 –축 복 들 –
2. 내 삶 에 행 하 신 일 –   어 둠 물 리 치 고 빛 –주 셨 네 –
    수 치 와 죄 사 하 고 –   고 통 과 질 병 을 치 –유 했 네 –

Thank You Lord   thank You Lord   with a grate-ful heart

감 사 해 –   감 사 해 –   감 사 의 마 음 –

with a song of praise   with an out stretched arm   I will bless Your name

찬 양 의 노 래 –   두 팔 을 들 어 –   주 를 송 축 해 –

Thank You Lord   I just want to thank You Lord   Thank You Lord

감 사 해 –   오 직 주 께 감 사 해 –   – 감 – 사 해 –

F

224 This Is The Day

(이 날은)

Les Garrett

This is the day This is the day that the Lord has made That the Lord has made
이 날 - 은 이 날 - 은 주 의 지 으 신 주 의 날 일 세

We will re-joice We will re-joice and be glad in it and be glad in it
기 뻐 하 고 기 뻐 하 며 즐 거 워 하 세 즐 거 워 하 세

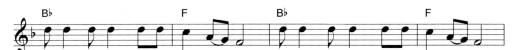

This is the day that the Lord has made We will re-joice and be glad in it
이 날 은 주 의 날 일 - 세 기 뻐 하 고 즐 거 워 하 - 세

This is the day this is the day that the Lord has made
이 날 - 은 이 날 - 은 주 의 날 일 세

We Are Your People

(우리는 주의 백성이오니)

David Fellingham

We are Your peo - ple who are call'd by Your name
우리는 주의 백성이 - 오 니 -

We call up - on You now to de-clare Your fame
주 의 그 큰 이 름 선 포 합 - 니 다 -

In this na-tion of dark - ness You've call'd us to be light.
이 곳 어 두 운 세 상 에 빛 으 로 부 르 셨 네

As we seek Your face, Lord. Stir - up Your might.
주 의 얼 굴 구 할 때 역 사 하 소 서

Build Your church and heal this land, -
- 교 회 를 세 우 시 고 -

let Your king - - dom come.
이 땅 고 쳐 주 소 서 -

Build Your church and heal this land
주 님 나 라 임 - 하 시 고

let Your will - - be done.
주 뜻 이 뤄 지 이 다

226 We've Come To Bless Your Name

(주님의 은혜로)

Don Moen

We're here be-cause of grace   A part of Your great plan;
Lord, You've made a way   be-cause of Your great love;
주 님 의은-혜 로 -   큰 계 획가-운 데 -
주 사 랑가-운 데 -   내 길 을여-시 고 -

we have come to seek Your face   Not the won-ders of Your hand
And our hearts are filled with praise   For all that You have done
주 의 얼 굴구-하 며 -   주 께 나 아갑-니 다 - -
주 의 행 하신-일 을 -   찬 양 하 게하-시 네 - -

And yes, we need Your touch   But You've giv-en us so much
And there is none like You   so faith-ful and so true
그 베 푸 신-은 혜 -   기 억 할때-마 다 -
주 같 이참-되 고 -   신 실 하신분-없 네 -

that we just want to thank You   for all You've done for us
that we just want to thank You   For all You've brought us through
주 내 게 행-하 신 -일 -   감 사 드 립-니 다 -
날 인 도하-신 주 -께 -   감 사 드 립-니 다 -

we've come to bless Your name   King of kings and Lord of lords
주 이 름 송 축 하 -리 -   왕 의 왕-또 주 -의 주

we've come to give You praise   You are the One that we a-dore
주 이 름 찬 양 하 -리 -   주 님 께 경-배 드 -리 리 -

We've Come To Bless Your Name

O Lord cleanse our hearts with fire   And fill us with de - sire
나 를 씻 어 주 - 시 고 -   주 임 재 하 - 심 만

for Your courts   and for Your pres-ence in   our lives
- 내 - 삶 에 -   가 득 하 게 하 - 소 서 -

White As Snow
(눈 보다 더 희게)

227

F

Leon Olguin

White as snow   white as snow   though my sins   were as   scar - let
눈 보 다 -   더 희 게 -   나 의 죄   씻 으 셨 네

Lord I know   Lord I know   that I'm clean   and for - giv - en
날 용 서 -   하 시 고 -   정 결 한   맘 주 셨 네

Through the pow - er of Your blood,   through the won - der of Your love,
보 혈 의 능 력 으 로 -   놀 라 운 사 랑 으 로 -

through faith in You I know that I can be   white as snow
주 님 날 용 서 하 사 내 모 든 죄 -   사 했 네 - -

228 With All My Heart
(온 맘 다해)

Babbie Mason

In this quiet place with you I bow be-fore Your throne I
You faith-fully sup-ply my needs ac-cord-ing to Your plan So
주 님 과 함 께 하 는 이 고 요 한 시 간 주
나 염 려 하 잖 아 도 내 쓸 것 아 시 니 나

bare the deep-est part of me to You and You a - lone I
help me Lord to seek Your face be - fore I seek Your hand And
님 의 보 좌 앞 에 내 마 음 을 쏟 네
오 직 주 의 얼 굴 구 하 게 하 소 서 다

keep no sec - rets for there is no thought You have not known I
trust You know what's best for me when I don't un - der - stand Then
모 든 것 아 시 는 주 님 께 감 출 것 없 네 내
이 해 할 수 없 을 때 라 도 감 사 하 며 날

bring my best and all the rest to You and lay them down
fol - low in o - be - di - ence in e - ve - ry cir-cum
맘 과 정 성 다 해 주 바 라 나 이 다
마 다 순 종 하 며 주 따 르 오 리

stance with all my heart I want to love You Lord I live my
다 온 맘 다 해 사 랑 합 니 다 온 맘 다

life each day to know You more all that's in me is Yours come-
해 주 알 기 원 하 네 내 모 든 삶 당 신 것

plete - ly I'll serve you on — ly With all my heart
이 니 주 만 섬 기 리 온 맘 다 해

You Shall Love The Lord

229

(온 맘 다해 주 사랑하라)

Jimmy Owens

230 Blow The Trumpet In Zion

(저 성벽을 향해)

Craig Terndrup

They ush on the ci - ty they run on the wall　Great is the ar - my that
저　성 - 벽을 - 향해 전진하라 -　　주 님 이 - 우 리

car-ries out His word They　car-ries out His word The Lord　ut-ters His
대 장 되 신 다 저　대 장 되 신 다 주 가　명 령 하

voice　be-fore His ar - my　The Lord ut-ters His voice　be-
네　강 한 군 사 - 들 아　주 가 명 령 하 네　강

fore His ar - my　Blow the trum-pet Zi - on　Zi - on
한　군 사 들 아　나 팔 소 리 시 온 성 에

Sound the a-larm on My　ho - ly moun-tain　Blow the trum-pet
크 - 게 울 려 거 - 룩 한 성 에　나 팔 소 리

Zi - on Zi - on　sound the a - larm　larm
시 온 성 에　울 - 려 라　라

For The Lord Is Marching On

(주께서 전진해 온다)

231

Bonnie Low

For the Lord is march-ing on and His ar-my is
주 께 서 전 진 해 온 다 _ 그 의 강 한 승 리

ev-er strong And His glo-ry shall be seen up-on our land.
의 군 대 _ 그 의 영 광 찬 란 하 게 비 치 _ _ 네 _

Raise the an-them sing the vic-tor's song Praise the Lord for the
찬 양 하 세 승 리 의 노 래 주 찬 양 승 리

bat-tle's won No wea-pon formed a-gainst us shall stand
의 찬 양 _ 누 가 당 할 손 가 주 님 의 군 _ 대

For the cap-tain of the host is Je-sus. We're
우 리 대 장 되 신 구 주 예 수 나

fol-low-ing in His foot-steps. No foe can stand a-
주 님 의 뒤 따 르 면 누 가 당 할 손 가

gainst us in the fray. For the fray.
주 님 의 군 대 우 리 대

F

232 Saviour King
(왕 되신 주)

Marty Sampson & Mia Fieldes

Saviour King

to car-ry this　The hea-vy cross　our weight of　sin
사 하 시 려　그 십 자 가 -　지 신 주 - -님 -

I love You Lord　I wor-ship You　Hope which was lost
사 랑 해 요　경 배 해 - 요　산 소 망 - 이 -

now stands re-newed　I give my　life　to ho-nour this
되 신 주 - 님　내 삶 다 - 해　찬 양 하 - 리

The love of　Christ　the Sa-viour　King
주 의 사 - 랑 -　왕 되 신 - 주

Fine

Play 3 X

Let now our hearts burn with a flame Afire consu-ming all for Your Son's ho-ly Name
성 령 의 불 꽃 임 하 사　우 리 맘 태 우 소 서　주 이 름　위 하 여

And with the hea-vens we de-clare　You are our King　we love You
하 늘 이 함 께 선 포 해 -　주 나 - 의 왕 -　사 랑 해 -

D.S. al Fine

Words and Music by Marty Sampson, Mia Fieldes
© 2019 Hillsong Music Publishing Australia (admin in Korea by Universal Music Publishing/ CAIOS)

233 Rock Of My Salvation

(주님은 나의 구원의 반석)

Teresa Muller

You are the Rock of my sal-va-tion, You are the strength of my life
주님은 나-의 구원 - 의 반-석 - 나의 생명 - 의 능 력

You are my hope and my in - spir-a - tion, Lord, un-to You will I cry.
나의 소망 - 나의 힘 - 되시-네 - 내가 주께 - 외치 리

I be - lieve in You be - lieve in You for Your faith-ful love to me
나는 신 뢰해 - 주 신 뢰해 - 성실 하신 그 사랑 -

You have been my help in time of need; Lord, un-to You will I cleave
환난 때 마다 - 도움 되셨네 - 주 님만 의지하리 -

You are the Rock of my sal-va-tion You are the strength of my life
주님은 나 -의 구원 - 의 반-석 - 나의 생 명 -의 능 력

You are my hope and my in - spir-a - tion, Lord, un-to You will I cry.
나의 소망 - 나의 힘 - 되시네 - 주 님만 의 -지하 리

Arise And Sing
(일어나 찬양)

234

Mel Ray

A - rise and sing ye chil-dren of Zi-on For the Lord has de-liv-ered Thee
일 어 나 라 찬 양 을 드 리 라 우 릴 구 원 하 신 주 께

A - rise and sing ye chil-dren of Zi-on For the Lord has de-liv-ered Thee
일 어 나 라 찬 양 을 드 리 라 우 릴 구 원 하 신 주 께

O-pen up your hearts and re-joice be-fore Him   O-pen up your hearts and re-
마 음 열 고 주 님 앞 에 기 뻐 해   마 음 열 고 주 님 앞

joice   be - fore Him   O-pen up your hearts   and   re -
에   기 뻐 해   마 음 열 고 주   님   앞

joice   be - fore Him for the king   is   your   God
에   기 뻐 해 주 님 은   우 리   왕

G

235

10,000 reasons
(송축해 내 영혼 / Bless the Lord)

Matt Redman & Jonas Myrin

The sun comes up, it's a new day dawn - ing   It's time to sing Your song
해 가 뜨 는 새 아 침 밝 았 네   이 제 다 시 주 님

a - gain   What - ev - er may pass,   and   what-ever lies be - fore   me
- 찬 양 -   무 슨 일 이 - 나   어 떤   일 이 내 게   놓 여 도

Let me be singing when the eve - ning   comes   Bless the
저 녁 이 올 땐 나 는   노   래   해   송 축

Lord, O my soul   O   my   soul   Worship His ho - ly name   Sing like
해 내 영 혼   내 - 영 혼 아   거 룩 하 신 - 이 름 -   이 전

nev - er be - fore   O   my soul   I'll worship Your ho - ly   name
에 없 었 던   노 래 로   나 주 님 을 경 - 배 해 -

You're rich in love, and You're slow to   ang - er Your name is great, and Your
And on that day when my strength is fail - ing The end draws near and my
노 하 기 를 더 디 하 시 는 주 그 의 크 신 사 랑
곧 그 날 에 나 의 힘 다 하 고 나 의 삶 의 여 정

heart is kind   For all Your goodness I will   keep on   sing - ing
time has come   Still my soul will sing Your praise un - end - ing
넘 치 네 - 주 의 선 하 심 내 가 노 래 하 리 -
마 칠 때 - 끝 없 는 찬 양 - 나 드 리 리 라 -

10,000 reasons

Ten	thousand	reasons	for	my	heart	to	find
Ten	thousand	years and	then	for -	ev -	er -	more
수	많 은	이 유	로	나	노	래	해
수	많 은	세 월	지	나	영	원	히

O.T. : 10,000 Reasons (Bless The Lord) / O.W. : Matt Redman, Jonas Myrin
O.P. : worshiptogether.com Songs, sixsteps Music, Atlas Mountain Songs, Thankyou Music Ltd / S.P. : Universal Music Publishing Korea, CAIOS
Adm. : Capitol CMG Publishing / All rights reserved. Used by permission.

G

236

Alive In Us
(크신 사랑 온 땅 찬양해)

Reuben Morgan, Jason Ingram

Great is Your love. Let the whole earth sing   Let the whole earth sing
You out-shine the sun You are glo-ri-ous   You are glo-ri-ous
크 신 사 랑 온 땅 찬 양 - 해 온 땅 찬 양 - 해 -
주 빛 비 추 사 영 광 찬 란 - 해 영 광 찬 란 - 해 -

You reached for us, from on heaven's throne. when we had no hope.
Lord o-ver all You have made us new we owe it all to You
희 망 없 는 우 리 를 위 - 해 찾 아 오 신 - 주 -
만 유 의 주 구 원 의 주 - 님 우 리 삶 의 주 - 인 -

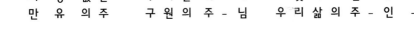

You are the Way. There is no oth-er. You are the Way. There is no oth-er.
in ev-ery-thing be ex-alt-ed in ev-ery-thing be ex-alt-ed
주 님 만 이 내 길 되 시 네 - 주 님 만 이 내 길 되 시 네 -
우 리 찬 양 받 으 소 서 - 우 리 찬 양 받 으 소 서 -

You rose from death, to vic-to-ry. You reign in life, oh Maj-es-ty,
부 활 하 신 승 리 의 주 - 삶 을 다 스 리 시 는 - 주

Your Name be high and lift-ed up Je-sus, Je-sus a-live in us.
그 이 름 높 여 드 리 리 - 예 - 수 예 - 수 우 리 - 의 주 -

1. C   G   Em   C

- -

Alive In Us

Written by Jason Ingram, Reuben Morgan
© 2011 Hillsong Music Publishing Australia (admin in Korea by Universal Music Publishing/ CAIOS)

237

All Who Are Thirsty

(목마른 자들)

Brenton Brown & Glenn Robertson

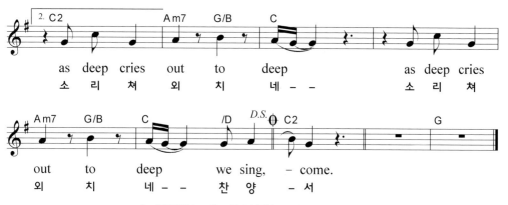

as deep cries out to deep　　　as deep cries
소 리 쳐 외 치 네 — —　　　소 리 쳐

out to deep we sing, – come.
외 치 네 — — 찬 양 – 서

All That I Can Do

(내가 할 수 있는 것은)

238

G

Ted Sandquist

And all that I can do　　is thank him　All that I can do　　is pray
내 가 할 수 있 – 는 것 은　　오 직 감 사 와 – 기 도

All that I can do　　is lift my hands　to sing his praise
두 손 을 높 이 – 들 고 주 께 – 찬 양 하 네

239 Amazing Grace (My Chains Are Gone)

(나 같은 죄인 살리신)

Loue Giglio, Chris Tomlin, John Newton & John P. Rees

A - maz - ing grace! how sweet the sound! That saved a
Twas grace that taught my heart to fear, And grace my
Thro' man - y dan - gers, toils, and snares I have al -
When we've been there ten thou - sand years, Bright shin - ing

나 같은 – 죄 인 살 리 신 주 은 혜 –
큰 죄 악 – 에 서 건 지 신 주 은 혜 –
이 제 껏 – 내 가 산 것 도 주 님 의 –
거 기 서 – 우 리 영 원 히 주 님 의 –

wretch like me! I once was lost, but now I'm
fears re - lieved. How pre - cious did that grace ap -
read - y come. Tis grace hath - bro't me safe thus
as the sun, We've no less days to sing God's

놀 라 워 잃 었 – 던 – 생 명 찾 – 았 –
고 마 워 나 처 – 음 – 믿 은 그 – 시 –
은 혜 라 또 나 – 를 – 장 차 본 – 향 –
은 혜 로 해 처 – 럼 – 밝 게 살 – 면 –

found; Was blind, but now I see. My chains are
pear The hour I first be - lieved!
far, And grace will lead me home.
praise Than when we first be - gun.

고 광 명 을 – 얻 었 네 나 의 결
간 귀 하 고 – 귀 하 다
에 인 도 해 – 주 시 리
서 주 찬 양 – 하 리 라

gone, I've been set free. My God, my Sav - ior has ran somed
– 박 푸 셨 도 – 다 나 의 구 세 주 대 속 – 했 –

Amazing Grace (My Chains Are Gone)

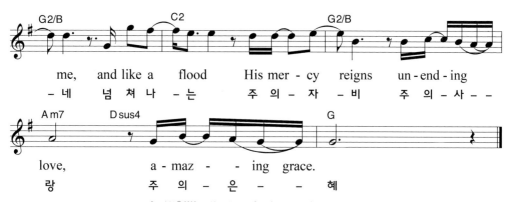

me, and like a flood His mer - cy reigns un - end - ing
– 네 넘쳐나 – 는 주 의 – 자 – 비 주 의 – 사 – –

love, a - maz – - ing grace.
랑 주 의 – 은 – – 혜

G

240

All Over The World

(온 세계 위에)

Terry Butler

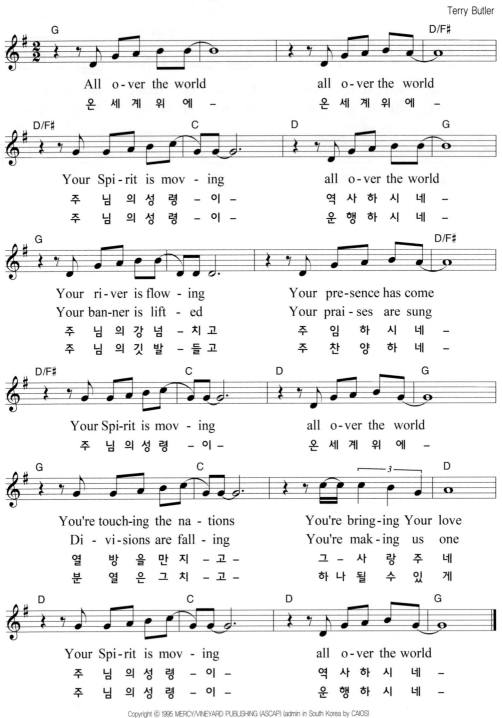

All o-ver the world   all o-ver the world
온 세 계 위 에 –   온 세 계 위 에 –

Your Spi-rit is mov - ing   all o-ver the world
주 님 의 성 령 – 이 –   역 사 하 시 네 –
주 님 의 성 령 – 이 –   운 행 하 시 네 –

Your ri-ver is flow - ing   Your pre-sence has come
Your ban-ner is lift - ed   Your prai - ses are sung
주 님 의 강 넘 – 치 고   주 임 하 시 네 –
주 님 의 깃 발 – 들 고   주 찬 양 하 네 –

Your Spi-rit is mov - ing   all o-ver the world
주 님 의 성 령 – 이 –   온 세 계 위 에 –

You're touch-ing the na - tions   You're bring-ing Your love
Di - vi -sions are fall - ing   You're mak-ing us one
열 방 을 만 지 – 고 –   그 – 사 랑 주 네
분 열 은 그 치 – 고 –   하 나 될 수 있 게

Your Spi-rit is mov - ing   all o-ver the world
주 님 의 성 령 – 이 –   역 사 하 시 네 –
주 님 의 성 령 – 이 –   운 행 하 시 네 –

Arms Of Love

(사랑의 노래 드리네)

241

Craig Musseau

242 Awesome Is The Lord Most High

(높고 놀라우신 주)

Jesse Reeves, Cary Pierce, Jon Abel & Chris Tomlin

Great are You, Lord, might - y in strength,
Where You send us, God, we will go.
위 대 하 - 신 전 능 - 의 주 -
보 내 신 - 곳 우 리 - 가 리 -

You are faith - ful and You will ev - er be,
You're the an - swer we want the world to know,
신 실 하 - 고 변 함 없 으 - 시 네 -
구 주 되 - 심 세 상 알 기 - 원 해 -

We will praise You all of our days,
We will trust You when You call our name,
내 평 생 - 에 찬 양 - 하 리 -
부 르 심 - 을 신 뢰 - 하 며 -

it's for Your glo - ry we of - fer ev - 'ry - thing. Raise your
Where You lead us we'll fol - low all the way
주 영 광 위 - 해 나 모 두 드 - 리 리 - 모 든
주 의 - 길 - 을 다 따 라 가 - 리 라 -

hands all you na - tions, shout to God all cre - a - tion, how
나 라 만 물 - 아 두 손 들 고 외 쳐 라 - 가 장

awe - some is the Lord most high. We will
높 고 - 놀 라 우 신 - 주 - 우 리

Awesome Is The Lord Most High

praise you to-geth - er, for now and for-ev - er. How
함 께 찬 양 – 해 지 금 부 터 – 영 원 – 히 – 가 장

awe - some is the Lord most high. *Fine*
높 고 – 놀 라 우 신 – 주 –

Hal - le-lu - jah, Hal - le-lu - jah, how awe-some is the
할 렐 루 – 야 – 할 렐 루 – 야 – 가 장 높 고 – 놀 라

Lord most high. *D.S.* Raise Your
우 신 – 주 – 모 든

O.T. : Awesome Is The Lord Most High / O.W. : Jesse Reeves, Chris Tomlin, Carl Richard Pierce, Jon Abel
O.P. : Rising Springs Music, worshiptogether.com Songs, Vamos Publishing, 45 Degrees Music, Bridge Building Music, Popular Purple Publishing
S.P. : Universal Music Publishing Korea, CAIOS
Adm. : Capitol CMG Publishing / All rights reserved, Used by permission.

243

Be Magnified
(나는 주를 작게 보았네)

Lynn DeShazo

I have made You too small in my eyes　O Lord,　for-give me
I have leaned on the wis-dom of men　O Lord,　for-give me
나는 주를 작게 보았네 － － 용서 － 하소서 －
사람들을 의지했던 나 － － 용서 － 하소서 －

And I have be-lieved in a lie　that You were un-a-ble to help me.
And I have re-spond-ed to them　In-stead of Your light and Your mer-cy.
나를 － 도울 수 － 없다는 － － 거짓 － 말을 믿 － 고 있었 － 네 －
주의 － 자비와 － 빛보다 － － 사람 － 들에게 － 의지했 － 네 －

But now,　O Lord, I see　my wrong　Heal my heart and show Your-self strong
이제 － 내잘 － 못알 － 았네 － － 내 마음 치료 － 하소서 －
이제 － 내잘 － 못알 － 았네 － － 주 능력 보여 － 주소서 －

And in my eyes and with my song　O － － Lord, be mag-ni-fied,　O － －
나의 눈과 노래 － 안에 광 － － 대 하 신 － 주 님 － － 광 － －

Lord, be mag-ni-fied.　Be mag-ni-fied, O Lord
대 하 신 － 주 님 － － 광 대 하 신 － 주 님 －

You are high-ly ex-alt-ed　And there is noth-ing You can't do
주는 높이 들리리 － 리 － 능 치 못할 일 없 － 으 리 －

Be Magnified

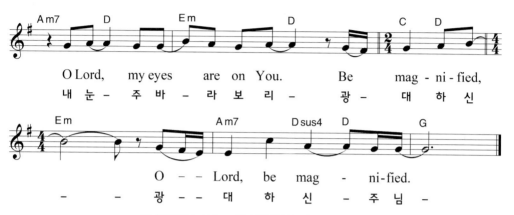

O Lord, my eyes are on You. Be mag - ni - fied,
내 눈 – 주바 – 라보리 – 광 – 대 하 신

O – – Lord, be mag – ni - fied.
– – 광 – – 대 하 신 – 주 님 –

G

244

Because Of Your Love
(주 사랑으로)

Brenton Brown & Paul Baloche

As we come in-to Your pres-ence, we re-mem-ber ev-'ry bless-ing that You've
grat-i-tude and prais-es for com-pas-sion so a-maz-ing, Lord, we've
주 계 신 곳 나 아 갈 때 우 리 에 게 부 으 시 는 주 의
하 신 모 든 일 들 우 리 함 께 찬 양 하 며 크 신

1. poured out so free-ly from a-bove
은 혜 늘 기 억 합 니 다

2. Lift-ing come to give You thanks
주 행 긍 휼 하 심 다

for all You've-done.
감 사 하 리

Be-cause of Your love,
주 사 랑 으 로

we're for-giv-en
용 서 받 고

Be-cause of Your love,
주 사 랑 으 로

our hearts are clean
정 케 되 네

We lift You up
찬 양 하 리

with songs of free-dom
자 유 의 노 래

For-ev-er we're changed
새 롭 게 되 리

D.S.

Be-cause of Your love
주 사 랑 으 로

Yeah
예

Yeah
예

Yeah
예

O.T. : Because Of Your Love / O.W. : Brenton Brown, Paul Baloche
O.P. : Thankyou Music Ltd / S.P. : Universal Music Publishing Korea, CAIOS
Adm. : Capitol CMG Publishing / All rights reserved. Used by permission.

Celebrate Come On And Celebrate 245
(다 와서 찬양해)

Trish Morgan & Dave Bankhead

Come on and cle - e - brate,
다 와 서 찬 양 해 –
His gift of love we will
사 랑 을 주 신 주

cel - e - brate.
찬 양 해 –
The Son of God who loved us
사 랑 의 우 리 주 님 –

and gave us life.
생 명 주 셨 네 –
We'll shout Your
소 리 쳐

praise O King,
찬 양 해 –
You give us joy no - thing else can bring.
기 쁨 을 주 시 는 우 리 왕 –

We'll give to You our of - fer - ing
찬 양 의 제 사 드 리 며 –
in cel - e - bra - tion praise.
주 님 께 경 배 해

Come on and cel - e - brate
다 와 서 찬 양 해 –
cel - e - brate
찬 양 해 –

cel - e - brate and sing.
찬 양 해 – 주 님
1. cel - e - brate and sing.
찬 양 해 주 님
to the King.
우 리 왕 –

2. cel - e - brate and sing to the King.
찬 양 해 주 님 우 리 왕 – –

G

O.T. : Celebrate Come On And Celebrate / O.W. : Trish Morgan, Dave Bankhead
O.P. : Thankyou Music Ltd / S.P. : Universal Music Publishing Korea, CAIOS
Adm. : Capitol CMG Publishing / All rights reserved. Used by permission.

246

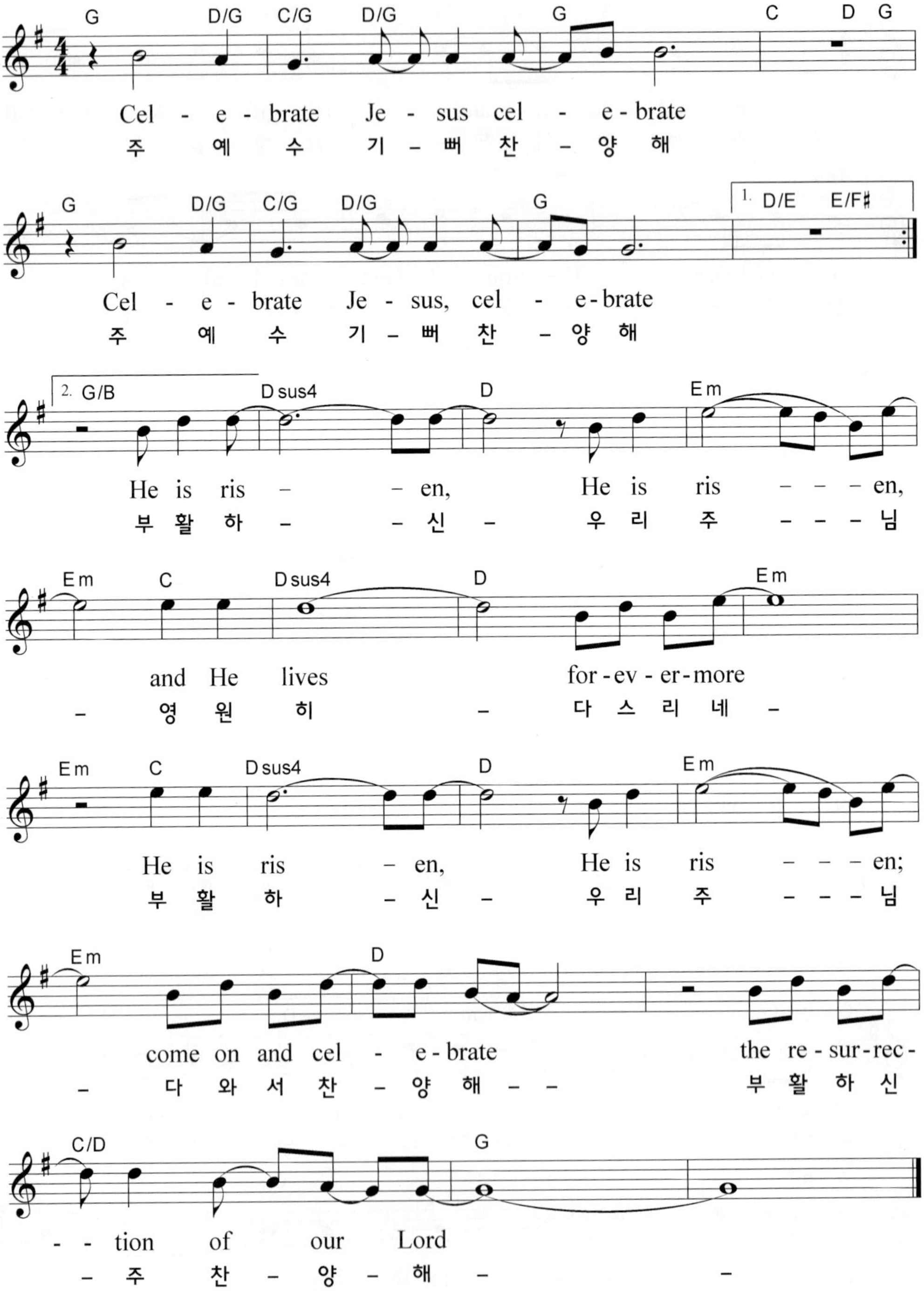

Celebrate Jesus Celebrate

(주 예수 기뻐 찬양해)

Gary Oliver

G D/G C/G D/G G C D G
Cel - e - brate Je - sus cel - e - brate
주 예 수 기 – 뻐 찬 – 양 해
G D/G C/G D/G G 1. D/E E/F♯
Cel - e - brate Je - sus, cel - e - brate
주 예 수 기 – 뻐 찬 – 양 해
2. G/B Dsus4 D Em
He is ris – – en, He is ris – – – en,
부 활 하 – – 신 – 우 리 주 – – – 님
Em C Dsus4 D Em
and He lives for - ev - er - more
– 영 원 히 – 다 스 리 네 –
Em C Dsus4 D Em
He is ris – en, He is ris – – – en;
부 활 하 – 신 – 우 리 주 – – – 님
Em D
come on and cel - e - brate the re - sur - rec -
– 다 와 서 찬 – 양 해 – – 부 활 하 신
C/D G
- - tion of our Lord
– 주 찬 – 양 – 해 – –

Create In Me A Clean Heart

(정결한 맘 주시옵소서)

247

Keith Green

Cre - ate in me a clean – heart Oh, – – God
정 결 한 맘 주 시 옵 소 서 오 주 님

and re-new a right spi-rit with-in me Cre
정 직 한 영 을 새 롭 게 하 소 서 정 나 를

Cast me not a - way from Thy pre-sence, oh Lord, and
주 님 앞 에 서 멀 리 하 지 마 시 고 주 의

take not thy Ho - ly spir - it from me Re -
성 령 을 거 두 지 마 옵 소 서 그

store un - to me the joy of Thy sal - va - tion
구 원 의 기 쁨 다 시 회 복 시 키 시 고

and re - new a right spi - rit with in me
변 치 않 는 맘 내 안 에 주 소 서

248

Church On Fire

(성령의 불타는 교회)

Russell Fragar

G7

The Ho-ly Spir - it is here and His pow - er is real any-
light that shines to make the dark dis - ap - ppear There's a
성 령 님 이 임 하 시 면 능 력 이 나 타 나 – 모
– – 을 물 리 치 는 빛 이 있 네 – 능

C7

- thing can happ - en and it pro - ba - bly will some -
pow - er at work but the - re's noth - ing to fear
– 든 것 이 일 어 날 수 있 게 되 죠 – 참
– 력 힘 입 어 – 난 두 렵 지 않 네 –

A7　　**D7**　　**G**

- thing ve - ry good some-thing good is go-ing on a - round here
– 선 한 것 이 선 한 것 이 여 기 일 어 나 – 네 –

1. G　　**2. G**　　**C/G**

Well there's a　　This is a church on fire
어 두 움　　성 령 의 불 타 는

G　　**D/F#**　　**Em**

This is the Ho - ly Spir - it's flame We have a
– 회 – 성 령 의 불 꽃 임 – 하 네 – 온 마 음

C/G　　**G**　　**Am7**　　**D7**

burn - ing de - sire to lift up Je - sus's name Let
다 하 여 – – 서 주 이 름 높 이 세 – 우

Church On Fire

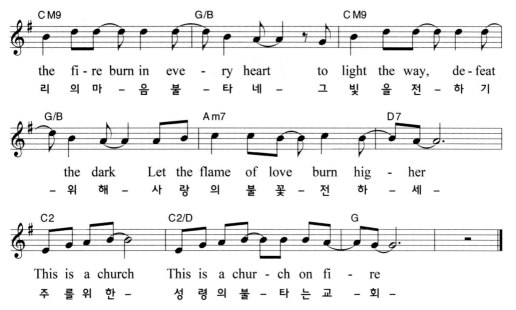

the fi - re burn in eve - ry heart   to light the way, de - feat
리 의 마 – 음 불 – 타 네 –   그 빛 을 전 – 하 기

the dark   Let the flame of love   burn hig - her
– 위 해 – 사 랑 의 불 꽃 – 전 하 – 세 –

This is a church   This is a chur - ch on fi - re
주 를 위 한 – 성 령 의 불 – 타 는 교 – 회 –

Words and Music by Russell Fragar
© 1997 Hillsong Music Publishing Australia (admin in Korea by Universal Music Publishing/ CAIOS)

G

249 Every Move I Make

(내 모든 삶의 행동 주 안에)

David Ruis

Ev - 'ry move I make, I make in You You make me move, Je - sus
내 모든 삶의 행동 주 안 에 주 님 안 - 에 있 네

ev - 'ry breath I take, I breathe in You.
나 의 숨 쉬 는 순 간 들 도

Ev - 'ry step I take, I take in You, You are my way, Je - sus,
내 모 든 삶 의 걸 음 주 안 에 내 길 도 - 주 안 에

ev - 'ry breath I take, I breathe in You.
나 의 숨 쉬 는 순 간 들 도

La la la la la la la la la la la la
라 라 라 라 - 라 라 라 라 라 라 - 라 라

Waves of mer - cy, waves of grace, ev - 'ry - where I look,
자 비 와 은 혜 의 물 결 어 디 서 나 주

I see Your face; You love has cap - tured me,
- 얼 굴 - 보 네 - 주 사 랑 날 붙 드 네

O, my God, this love how can it be?
오 놀 라 운 주 - 님 의 사 랑 -

Glory

(영광 높이 계신 주께)

Danny Daniels

250

Glo - ry glo - ry in the high - est glo - ry
영 광 – 높 이 계 신 주 께 영 광 –

to the Al - might - y glo - ry to the Lamb of God and
전 능 의 구 주 어 린 양 께 영 – 광 을 – 내

glo - ry to the liv - ing word glo - ry to the Lamb
살 아 계 신 주 – 님 께 – 어 린 양 께 영 광 –

I give Glo - ry glo - ry glo - ry
주 께 – 영 광 – 영 광 – 영 광 –

glo - ry glo - ry glo - ry to the Lamb
영 광 – – 영 광 – 영 광 어 린 – 양 –

I give glo - ry to the Lamb
주 께 영 – 광 어 – 린 양 – –

251 Famous One You Are The Lord

(당신은 주)

Jesse Reeves & Chris Tomlin

You   are the Lord,   the fa-mous One,   fa-mous One
당 – 신 은 주 –   위 대 하 – 신   그 이 – 름

great   is Your name in all   the earth.   The
온 – 땅 에 널 리 퍼 – 지 네   하

heav – ens de-clare   You're glo-ri-ous,   glo-ri-ous
늘 – 도 찬 양 – – 주   영 광 의 – –   그 이 름 – –

great   is Your fame be – yond   the earth.   *Fine*
온 – 땅 에 널 리 퍼 – 지 네

And for
The
주 가
새

all   You've done   and yet to do,   with
Morn – ing Star   is shin-ing through,   and
행 – 하 신 – 모 든 일 들 –   온
벽 – 하 늘 – 빛 나 는 별 –   다

ev – 'ry breath   I'm   prais-ing You.   De-
ev – 'ry eye   is   watch-ing You.   Re-
힘 – 다 해 – – 주 – 찬 양 해   모
눈 – 들 어 – – 주 – 를 보 네   주

Famous One You Are The Lord

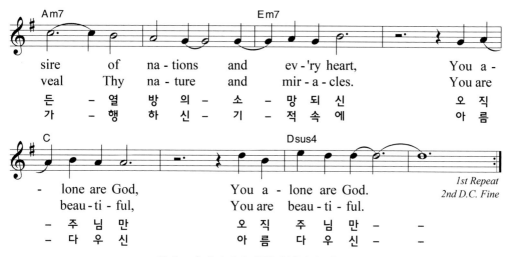

sire of na-tions and ev-'ry heart, You a-
veal Thy na-ture and mir-a-cles. You are

든 – 열 방 의 – 소 – 망 되 신 오 직
가 – 행 하 신 – 기 – 적 속 에 아 름

- lone are God, You a-lone are God.
beau-ti-ful, You are beau-ti-ful.

1st Repeat
2nd D.C. Fine

– 주 님 만 오 직 주 님 만 – –
– 다 우 신 아 름 다 우 신 – –

O.T. : Famous One You Are The Lord / O.W. : Chris Tomlin, Jesse Reeves
O.P. : Rising Springs Music, worshiptogether.com Songs, Vamos Publishing / S.P. : Universal Music Publishing Korea, CAIOS
Adm. : Capitol CMG Publishing / All rights reserved. Used by permission.

G

252 Freedom

(주의 영이 계신 곳에)

Darrell Evans

Where the Spir-it of the Lord – is, there is free-dom   where the
주 의 영 이계신 곳 – 에 자 유 함 있네   주 의

there is peace,   there is love,   there is joy.
평 – 화   사 – 랑   기 – 쁨 –

It is for free - dom You've set us free
주 내게 자 – 유 주 셨 네 –

It is for free - dom You've set us free   I'm free,
자 유 케 하 – 기 위 하 여 –   자 유

O, I'm   free,   O, I'm   free,   I'm   free,
난 자 유   자 유   난 자 유

So, we will walk in Your free-dom, walk in Your lib-er-ty
주 의 자 유 함 안 에 우 리 걸 어 가 리

We will walk in Your free-dom, walk in Your lib-er-ty
주 의 자 유 함 안 에 우 리 걸 어 가 리

Freedom

We will dance in Your free-dom, dance in Your lib - er - ty
주 의 자 유 함 안 에 우 리 춤 을 추 리

Where the Spir-it of the Lord – is there is free - dom
주 의 영 이 계 신 곳 – 에 자 유 함 있 네

Where the Spir-it of the Lord is, there is free-dom
주 의 영 이 계 신 곳 – 에 자 유 함 있 네

Where the
주 의

It is for free - dom You've set us free
주 내 게 자 – 유 주 셨 네 –

It is for free - dom You've set us free
자 유 케 하 – 기 위 하 여 –

and I'm free.
자 유

G

253 Give Us Clean Hands

(깨끗한 손 주옵소서)

Charlie Hall

Give Us Clean Hands

a gen-er-a-tion that seeks, that seeks Your face

주의 얼굴 찾게 하옵 소 서

O – God of Ja - - cob

오 – 야 곱 의 – 하 나 – 님 –

O.T. : Give Us Clean Hands / O.W. : Charlie Hall
O.P. : worshiptogether.com Songs, sixsteps Music / S.P. : Universal Music Publishing Korea, CAIOS
Adm. : Capitol CMG Publishing / All rights reserved, Used by permission,

G

254

Glory Glory Lord
(영광 주님께)

Robert D Fitts

Glo - ry, glo - ry Lord,　　we give you glo - ry, Lord
영 광 주 님 께 -　　주 님 께 영 광 을 - -

Glo - ry, glo - ry Lord,　You are the might - y God.
영 광 주 님 께 - 당 신 은 능 력 의 주

You are the might-y God.　　You who go down to the sea,
당 신 은 능 력 의 주　　산 위 에 올 라 가 서

You who live in the is - lands,　　If you live in the ci - ty,
넓 은 바 다 를 향 해　　거 리 한 가 운 데 서

Lift Your voice and sing out.　Sing to the Lord a new song,
소 리 높 여 주 찬 양　새 노 래 로 주 찬 - 양

Sing His praise to the ends of the earth　　Let ev' - ry na - tion tell
땅 끝 까 - 지 주 이 름 높 여 -　　모 든 열 방 들 나

it,　　Till ev' - ry man has heard.
- 와　　소 리 높 여 주 찬 양

Glory Glory Lord

You are the liv-ing God,
주　　　당 신 은 능 력 의 주

You are the on-ly God,
당 신 은 능 력 의

You are the might-y God!
주　　　당 신 은 능 력 의 주 　　　－

O.T. : Glory Glory Lord / O.W. : Robert D, Fitts
O.P. : Universal Music – Brentwood Benson Publ, / S.P. : Universal Music Publishing Korea, CAIOS
Adm, : Capitol CMG Publishing / All rights reserved, Used by permission,

G

255 God Will Make A Way
(나의 가는 길)

Don Moen

God will make a way, where there seems to be no way
나의 가-는 길 - 주 님 인 도 하-시 네

He works in ways we can-not see He will make a way
- 그 는 보 이 지 - 않 아 도 - 날 위 해 - 일 하

for me He will be my guide, hold me
- 시 네 - 주 나 의 - 인 도 - 자 항 상

close-ly to His side With love and strength for each new day
함 께 하 - 시 네 - 사 랑 과 힘 - 베 푸 시 며 -

He will make a way, He will make a way
인 도 하 - 시 네 - 인 도 하 - 시 - 네

Fine

By a road-way in the wil-der-ness He'll
광 야 에 길 을 - 만 드 - 시 고 - 날

lead me and riv-ers in the des-ert will I see.
인 도 해 사 막 에 강 - 만 드 - 신 것 - 보 라

God Will Make A Way

Heav-en and earth will fade, but His
하 늘 과 땅 – 변 해 – 도 주 의

Word will still re - main He will do
말 씀 영 – 원 히 – 내 삶 속 에 – 새

some - thing new to - day,
일 을 행 – 하 리 –

D.C.

G

256

Great Awakening

(모든 민족에게)

Ray Goudie/Dave Bankhead & Steve Bassett

Lord pour out Your Spir-it on all the peo-ples of the earth
Lord pour out Your Spir-it on all the na-tions of the world
모 든 민 족 에 게 - - 주 성 령 부 어 주 소 서 - - -
모 든 열 방 에 게 - - 주 성 령 부 어 주 소 서 - - -

Let Your sons and daugh-ters speak Your words of proph-e-sy
Let them see Your glo-ry let them fall in reve-rent awe
하 나 님 의 백 성 - - 주 의 말 씀 주 시 고 -
영 광 중 에 오 사 - - 주 경 외 하 게 하 시 고 -

Send us dreams and vi-sions re-veal the se-cret of Your heart
Show Your might-y pow-er shake the heav-ens and the earth
꿈 과 환 상 주 사 - 주 의 비 밀 알 리 소 서 - - -
크 신 능 력 으 로 - 땅 과 하 늘 흔 드 소 서 - - -

Lord our faith is ris-ing let all heav-en sound the com-ing of Your day
Lord the world is wait-ing let cre-a-tion see the com-ing of Your day
우 리 믿 사 오 니 - 하 늘 이 주 의 날 선 포 - 케 하 소 서 -
주 를 기 다 리 니 - 만 물 이 주 의 날 을 보 - 게 하 소 서 -

There's gon-na be a great a-wak-en-ing
그 날 엔 주 - 의 영 이 임 하 여 -

There's gon-na be a great re-vi-val in our land
큰 부 흥 이 - 땅 위 에 일 - 어 나 리 라

Great Awakening

There's gon - na be a great a - wak - en - ing and
모 든 영혼 – 깨 어 일 어 날 때 – 주

eve - ry - one who calls on Je - sus they will be saved
예 수 를 – 부 르 는 자 는 – 구 원 되 리 – – –

257

God Is Our Father

(주 우리 아버지)

Alex Simon & Freda Kimmey

God is our Fa - ther For He has made us His o - wn
주 우 리 아 – 버 지 우 리 는 그 분 의 자 – 녀

Made Je - sus our bro - ther And Hand in ha - nd we'll
예 수 우 리 – 형 제 손 에 손 잡 고 하 나 되 어

grow to - geth - er as one. Sing praise to the Lord,
함 께 걸 – 어 가 리 주 께 찬 송 해

with the tam - bou - rine Sing praise to the Lord, with clap ping
with the dan - cing feet Sing praise to the
탬 버 린 으 로 주 께 찬 송 해 손 뼉 쳐
춤 을 추 면 서 주 께 찬 송

Lord, with our voi - ce La la la la la la la la la
해 – 목 소 리 로 랄 랄 라 라 랄 라 라 – 랄 라

La la la la la la la la la la la la la la la la la
랄 랄 라 라 랄 라 라 – 라 랄 랄 라 라 랄 라 라 – 랄 라

la la la la la la la la la la
랄 랄 랄 랄 랄 라 라 – 라 랄 라 –

Hallelujah

258

(주 사랑 놀라와)

Brian Doerksen & Brenton Brown

G

259

Hail To The King

(이 땅 위에 오신)

Larry Hampton

You came to us a man, in ve-ry na-ture God.
We eag-er-ly a-wait the com-ing of the day.
이 땅 위에 오신 — 하 나 님의 — 본체 —
우 리 고대 하 네 — 주 님 오 실 — 그 날 —

Pierced for our in-i-qui-ties as You hung up-on the Cross
the glo-ry of the ris-en King will shine up-on the earth.
십 자 가 — 에 달 — 리 사 우 리 죄 사 하 — 셨 네 —
다 시 사 신 — 왕 의 — 영 광 이 땅 을 비 — 추 네 —

But God ex-alt-ed You to the high-est place
Then riv-al thrones will fall be-fore the Lord of all,
하 나 님 이 — 그 를 — 지 극 히 — 높 여 —
사 단 의 권 — 세 는 — 주 앞 에 무 — 너 져 —

and gave to You the right to bear the name a-bove all names.
and hail sup-reme au-thor-i-ty to True and Liv-ing God.
모 든 이 름 — 위 에 — 뛰 어 — 난 이 름 을 — 주 사 —
생 명 과 진 — 리 의 — 주 권 — 세 가 장 높 — 도 다

that at the name of Je-sus we should bow,
우 리 예 수 이 름 앞 에 절 하 고

ev'-ry tongue con-fess that You are Lord.
모 든 입 이 주 를 시 인 — 해

Hail To The King

when You come in glo - ry for the world to see,
영 광 중 에 오 실 주 를 보 리 라

we will sing "Hail to the King
선 포 - 해 - 왕 께 만 세 -

in all His splen - dor and ma - jes - ty
존 귀 와 위 엄 - 을 찬 양 해

Hail to the King of kings, Lord Je - sus, Our God."
왕 의 왕 께 만 세 주 예 - 수 하 나 님 -

G

260 Hallelujah To The Lamb

(모든 민족과 방언들 가운데)

Debbye Graafsma & Don Moen

Lord I stand in the midst of a mul-ti-tude of those from ev-'ry tribe and tongue.
Lord we stand by grace in Your pre-sence, cleansed by the blood of the Lamb.

모 든 민족과 방언들 가운데 수 많 은 주 – 백 성 모 였 –
어 린 양 피 로 씻 어 진 우 리 들 은 혜 로 주 – 앞 에 서 있 –

We are Your peo-ple re-deemed by Your blood pur-chased from
We are Your child-ren, called by Your name hum-bly we

네 주 의 – 보 혈 과 – 그 사 랑 – 으 로 친 백 – 성
네 주 이 – 름 으 로 – 자 녀 된 – 우 리 겸 손 – 히

death by Your love. There are no words good e-nough to
bow and we pray. Re-lease Your power to work in us and

삼 – 으 셨 네 – 주 를 향 한 감 사 와 – 찬
구 – 하 오 니 – 주 의 능 력 우 리 게 – 베

thank – You there are no words to ex-press my praise – – but I will
through us till we are changed to be more like You, Then all the

양 – 을 말 로 다 표 현 할 수 없 네 – – 다 만 – 내
푸 – 사 주 를 더 욱 닮 게 하 소 서 – – 그 때 – 에

lift up my voice and sing from my heart with all of my strength
na-tions will see Your glo-ry re-vealed and wor – ship you

소 리 높 혀 – 온 맘 을 다 해 – 찬 양 – 하 리 라 –
모 든 나 라 – 주 영 광 보 며 – 경 배 – 하 리 라 –

Hallelujah To The Lamb

Hal-le - lu-jah, Hal-le - lu-jah, Ha-le - lu-jah, to the Lamb Hal-le-
할 렐 루 야 할 렐 루 야 할 렐 루 야 어린 양 할 렐

lu - jah, hal-le - lu - jah, by the blood of Christ we stand. - Ev-'ry
루 야 할 렐 루 야 주의 보 혈 덮 으 사 - 모 든

tong - ue, ev-'ry tri-be ev-'ry peo-ple, ev-'ry land giv-ing
족 속 모 든 방 언 모 든 백 성 열 방 이 모 든

glo - ry gi-ving hon-or gi-ving praise un-to the Lamb - of God
영 광 모 든 존 귀 모 든 찬 양 주 께 드 - 리 네

Fine

Ev' - ry knee shall bow,
무 릎 꿇 - 고 서 -

ev'-ry tongue con-fess that You are Lord of all Hal-le
다 함 께 - 고 백 해 만 유 의 주 님 - 할 렐

261 Heaven Is In My Heart

(주님 나라 임하리)

Graham Kendrick

O, — — — — — — — heav-en is in my heart.
오 — — — — — — — 주 님 나 라 임 하 리

last time to Coda

O, — — — — — — — heav-en is in my heart.
오 — — — — — — — 주 님 나 라 임 하 리

The king - dom of our God is here,
His pre - cious life on me He spent,
We are a tem - ple for His throne,
주 이 름 거 - 룩 하 - 도 다 -
호 흡 이 있 - 는 자 - 들 아 -
민 족 과 열 - 방 나 - 아 와 -

Heav-en is in my heart. The pres-ence of His maj - es - ty,
To give me life with-out an end,
And Christ is the foun - da - tion stone,
주 님 나 라 임 하 리 그 뜻 이 이 - 뤄 지 - 이 다 -
주 이 름 찬 - 양 하 - 여 라 -
주 의 이 름 - 부 르 리 라 -

Heav-en is in my heart. And in His pres-ence joy a-bounds,
In Christ is all my con - fi-dence,
He will re - turn to take us home,
주 님 나 라 임 하 리 악 에 서 승 - 리 하 - 셨 네 -
존 귀 와 영 - 광 능 - - 력 -
온 세 상 에 - 전 파 - 하 라 -

Heaven Is In My Heart

Heav-en is in my heart.

The light of ho-li-ness sur-rounds,
The hope of my in her-i-tance,
The Spi-rit and the Bride say,"Come",

주 님 나 라 임 하 리

영 광 이 주 – 께 있 – 도 다 –
구 원 이 주 – 께 있 – 도 다 –
땅 끝 까 지 이 르 – 도 다 –

Heav-en is in my heart. Heav-en is in my heart.

주 님 나 라 임 하 리   주 님 나 라 임 하 리

D.C.

G

He Is Lord

(우리 주 우리 주 죽음에서)

262

He is Lord, He is Lord He has ri-sen from the dead And He is Lord
우 리 주 우 리 주 죽 음 에 서 부 활 하 신 우 리 주

Eve-ry knee shall bow Eve-ry tongue con-fess That Je-sus Christ is Lord
모 두 절 하 고 모 두 외 치 세 예 수 는 우 리 주

263

He Is The King

(예수는 왕 예수는 주)

Don Moen, Rev John F Stocker & Tom Ewing

He is the King He is the Lord He is the One who deli - vers
예 수 는 왕 - 예 수 는 주 - 예 수 는 날 - 구 원 하 신

me He is the King He is the Lord He is the One
주 - - - 예 수 는 왕 - 예 수 는 주 - 예 수 는 날

who deli - vers me Hail to the King Hail to the Lord
- 구 원 하 신 - 주 왕 께 만 세 - 주 께 만 세

Hail to the One who de - li - vers me Hail to the King
- 날 구 원 하 신 주 님 께 만 세 - - - 왕 께 만 세

Fine

Hail to the Lord Hail to the Lord who de - li - vers me
- 주 께 만 세 - 날 구 원 하 신 주 님 께 만 - 세

Je - sus strong and migh - ty King Rul - ing o - ver all the king - doms of this
강 하 고 능 하 신 왕 세 상 모 - 든 나 라 다 - 스 리 시

world Lift Your voice to Him and sing He's the Lord
네 소 리 높 여 찬 양 해 그 는 만

of every - thing He is the King of kings He is the Lord
- - 유 의 주 - 그 는 만 왕 의 왕 예 수 는 왕

D.S.

He Is The King Of Kings

(만왕의 왕 예수)

Virgil O Meares

He is the King of kings. He is the Lord
만 왕 의 왕 예 수 - 만 유 의 주

of lords. His name is Je-sus, Je-sus, Je-sus, Je-sus
예 수 - 그 이 름 예 수 예 수 예 수 예 수

O He is the King.
오 - - 예 수 는 왕 -

G

265

Here Is Love

(바다 같은 주의 사랑)

Matt Redman (Arr.)

Here is love vast as the o-cean, lov-ing kind-ness as the flood when the
mount of cru-ci-fi-xion, foun-tains o-pened deep and wide. Through the

바 다 같 은 주 의 사 랑 내 맘 속 에 넘 치 네 생 명
박 힌 언 덕 위 에 생 명 의 문 열 렸 네 깊 고

prince of life our ran-som shed for us His pre-cious blood
flood-gates of God's mer-cy flowed a vast and grac-ious

의 주 우 릴 위 해 보 혈 흘 려 주 셨 네
넓 은 은 혜 의 샘 강 과 같 이 흐 르

when the blood. Who His love will not re-mem-ber? Who can
바 다 네 영 원 하 신 주 의 사 랑 어 찌

cease to sing His praise? He can nev-er be for-got-ten, Through-out
우 리 잊 으 리 생 명 주 신 주 님 만 을 영 원

heaven's e-ter-nal days.
히 찬 양 하 리

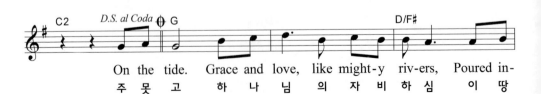

On the tide. Grace and love, like might-y riv-ers, Poured in-
주 못 고 하 나 님 의 자 비 하 심 이 땅

Here Is Love

ces - sant from a - bove. And heaven's peace and per-fect jus-tice Kissed a
위 에 넘치네 평 강 의 왕 주님예 수 세 상

guilt - y world in love.　No love is high-er,
죄 구 속 했 네　더 높은사 랑

no love is wid-er, no love is deep-er, no love is tru-er. No love is high-er,
더 높은사 랑 더 깊은사 랑 진 실한사랑 더 높은사 랑

no love is wid - er,　no love is like Your love, O Lord.
더 넓은사 랑　주 같은 사 랑 없 - 네 -

love, O Lord.　Here is　love　vast as the o-cean,
없 - 네 - 바 다 같 은 주 의 사 랑 -

Here is love vast as the o-cean,　Here is
바 다 같은 주의 사 랑 -　바 다

G

266

Hold Me Lord

(주님의 손으로)

Danny Daniels

Hold me Lord, in Your arms. Fill me Lord, with Your Spir - it
주님의 - 손 으로 - 나 -를 - 붙 드 소 서
주님의 - 사랑으로 - 나 -를 - 만 지 소 서

Touch my heart, with Your love Let my life glo - ri - fy Your Name,
주님의 - 성 령으로 나 -를 - 채 워 주 소 서 -
내 삶을 - 드림으로 주님께 - 영 광 돌 리 리 -

Sing-ing al - le - lu - ia. Sing-ing al - le - lu - ia.
찬양 할 렐 - -루 야 - 찬양 할 렐 - -루 야 -

Sing-ing al - le - lu - ia Sing-ing al - le - lu - ia,
찬양 할 렐 - -루 야 - 찬양 할 렐 루 야

al - le - lu - ia al - le - lu - ia al - le - lu - ia, al - le - lu
할 렐 루 - 야 - 할 렐 루 - - - - 할 렐 루 - 야 - 할 렐 루

Holy And Anointed One

(예수 예수 거룩한)

John Barnett

267

Je - sus Je - sus
예 - 수 예 - 수

Ho - ly and a - noin - ted One Je - sus
Ri - sen and ex - alt - ed One Je - sus
거 룩 한 - 기 름 부 음 받 은 예 - - 수
영 원 히 - 높 임 받 으 실 예 - -

sus Your name is like ho - ney on my lips Your Spi - rit like wa-
수 주 이 름 내 입 술 에 꿀 - 같 고 - 주 성 령 내 영

- ter to my soul Your word is a lamp un - to my feet
혼 을 적 - 시 네 - 주 말 씀 내 길 에 빛 과 - 같 네

Je - sus I lo - ve You I lo - ve You
- 예 수 주 님 - - 을 - 사 랑 해 요

G

268 Hosanna

(호산나)

Brenton Brown & Paul Baloche

Praise is ris - ing Eyes are turn - ing to You –
Hear the sound of hearts re - turn - ing to You –
찬 – 양 중 – 에 눈 을 들 – 어 – 주 를 –
주 – 께 드 – 린 마 음 다 – 한 – 기 도 –

We turn to You Hope is stir - ring
We turn to You In Your king - dom
주 를 보 네 – 소 – 망 중 – 에
들 으 소 서 – 주 – 의 나 – 라

Hearts are yearn - ing for You We long for You
bro - ken lives are made new You make us new
마 – 음 다 – 해 – 주 만 – 나 바 라 네 –
상 – 한 영 – 혼 – 들 을 – 새 롭 게 해 –

When we see You we find strength to face the day
주 님 을 볼 – 때 나 에 게 – 힘 주 시 네

In Your Pre - sence all our fears are washed a - way washed a - way
주 님 안 – 에 모 든 두 – 렴 – 사 라 져 사 라 져

Ho - sa – – na Ho - san – – – – – na
– 호 산 – – 나 호 산 – – – – – 나

Hosanna

You are the God who saves us Wor-thy of all
구 원 의 주 – 하 나 – 님 – 찬 양 받 으

our prais - es Ho - san – – na Ho -
– 실 주 – 님 – 호 산 – – 나 호

san – – – – – na come have Your way a - mong us
산 – – – – 나 – 내 안 에 임 – 하 셔 – 서

we wel-come You here Lord Je - sus
– 주 님 의 뜻 이 – 루 소 – 서 –

O.T. : Hosanna (Praise Is Rising) / O.W. : Brenton Brown, Paul Baloche
O.P. : Thankyou Music Ltd / S.P. : Universal Music Publishing Korea, CAIOS
Adm. : Capitol CMG Publishing / All rights reserved, Used by permission,

G

269 Hosanna

(호산나)

Carl Tuttle

Ho - san - na! Ho - san - na! Ho-san-na in the high - est!
Glo - ry! Glo - ry! Glo-ry to the King of Kings!

호 산 - 나 호 산 - 나 호 산 나 높은 곳 에 서
영 - 광 영 - 광 왕 의 왕 께 영 광 을

Ho - san - na! Ho - san - na! Ho-san-na in the high - est!
Glo - ry! Glo - ry! Glo-ry to the King of Kings!

호 산 - 나 호 산 - 나 호 산 나 높은 곳 에 서
영 - 광 영 - 광 왕 의 왕 께 영 광 을

Lord, we lift up Your name, with hearts full of praise;

주 의 이 름 높 여 - 다 찬 양 하 라 -

Be ex-alt-ed, oh Lord, my God! Ho-san-na in the high - est!
Glo-ry to the King of Kings!

귀 하 신 주 나 의 하 나 님 호 산 나 높 이 외 치 세
주 님 께 영 광 돌 리 세

Hosanna To The Son Of David

270

(당신은 영광의 왕)

Mavis Ford

You are the King of glo-ry You are the prince of
당 신 은 영 광 의 – 왕 당 신 은 평 강 의

Peace. You are the Lord of Hea-ven and Earth.
왕 당 신 은 하 늘 과 땅 의 주

You are the son of righte-ous-ness. An-gels bow down be-
당 신 은 정 의 의 아 들 천 사 가 무 릎

fore You wor-ship and a-dore. You For
꿇 – 고 예 배 하 며 경 배 하 네

You have the words of eter-nal life. You are Je-sus Christ the
영 원 한 생 명 의 말 – 씀 당 신 은 예 수 그리스도

Lord. Ho-san-na to the Son of Da-vid. Ho-
주 호 산 나 다 윗 의 – 자 손 – 께 호

san-na to the King of kings. Glo-ry in the highest
산 나 불 러 왕 중 의 왕 높 은 하 늘 엔

Hea – – ven for Je-sus the Mes-si- ah reigns.
영 광 을 – 예 수 주 메 시 아 – 네

G

271 I Give You My Heart

(주를 높이기 원합니다)

Reuben Morgan

This is my de-sire to hon - or You,
All I have with-in me I give You praise.
주를 높 - 이 기 - - - - - 원 합 니 다
내 안 의 - 모 든 - - 것 - - 찬 양 하 리

Lord, with all my heart I wor-ship You
온 마 음 - 다 해 - - - 경 배 하 리 -
오 직 주 - 님 만 - - - 높 이 리

1. F2 F C6 C/D

2. F2 F C6 C/D G

Lord, I give You my heart I give You my soul,
나 의 맘 과 영 혼 - 다 주 께 드 - 려

I live for You a - lone, Eve-ry breath that I take,
주 위 해 살 리 라 - 나 의 모 든 호 - 흡

eve-ry mo-ment I'm a-wake Lord, have Your way in me
삶 의 모 든 순 - 간 에 - - 주 뜻 이 루 소 서

Lord, I give You my heart have Your way in me
나 의 맘 과 영 혼 뜻 이 루 소 서 -

I Just Keep Trusting The Lord 272

(나 주의 믿음 갖고)

John W. Peterson

I just keep trus-ting my Lord as I walk a - long
나 주의 믿 음 갖 고 홀 로 걸 어 도
내 주 는 선 한 목 자 나 를 인 도 해

I just keep trus-ting my Lord and He gave a song
나 주 의 믿 음 갖 고 노 래 부 르 네
사 망 의 골 짜 기 로 다 닐 지 라 도

Though the storm clouds dark-en the sky over the heaven-ly trail
폭 풍 구 름 몰 아 치 고 하 늘 덮 어 도
주 님 께 서 나 의 길 을 인 도 하 시 니

I just keep trus-ting my Lord He will ne-ver fail
나 주 의 믿 음 갖 고 실 망 치 않 네
나 주 를 따 라 가 리 언 제 까 지 나

Fine

He's a faith-ful friend such a faith-ful friend
주 는 내 친 구 진 실 한 친 구
주 는 내 목 자 선 하 신 목 자

D.S. al Fine

I can count on Him to the ve-ry end
세 상 끝 까 지 주 의 지 하 리
어 디 가 든 지 함 께 하 시 네

273 I Want To Be Where You Are

(주님 곁에 있기 원해요)

Don Moen

I Want To Be Where You Are

G

274 I Love To Be In Your Presence
(주 임재하시는 곳에)

Paul Baloche & ED Kerr

I love to be in Your pres - ence, with Your peo-
주 임 재 하 시 - 는 곳 - 에 - 우 리 함

- ple sing - ing prais - es   I love to stand and re - joice,
- 께 - 찬 양 하 - - 리   일 어 나 기 - 쁨 으 로

lift my hands   and raise   my voice.   I
- 소 리 높 - 여 찬 - - 양 해 -   주 -

You set my feet to danc - ing,   You fill my heart with song   You give me
내 영 혼 노 래 하 - 며   춤 추 게 하 시 네 -   기 쁨 의

rea - son to re - joice,   re - joice,   I   Lift my hands,
이 유 되 시 는 - 주 님 - - - -   주 - 두 손 을

lift my hands,   lift my hands and raise   my voice.
- 들 고 서 -   소 리 높 - 여 찬 - - 양 해 -

In The Secret

(은밀한 곳 조용한 곳에)

Andy Park

275

In the se - cret, in the qui - et place
I am reach - ing for the high - est goal,
은 밀 한 - 곳 조 용 한 - 곳 에 -
주 께 받 - 을 상 을 바 라 며 -

in the still - ness You are there
that I might re - cieve the prize
주 님 그 - 곳 에 계 시 네
저 높 은 곳 에 올 라 - 가

In the se - cret, in the qui - et ho - ur I wait on - ly for You
press-ing on-ward, push-ing ev' - ry hin-drance a-side out of my way
은 밀 하 - 게 조 용 하 - 게 주 - 님 만 을 - 기 - 다 리 리 - -
어 려 움 - 과 모 든 장 - 애 물 - 리 치 고 달 - 려 가 리 - -

'cause I want to know You more
주 를 더 알 기 - 원 - - 하 - 네 - - -

I want to know You I want to hear Your voice
I want to touch You I want to see Your face
주 알 기 원 - 해 그 음 성 듣 기 - - 를
주 보 기 원 - 해 주 님 을 만 나 - - 길

I want to know You more
I want to know You more
간 절 히 원 - 하 네 -
간 절 히 원 - 하 네 -

G

276 I Will Celebrate

(나는 주님을 찬양하리라)

Rita Baloche

I will cel-e-brate sing un-to the Lord
나 – 는 주 님 을 – 찬 – 양 하 리 라 –

sing to the Lord a new song
새 – 노 래 로 – 주 찬 – 양 – – – –

I will cel-e-brate sing un-to the Lord
나 – 는 주 님 을 – 찬 – 양 하 리 라 –

sing to the Lord a new song
새 – 노 래 로 – 주 찬 양 –

Fine

With my heart re-joic-ing with-
– 온 맘 과 – 뜻 다 하 – 여

in with my mind fo-cusde on Him With my
서 주 님 을 – 기 뻐 – 하 리 두 손

hands raised to the heav-ens all I am
을 – 높 이 – 들 고 서 주 님 을 –

wor-ship-ing Him
경 배 – 하 리 –

D.C.

I Will Rejoice

(나 기뻐하리)

Brent Chambers

I will re-joice I will re-joice I will re-joice
나 기 뻐 하 리 – 나 기 뻐 하 리 – 나 기 뻐 하 리

for I've made my choice to re-joice in the Lord
– 나 주 안 – 에 – 서 – 기 뻐 하 – 리 – 라 –

to re-joice in the Lord The en-em-y whis-pered in-to
– 기 뻐 하 – 리 – 라 – 원 수 가 나 를 – 무 너 뜨
환 경 에 지 배 – 를 받 지

my mind de-ter-mined to wear me down A-
– 리 려 고 – 내 마 음 에 속 – 삭 – 였 – 네 내
– 않 – 고 – 내 팔 의 힘 과 – 목 – 소 – 리 느

lert in the Spi - rit I am not blind my con-
영 이 깨 어 – 넘 어 지 지 않 고 나 의
끼 는 감 정 – 과 상 관 없 이 – 내 마

fess-ion of faith has the en-em-y bound
믿 음 의 고 – 백 이 원 수 를 – 묶 네 –
음 기 뻐 하 – 기 로 결 심 을 – 했 네 –

278 I Will Run To You

(주 말씀 향하여)

Darlene Zschech

I Will Stand
(예수의 이름으로)

279

Chris Bowater

280 I'll Always Love You I Just Want To Love
(주 사랑해요)

Tim Hughes

I   just want to   love   I   just want to   sing
Ev' - ry - day I'll   come   spend   my life with   You
갈 – 급한 내 –맘 –   만 – 지 시 는 주 –
매 – 일 주 님 – 과 –   함 – 께 지 내 – 며 –

To   the one a - bove   who has touched this thirst - y soul
Learn - ing of Your heart   What You're call - ing   me   to do
사 – 랑 과 노 – 래 –   드 리 기 원 합 니 다 –
주 – 의 부 르 – 심 –   주 마 음 알 기 원 해 –

I   just want to   love   I   just want to   sing
Ev' - ry day I'll   come   spend   my life with   You
주 – 사 랑 해 – 요 –   주 – 찬 양 해 – 요 –
내 – 모 든 호 – 흡 –   주 – 께 속 했 – 네 –

To   the one a - bove   Who has touched this thirst-y soul   and now I'll
Learn - ing of Your heart   What You're call-ing me to do   My ev' - ry
높 – 고 거 룩 – 한 –   주 날 만 져 주 시 니 –   이 전 과
주 – 의 부 르 – 심 –   주 마 음 알 기 원 해 –   내 생 명

ne - ver be the same   I'll al-ways love   You
breath be - longs to you
같 지 않 으 리 –   주 사 랑 해 – 요 –
주 께 속 했 네 –

I'll Always Love You I Just Want To Love

I'll al-ways sing to You Je - sus I long to wor-
영원히찬 - 양 - 해 - 예 - 수 - 신 령 과 진

- ship You in spir - it and in truth
- 정 - 으 - 로 - 경 - 배 - 드 - 려 - 요 -

And with the song we'll lift the name of Je - sus
예 수 이 름 - 높 이 올 려 - 드 리 - 세

high - - - er And with a shout we'll raise up one
한 목 소 리 로 - - 소 리 높 여 - 모 두 외 치

voice
- 세 -

G

O.T. : I'll Always Love You I Just Want To Love / O.W. : Tim Hughes
O.P. : Thankyou Music Ltd / S.P. : Universal Music Publishing Korea, CAIOS
Adm. : Capitol CMG Publishing / All rights reserved. Used by permission.

281 I Worship You Almighty God
(경배하리 주 하나님)

Sondra Corbett-Wood

G2　G　D/E　Em　Bm7　Am7　C/D　G　C2/D

I wor - ship You, Al-might-y God　There is none like You
경 배 하 리 주 하 나 님　전 능 하 신 주

G2　G　D/E　Em　Bm7　Am7

I wor - ship You,　O Prince of Peace
경 배 하 리 평 화 의 - 왕 -

CM7/D　D　C/G　GM7　Em7

that is what I want to do, I give You praise
주 를 사 랑 합 니 다 찬 양 하 세 -

Am　D　C/D

for you are my right - eous-ness
누 가 주 와 같 으 리 -

D G2　G　D/E　Em　Bm7　Am7　C/D D7　G

I wor - ship You, Al-might-y God　there is none like You
경 배 하 리 주 하 나 님　전 능 하 신 주

I'm So Glad Jesus Lifted Me

(오 이 기쁨)

283 Jesus, Lover Of My Soul

(예수 내 영혼의 사랑)

Daniel Grul/John Ezzy & Steve McPherson

Je - sus, lov - er of my soul, Je - sus I will
예 수 - 내 영혼의사 랑 - - 예 수 - 나 는

never let You go. You've tak - en me from the mi - ry clay,
포 기 할수없네 - - 수 렁 에서 - 날 건 지 - 시고 - -

you've set my feet up - on the rock, and now I know
주 님 의 반 석 위 - 에 날 세 우 셨 네 - -

I love You. I need You. Though my world may fall, I'll
주 - 님 만 사 랑 - 해 결 코 주 님 을 - 나

na - ver let You go. My Sa - viour, my clos - est friend,
떠 나 지 - 않 으 - 리 내 구 주 나 의 친 구 -

I will wor - ship You un - till the ve - ry end.
세 상 끝 날 까 - 지 주 만 섬 - 기 리 - -

Jesus At Your Name

(지존하신 주님 이름 앞에)

284

Chris Bowater

G

285 Jesus We Celebrate Your Victory

(예수 주 승리하심 찬양해)

John Gibson

Je - sus, We ce - le - brate Your vic - to - ry
예 – 수 주 승리하 – 심 찬 – 양 해 –

Je - sus, We re - vel in Your love
예 – 수 주 사 랑 놀 – 라 와 –

Je - sus, We re - joice, You've set us free
예 – 수 자 유 주 – 심 기 – 뻐 해 –

Je - sus, Your death has brought us life
예 – 수 생 명 – 을 주 – 셨 네

Fine

It was for free - dom that Christ has set us free no
His Spi - rit in us re - lea - ses us from fear the
구 원 의 주 – 님 – 자 유 케 하 셨 네 – 모
주 님 의 성 – 령 – 내 안 에 계 시 니 – 담 대

long - er to be sub - ject to a yoke of sla - ve - ry
way to Him is o - pen With bold - ness we draw near
든 죄 의 – 멍 에 – 를 – 주 가 깨 뜨 리 – 셨 네 –
히 주 께 – 나 갈 – – – 담 력 을 얻 었 – 네 –

Jesus We Celebrate Your Victory

So we're re-joic-ing in God's vic-to-ry Our
And in His pre-sence, our pro-blems dis-a-ppear
우 리 기 뻐 –해– 승 리 의 주 님 – 우
주 임 재 안 –에서 문 제 는 사 라 져 –

hearts re-spond-ing to His love
리 마 음 주 께 향 하 네 –

D.C.

O.T. : Jesus, We Celebrate Your Victory / O.W. : John Gibson
O.P. : Thankyou Music Ltd / S.P. : Universal Music Publishing Korea, CAIOS
Adm. : Capitol CMG Publishing / All rights reserved, Used by permission.

G

286 Joy In The Holy Ghost

(내 맘 속에 거하시는)

Russell Fragar

Joy In The Holy Ghost

It's like a ri-ver and you'll ne-ver run it dry. We've got pow-
결코-마르-지 않-는 강-과 같-으 니- 사 망 권

-er o-ver fear and death and hearts filled up with joy.   The
-세 두-렴 이-기 네-큰 기-쁨 넘-치 리-   -   내

King of Kings Bless The Lord O My Soul 287

(찬양하라 내 영혼아)

Margaret Evans

Ble-ss the Lord   O, my soul   Ble-ss the Lord   O, my
찬 양 하 라   내 영 혼 아   찬 양 하 라   내 영 혼

Lord   And all that is with-in me Bless His Ho - ly Name
아   내 속 에 있는 것들 아 다 찬 양 하 라

G

288 Kindness

(친절하신 주님)

Chris Tomlin, Louie Giglio, Jesse Reeves

O - pen up the skies of mer - cy.
We can feel Your mer - - - - cy fall - ing.
1.2. 자 비 의 — 하 늘 — — — — 여 시 고 —
3. 자 비 를 — 내 려 — — — — 주 시 네 —

and rain down the cleans - ing flood heal - ing wa - ters
You are turn - ing our hearts back a - gain hear our prais - es
은 혜 — — 내 리 소 서 — 생 명 수 — 가
우 리 심 령 — 회 복 케 하 니 하 늘 향 — 해

rise a-round us, And hear our cries Lord let 'em rise.
rise to hea - ven, And draw us near, Lord,
솟 아 — 오 르 — 니 주 를 외 쳐 — 높 이 세 — — —
찬 양 을 올 리 — 세 더 가 까 — 이 —

let 'em rise. And it's Your kind - ness, Lord, that
meet us here. And it's Your kind - ness, Lord, that
높 이 세 — — 주 의 친 절 — 하 심 — 나
주 께 로 — — 주 의 친 절 — 하 심 — 나

leads us to re-pen-tance,Your fa-vor, Lord, is our de-sire. And it's Your
를 돌 이 — 키 시 고 그 사 랑 — 하 심 — 우 리 소 원 — 주 의

beau - ty, Lord, that makes us stand in sil - ence and Your
아 름 — 다 움 — 우 릴 잠 잠 — 케 하 — 니 주 사

love, Your love is bet - ter than life.
— 랑 — 생 명 보 다 — 귀 하 신 사 랑 —

Let Your Glory Fall

(창조의 아버지)

289

David Ruis

G

290 Lord Has Displayed His Glory

(주님의 영광 나타나셨네)

David Fellingham

The Lord has dis - play - ed His glo - ry The
주 님 의 － 영 광 나 － 타 나 셨 네 － 권

King - dom is com - ing in power the
능 으 － 로 임 하 － 셨 네 － 죽

Ho - ly Spi - rit bring - ing life from the dead How
음 에 서 날 － 살 리 신 주 성 령 － 놀

ex - cel - lent is our Lord God
라 우 － 신 주 하 나 님 －

Hal - le-
할 렐

let the blind see, let the deaf hear
눈 먼 자 는 － 눈 을 뜨 며 －

lu - jah let Your King - dom come Hal - le-
루 야 주 의 나 라 가 － － － 할 렐

Lord Has Displayed His Glory

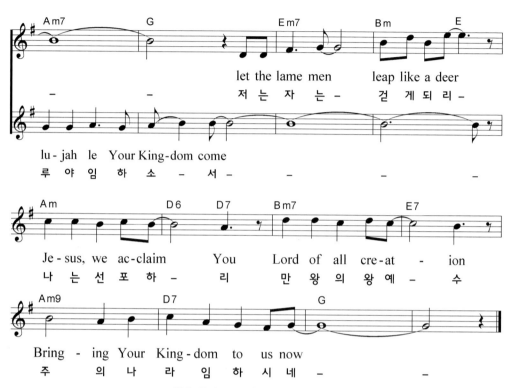

let the lame men　leap like a deer
저 는 자 는 –　걷 게 되 리 –

lu - jah le Your King - dom come
루 야 임 하 소 – 서 – – – –

Je - sus, we ac - claim　You　Lord of all cre - at - ion
나 는 선 포 하 – 리　만 왕 의 왕 예 – 수

Bring - ing Your King - dom to us now
주 의 나 라 임 하 시 네 – –

O.T. : Lord Has Displayed His Glory / O.W. : David Fellingham
O.P. : Thankyou Music Ltd / S.P. : Universal Music Publishing Korea, CAIOS
Adm. : Capitol CMG Publishing / All rights reserved. Used by permission.

G

291 Lord I Lift Your Name On High

(주의 이름 높이며)

Rick Doyle Founds

Lord, I lift You name on high
주 의 이 름 높 - 이 며

Lord, I love to sing Your
주 를 찬 양 하 - 나

Prais - es;
이 - 다

I'm so glad You're in   my life,
나 를 구 하 러 - 오 신

I'm so glad You came to save   us.
주 를 기 뻐 하 - 나 이 - 다

You came from heav-en to earth
하 늘 영 광 버 리 고

to show the way,   From the earth   to the cross   my debt to pay;
- 이 땅 위 에 - 십 자 가 - 를 지 시 고 - 죄 사 했 네

From the cross   to the grave   From the grave   to the sky
- 무 덤 에 - 서 일 어 나 - 하 늘 로 - 올 리 셨 네

Lord, I lift Your name on   high.
- 주 의 이 름 높 - 이 - 리 -

O.T. : Lord I Lift Your Name On High / O.W. : Rick Doyle Founds
O.P. : Universal Music – Brentwood Benson Publ. / S.P. : Universal Music Publishing Korea, CAIOS
Adm. : Capitol CMG Publishing / All rights reserved. Used by permission.

Lord I Love You

(사랑합니다 나의 기도 들으사)

Eddie Espinosa

292

Lord I love You. You a-lone did hear my cry.
사 랑 합 니 다 – 나 의 기 도 들 으 사

On-ly You can mend this bro-ken heart of mine.
– 주 님 만 이 상 한 맘 고 치 시 – 네

Yes, I love You. and there is no doubt.
사 랑 합 니 다 – 진 심 으 – 로

Lord, You've touch-ed me from the in-side out.
주 님 내 맘 깊 이 만 지 셨 네 –

G

293 Lord Of Lords, King Of Kings

(왕의 왕 주의 주)

Jessy Dixon, Randy Scruggs & John W.Thompson

Lord of lords　King of kings　Ma-ker of hea-ven and
Lord You're right-eous　in all Your ways　We bl-ess Your ho-ly
왕　의　왕 －　주　의　주 －　하　늘　과　땅 －　과
의　로　우　신　하　나　님 －　거　룩　한　주 －　의

earth and all　good things － － －　We give You glo
name and we will give You pra － － ise　We give You glo
모　든　것　지　으　신　주 － － －　영　광　돌　리
이　름　높　여　찬　양　하 － － 며 －　영　광　돌　리

－ － － － ry　Lord Je - ho - vah　Son of Man
－ － － － ry　You reign for - ever　in majes-ty
－ － － － 네　주　여　호 － 와　하　나　님 －
－ － － － 네　주　하　나 － 님　통　치　자 －

Pre - cious　Prin - ce of peace　and the great I － － Am
We praise You　and lift You up　for e - ter - ni － － ty
귀　하　신　평　강　의　왕 －　전　능　의　주 － － －
주　님　의　크　신　위　엄 －　선　포　하　며 － － －

We give You glo － － － － ry　Glo － ry to God
－ 영　광　돌　리 － － － 네　주 － 께　영　광 －

Lord Of Lords, King Of Kings

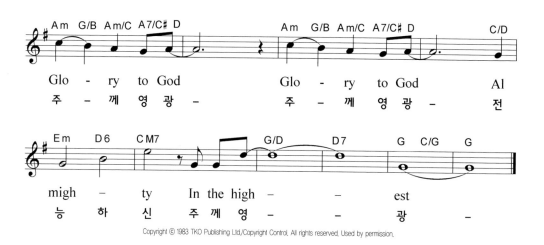

Glo - ry to God Glo - ry to God Al
주 - 께 영 광 – 주 - 께 영 광 – 전

migh - ty In the high – – est
능 하 신 주 께 영 – – 광 –

G

294 Mourning Into Dancing

(나의 슬픔을 주가 기쁨으로)

Tommy Walker

He's turned my mourn - ing in - to dan - cing a - gain He's
나 의 슬 픔 을 주 가 기 쁨 으 로 변

lift - ed my sor - row and I can't stay si - lent I must
화 시 키 시 네 잠 잠 할 수 없 네 기 뻐

sing for His joy has come where there
춤 추 며 찬 양 해 상 처

Fine

once was on - ly hurt He gave his heal - ing hand
뿐 인 내 영 혼 위 로 해 주 셨 네

Where there once was on - ly pa - in He brought
고 통 중 에 있 을 때 주 님

com - fort like a friend I feel the sweet - ness of His love
평 안 주 셨 네 주 사 랑 어 둠 이 김 을

pier - cing my dark - ness I see the
나 는 느 끼 네 - - - 주 의 빛

bright and morn - ing sun As it ush - ers in His
비 춰 주 시 니 내 마 음 기 뻐 주

Mourning Into Dancing

joy - ful glad - ness Your an - ger lasts for a
찬 양 하 네 때 론 주 님 – 분 노

mo - ment in time But Your fa - vor is here
하 실 지 라 도 – 주 의 은 혜 와 사 랑

and will be on me for all my life time
– 나 의 평 생 에 내 게 임 하 네

G

295 Magnificent
(주 광대하시네)

Raymond Badham

My Delight

(아버지 주 나의 기업 되시네)

296

Andy Park

Fa - ther,   You are   my por - tion   in this life,
Je - sus,   You are   my trea - sure in this life,
아 버 지   주 나   의 기   업   되 시   네
예 - 수   내 삶   의 보 - 배   되 시   네

And You are   my   hope and my   de - light
And You are   so   pure   and so kind,
주 님 은   내 - 소 망 내 기 쁨
주 님 은   온 유 하 고 순 결 해

And I   lo - ve You,   Yes, I   lo - ve You,
사 랑 합 니 다   사 랑 합 니 다

Lord, I lo - ve You,   My de - light.
나 의 기 - 쁨   주 님 을   -

G

297 My Heart Is Steadfast

(시편 57편)

My heart is stead-fast O God, my heart is
오 주 여 나의 마 – 음 이 주 께 로

stead-fast I will sing and make mel-o-dy
정 해 졌 – 으 니 나 – 는 주 찬 양 하 리 라 –

A-wake my soul a-wake O harp and lyre
깨 어 라 나의 영 – 혼 아 비 파 와 수 금 들 – 어

I will a-wake the dawn and sing mel-o-dy.
라 이 새 벽 에 내 가 – 찬 양 하 리 라 –

Mel-o-dy   mel-o-dy   Je-sus
Je - -sus   Je - -sus
멜 – 로 디   멜 – 로 디   예 수 님
예 – – 수   예 – – 수

is   my mel-o-dy.   my mel-o-dy.
은   나 의 노 래 –   나 의 노 래 –

My Life Is In You Lord

(생명 주께 있네)

Daniel Gardner

299

No Greater Love

(예수보다 더 큰 사랑)

Tommy Walker

There's no grea-ter love than Je-sus
예 수 보 다 더 큰 사 랑 –
There's no grea-ter love than He gives.
그 누 구 도 줄 수 없 네 –

There's no grea-terlove that frees us
우 리 에 게 자 유 주 신 –
so deep with-in
그 큰 사 – 랑

All the world's emp-ty plea - sures will soon. - - pass a - way
세 상 의 헛 된 보 – 화 – 곧 사 라 지 – – 지 만

But His love will last for-ev - er in my heart it shall re-main
영 원 한 주 의 사 – 랑 – 나 의 맘 에 남 – 으 리 –

We praise Your name. stand in awe of Your ne - ver en - ding
찬 양 하 세 영 원 히 변 치 않 는 그 사

love, love so great that it cov - ers all my sin and shame.
랑 위 대 – 한 – 그 사 랑 내 죄 씻 었 – 네

No grea - ter power, there is no grea - ter force in all the
세 상 모 든 능 력 과 권 세 보 다 강 하

No Greater Love

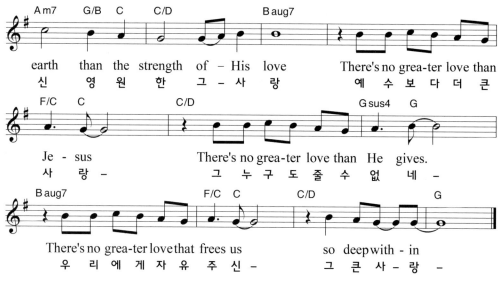

earth than the strength of – His love   There's no grea-ter love than
신   영   원   한   그 – 사   랑   예 수 보 다 더 큰

Je - sus   There's no grea-ter love than He gives.
사   랑 –   그 누 구 도 줄 수 없   네 –

There's no grea-ter love that frees us   so deep with - in
우 리 에 게 자 유 주 신 –   그 큰 사 – 랑 –

O.T. : No Greater Love / O.W. : Tommy Walker
O.P. : Universal Music – Brentwood Benson Songs / S.P. : Universal Music Publishing Korea, CAIOS
Adm. : Capitol CMG Publishing / All rights reserved. Used by permission.

G

300 O, How I Love Jesus

(햇빛이 찬란한 아침과)

John W. Peterson

I love Him in the mor - ning I love Him at noon time.
햇 빛 이 찬 란 한 아 침 과 한 낮 과 저 - 녁 에 -
주 나 를 위 - 해 죽 으 사 날 자 유 하 - 게 하 여
날 사 랑 하 - 신 주 예 수 그 아 름 다 - 운 이 름
주 나 를 사 - 랑 하 심 을 나 어 찌 표 - 현 하 리

I love Him in the e - ven - ing and all the night through
어 둡 고 깊 - 은 밤 에 도 주 님 - 만 사 랑 해
그 흘 린 보 - 배 피 로 써 날 정 - 결 케 했 네
내 귀 에 노 - 래 같 으 리 그 이 - 름 찬 양 해
내 맘 에 차 - 고 넘 치 니 주 님 - 만 사 랑 해

O, How I love Je - sus O, How I love Je - sus
오 사 랑 해 예 수 오 사 랑 해 예 수 -

O, How I love Je - sus Be - cau - se He first loved me.
오 주 님 이 먼 저 날 사 - 랑 하 셨 네 -

Oh How He Loves You And Me

301

(주님께서 주시는)

Kurt Kaiser

Oh, how He loves you and me
주 님 께 서 주 시 는 —

Oh, how He loves you and me
그 사 랑 놀 라 워 라 —

He gave His life what more could He give
그 의 생 명 주 — 시 기 까 지

Oh, how He loves you! Oh, how He loves me!
널 사 랑 하 네 날 사 랑 하 네

Oh, how He loves you and me
너 와 날 사 랑 하 네 —

G

302

One Thing I Ask

(내 마음의 한 소원)

Andy Park

One thing I ask   one   thing I   seek   that   I may
Hear me O Lord   hear me when I   cry   Lord   do not
내 마음 의   한 - 소원 은   주 님 집
들 으소 서   내 부르짖 음   주 얼굴

dwell in Your house O   Lord   All   of   my days
hide Your   face from   me   You have been my strength
에 거하 기 원하 네   내 - 모 든 날
을 가리 우 지 마 소 서   주는 - 나 의 힘

all   of my life   that   I may see You Lord
You have been my shield   and You will lift me   up
모 든 삶 동 안   주 님 을 보 고 파
주 는 내 방 패   주 나 를 높 이 네

One   thing I   ask one thing I de - sire   is to see You
나의 한   소 원 나의 한 갈 망 은   주님 보려네

I want to   see You   Lord let us   see You
is to see You   I want to   see You
주 님 보 려 네   주 님 보 려 네

Only You
(오직 주님만)

303

Andy Park

No-One   but You Lord   can sat-is-fy the long-ing in my heart
Fa - ther   I love you,   come sat-is-fy the long-ing in my heart
오 직 – 주 님 만 – 나 의 맘 의 – 갈 급 – 함 채 – 우 네 –

Noth-ing   I do Lord   can take the place of draw-ing near to You.
Fill me   over-whelm me, un - til I know Your love deep in my heart.
오 직 – 주 께 만 – 더 가 까 이 – 가 기 를 원 – 하 네

On - ly You   can fill my deep - est long - ing,   On - ly
주 님 만   내 갈 급 함 – 채 우 – 네 –   주 만

You can breathe in me new life,   On-ly You can fill my heart with laugh-
내 게 새 생 명 – 주 네 –   주 만 기 쁨 내 맘 에 – 주 시

- ter   On - ly You   can ans - wer my heart's cry
– 네 –   나 의 기 도 응 답 하 – 시 네

G

304 Only A God Like You
(나는 주만 높이리)

Tommy Walker

For the prai - es of man, I will nev - er, ev - er stand;
나 는 주 만 높 - 이 리 - 결 코 내 맘 변 - 치 않

For the king - doms of this world, I'll nev - er give
- 네 세 상 모 든 권 - 세 모 - 든 영 - 광 십

my heart a-way or shout my praise; My a - lle - giance and de-vo-
- 자 가 앞 에 다 버 리 고 나 의 충 성 과 - 내 헌

- tion, my heart's de - sire and all e - mo - tion, go to
- 신 내 모 든 소 망 오 - 직 예 - 수 나 무

serve the Man who died u - pon that tree.
에 달 려 - 죽 으 - 신 그 - 분 께 -

on - ly a God like You could be worth - y of my praise, and all
오 직 우 리 주 - 께 - 내 믿 음 - 소 망 찬 양 받 기

my hope and faith; To on-ly a King of all kings, do I bow
- 합 당 한 분 또 오 직 만 왕 - 의 왕 께 - 엎 드 려

my knee and sing give my ev'-ry-thing; my ev'-ry-thing; To
- 경 배 하 며 모 - 두 드 리 리 - 두 드 리 리 나

Only A God Like You

on-ly my Mak - er, my Fa - ther, my Sav - ior, Re - deem-er, Re - stor - er, Re - buil-
를 지으 시 - 고 아버 - 지 되 시 - 며 나 를 구 원 하 - 사 하 늘

- der, Re-war - der; To on-ly a God   like You,   do I give my praise,
- 의 상 주 - 실 오 직 우 리 주 - 님 께 - 나 찬 양 하 리

On - ly   a   God like   You,
오 직 우 리 주 - 께

on-ly a God like You,   on - ly a God like You.
오 직 우 리 주 - 께   오 직 우 리 주 - 께 -

305 Praise The Lamb
(어린 양 찬양)

Bruce Clewett

Praise The Lamb

Lord　　　　　　　He is Lord,　　　He is Lord
주　- - - - -　　그 는 주 - - - -　그 는 주

He is Lord　　　He is Lord　　　He is Lord
그 는 주 - - - -　그 는 주 - - - -　그 는 주

Reign In Me
(나의 주 다스리시네)

306

Chris Bowater

Reign in me　　　　Sov-'reign Lord　reign in me
나 의 주　　- 다 스 리　시 - 네　-

Reign in me　　　　Sov-'reign Lord　reign in me
나 의 주　　- 통 치 하　시 - 네　-

Cap-ti-vate my heart　　　let Your king-dom come
주 의 나 라 가　　-　임 할 때 까 지　-

es-tab-lish there Your throne　　let Your will be done
주 님 의 뜻 대 로　　-　날 붙 드 소 서　-

Fine

D.C.

G

307

Romans 16:19

(로마서 16장 19절)

Dale Mary Garratt/Ramon Lawrence Pink &
Graham Burt/John Mark Childers

Ro-mans Six-teen Nine-teen Says   Ro-mans Six-teen Nine-teen Says

Be ex-cel-lent   at what is good   be i-no-cent   of e-vil
선 한데는 -   지 혜 롭 고 -   악 한데는 -   미 련 하 라 -

Be ex-cel-lent   at what is good   be i-no-cent   of e-vil
선 한데는 -   지 혜 롭 고 -   악 한데는 -   미 련 하 라 -

And the God   of peace will soon   crush Sa-tan   Yes, God will crush him
평 강 의 주 님   속 히   사 단 을   너 희 발 아 래 에

un-der-neath your feet   And the God   of peace will soon crush Sa-tan   yes,
상 하 게 - 하 리   평 강 의   주 님 속 히   사 단 을 너 희

God   will crush him   un - der-neath   your feet
발   아 래 에   상 하 게 - 하 리

O.T. : Romans 16 : 19 / O.W. : Dale Mary Garratt , Ramon Lawrence Pink, Graham Burt, John Mark Childers
O.P. : Universal Music – Brentwood Benson Publ, / S.P. : Universal Music Publishing Korea, CAIOS
Adm. : Capitol CMG Publishing / All rights reserved, Used by permission.

Shout For Joy And Sing

(기뻐하며 왕께 노래 부르리)

David Fellingham

308

Shout for joy and sing your prai-ses to the King
기 뻐 하 며 왕 께 노 래 부 르 리

lift your voice and let your hal-le-lu-jahs ring;
소 리 높 여 할 렐 루 야 부 르 리

come be-fore His throne to wor-ship and a-dore,
주 님 앞 에 나 와 찬 양 드 리 며

en-ter joy-ful-ly now the pre-sence of the Lord.
우 리 주 님 과 함 께 기 뻐 하 리 라

You are my Cre-a-tor, You are my De-liv-'rer
나 의 창 조 자 나 의 구 원 자

You are my Re-deem-er, You are Lord and You are my Heal-er
가 장 귀 한 나 의 예 수 님 찬 양 합 니 다

You are my pro-vi-der. You are now my Shep-hard and my Guide.
나 의 치 료 자 나 의 선 한 목 자 되 신 주

Je-sus, Lord and King, I wor-ship You.
예 수 나 의 주 찬 양 하 리

309

Shout To The North

(믿음의 형제들이여)

Martin Smith

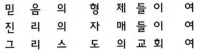

Men of faith, rise up and sing of the great and glo-rious King.
Rise up, wo - men of the truth, stand and sing to brok - en hearts.
Rise up, church, with bro - ken wings, fill this place with songs a - gain

믿 음 의 형 제 들 이 여 일 어 나 주 찬 양 하 라
진 리 의 자 매 들 이 여 일 어 나 빛 발 하 여 라
그 리 스 도 의 교 회 여 일 어 나 다 스 리 라 -

You are strong when you feel weak, in your bro - ken-ness com-plete.
Who can know the heal - ing pow'r of the awe-some King of love?
of our God who reigns on high, by His grace a - gain we'll fly.

위 대 하 신 영 광 의 왕 너 의 힘 이 되 시 리 라 - -
치 유 의 능 력 - 되 신 사 랑 의 왕 전 하 여 라 - -
전 능 하 신 만 왕 의 왕 영 광 을 선 포 하 라 - - -

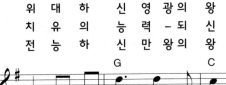

Shout! to the north and the south, sing to the east and the west
Shout! 동 과 서 쪽 에 서 sing! 남 과 북 쪽 까 지

Je - sus is Sa - vior to all, Lord of hea-ven and
예 수 구 원 - 의 주 하 늘 과 땅 의

earth. Lord of hea-ven and earth.
주 하 늘 과 땅 의 주 -

Someone Is Praying For You

(누군가 널 위해 기도하네)

Lanny Wolfe

When it seems that you prayed till your strength is all gone
당신이 지쳐서 — 기도할 수 없고

And your tears fall like rain-drops all the day long.
눈물이 빗물처럼 — 흘러내릴 때

Je-sus cares and He knows just how much you can bear; He'll speak your
주님은 우리 연약 함을 아시고 사랑으

name to some-one in prayer. some-one is pray-ing for
로 인도하시네 — 누군가 널 — 위 하

you Some-one is pray-ing for You. and when it
여 — 누군가 기 - 도 하 네 — 네 가 홀

seems you're all a - lone and yourheart would break in
로 외로워서 — 마음이 무너질

two, re-mem-ber some-one is pray-ing for You.
때 누군가 널 위 — 해 기 도 하 네 —

G

311 Sweeter Than The Air

(주님은 신실하고)

Scott Brenner & Andre Ashby

Faith-ful and true, You are there close by my side,
주 님 - 은 - 신 실 하 고 - 항 상 거 기

al-ways near What oth-er love can com-pare?
- 계 - 시 - 네 - 주 사 랑 을 뭐 - 라 할 까 -

Swee - ter than the air I brea-the is love for me
주 사 랑 - 이 내 생 명 보 다 귀 - 하 - 고

stron - ger than the rag-ing sea is your love for me
- 주 사 랑 - 이 파 도 보 다 더 강 - 해 - 요

Sea - sons chan-ge and though the flo-wers fade I know You
- 세 월 이 - 가 고 꽃 은 시 들 어 도 - 주 사 랑

nev - er change So faith - ful is Your love for me
- 영 원 해 - 주 님 - 사 랑 - 신 실 해 - 요 -

The Longer I Serve Him

(주 내 맘에 모신 후에)

312

William J. Gaither

Since I star-ted for the King-dom, Since my life He con-
주 내 맘 에 모 신 후 에 날 주 장 하 시
매 일 매 일 채 우 시 네 풍 성 한 그 은

trols; Since I gave my heart to Je-sus, The long-er I
네 - 주 께 내 맘 드 린 후 에 더 욱 섬 길
혜 - 매 일 내 길 더 빛 나 네

serve Him, the sweet-er He grows. The long-er I
수 - 록 - 더 귀 한 주 님 더 욱 섬 길

serve Him, the sweet-er He grows, The more that I love Him, more
수 록 더 귀 한 주 님 - 더 사 랑 할 수 록 주

love He bes-tows Each day is like hea-ven, my heart ov-er-
날 사 랑 해 매 일 내 맘 속 에 기 쁨 넘 치

flows, The long-er I serve Him, the sweet-er He grows.
네 더 욱 섬 길 수 록 - 더 귀 한 주 님

O.T. : The Longer I Serve Him / O.W. : William J. Gaither
O.P. : Hanna Street Music / S.P. : Universal Music Publishing Korea, CAIOS
Adm. : Capitol CMG Publishing / All rights reserved, Used by permission,

G

313 Thank You Lord

(감사해)

Dan Burgess

Thank You Lord

do And God's soft promp-ting can be eas - i - ly ig - nored.
리 주 님 의 성 령 나 를 인 도 하 시 리

I thank You Lord for the vic-'try that grow-ing brings,
모 두 감 사 해 실 망 속 에 서 새 힘 을

In sur-ren-der of ev - 'ry - thing life is so worth - while,
새 로 운 용 기 주 시 는 주 님 께 감 사

And I thank You Lord that when ev-'ry-thing's put in place,
또 감 사 드 리 세 - - - - 우 리 주 님 의 은 혜 로

Out in front I can see Your face and it's there You be - long.
받 은 구 원 을 감 사 해 주 님 을 찬 양 해

O.T. : Thank You, Lord / O.W. : Dan Burgess
O.P. : Bud John Songs / S.P. : Universal Music Publishing Korea, CAIOS
Adm. : Capitol CMG Publishing / All rights reserved. Used by permission.

G

314

The Happy Song
(나 기쁨의 노래하리)

Martin Smith

I could sing un-end-ing songs of how You saved my soul
나 기쁨의 노래하리 날구원하셨네 -

I could dance a thou-sand miles be-cause of Your great love
온 종일 나춤추리 그 사랑때문에 - - - 나

My heart is burst - in' Lord to tell of all You've done
내 마음 벅 - 차 네 주 행 한 일 - 볼 때 -

of how You changed my life and wiped a - way the past
어 둡 던 지 난 날 - 주 가 바 꿔 주 - 셨 네 -

I wan-na shout it out from ev - 'ry roof - top sing
높 은 곳 에 올 라 가 - 크 게 외 치 고 - 싶 네 -

For now I know that God is for me not a - gaint me
날 향 한 주 - 님 의 그 사 랑 모 두 에 게 나

I could sing un-end-ing songs of how You saved my soul
기 쁨 의 노 래 하 리 날 구 원 하 셨 네 -

Fine

I could dance a thou-sand miles be-cause of Your great love
온 종 일 나 춤 추 리 그 사 랑 때 문 에 - - 나 -

The happy song

Ev-'ry-bod-y's sing-in' now   'cause we'-re so hap-py
모 두 함 – 께 노 래 해 –   – 우 리 안 의 기 쁨 –

Ev-'ry-bod-y's danc-in's now   'cause we're so hap-py   If
모 두 함 – 께 춤 추 세   – 주 님 주 신 기 쁨 –   주 님

on - ly we could see Your face   and see You smil - in's o - ver us   and
얼 굴 볼 수 없 어 도 –   – 우 린 느 – 낄 수 있 죠

un-seen an - gels cel-e - brate   for joy is in this place!
우 리 안 – 의 이 기 쁨 –   – 다 주 님 주 – 신 – 것 –   나

G

315

The Name Of The Lord

(주의 이름 송축하리)

Clinton Utterbach

Bless-ed be the name of the Lord　bless-ed be the name of the Lord - - -
Glor - y to the name of the Lord　glor - y be the name of the Lord - - -
Hol - y is the name of the Lord　hol - y is the name of the Lord - - -
주　의　이 름　송 축　하 리 -　주 의　이 름　송 축 하 리 - - -
거 룩 하 신　주 의 이 름 -　거 룩 하 신　주 의 이 름 - - -
영 광 스 런　주 의 이 름 -　영 광 스 런　주 의 이 름 - - -

bless-ed be the name of the Lord　most　high
glor - y to the name of the Lord
hol - y is the name of the Lord
지　존 하 신　주 의 이 름 -　찬 - 양 -
거　룩 하 신　주 의 이 름 -
영　광 스 런　주 의 이 름 -

most high　*Fine*　The name of the Lord is　a strong tow - er
- 찬 - 양 - -　주 님 의 이 름 - 은 -　강 한 성 - 루 -

the right-eous run in - to　it　and they are saved
그 곳 에 달 려 - 간 - 자　안 전 - 하 리 -

The Name of the Lord　is　a strong tow - er
주 님 의 이 름 - 은 - -　강 한 성 - 루 -

D.C. al Fine

the right eous run in - to　it　and they are saved
그 곳 에 달 려 - 간 - 자　안 전 - 하 리 -

The Potter's Hand

(주의 손으로)

316

Darlene Zschech

317 There's Gonna Be A Revival
(부흥 있으리라)

Renee Morris

There's Gonna Be A Revival

G

318

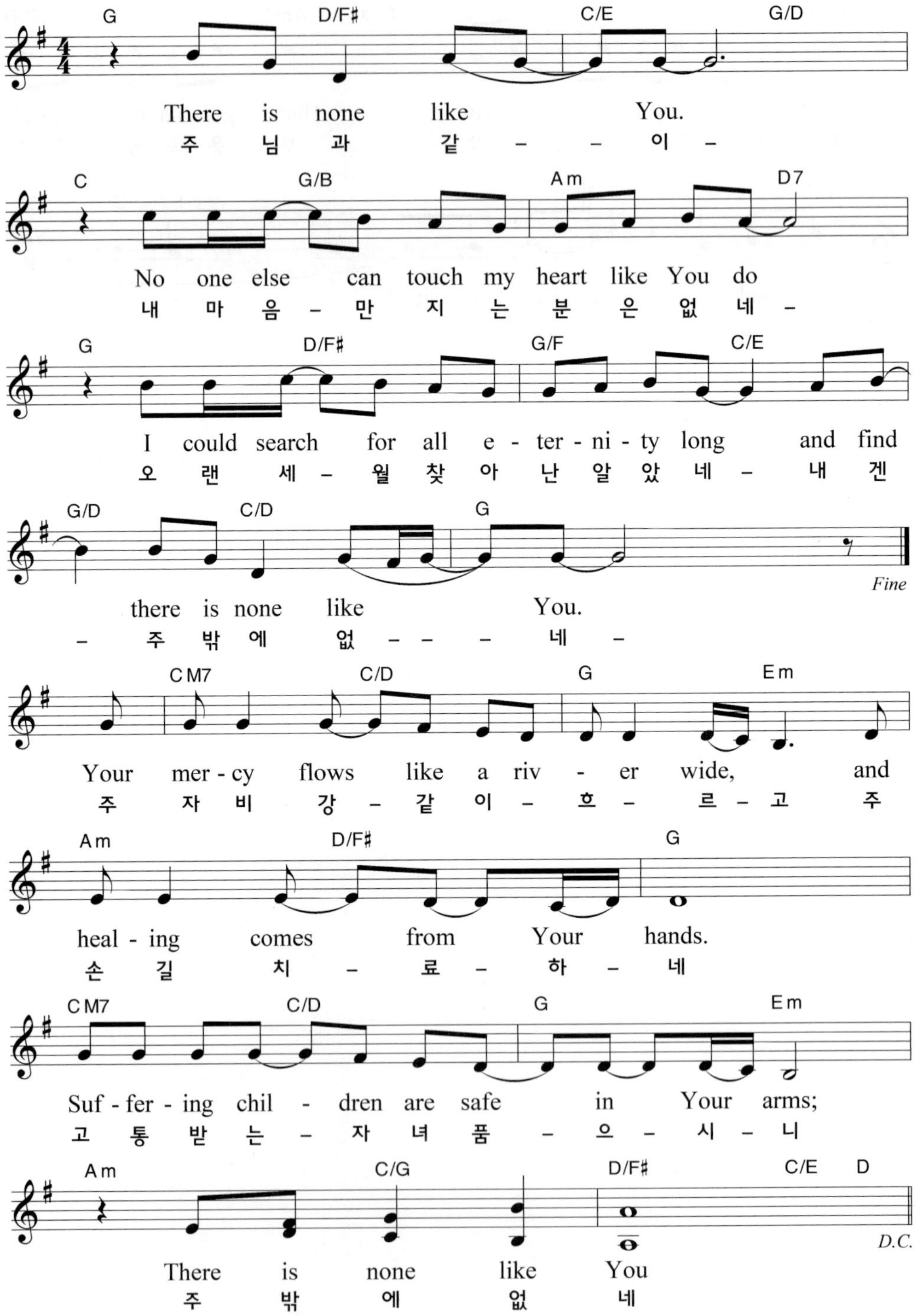

There Is None Like You

(주님과 같이)

Lenny LeBlanc

G D/F♯ C/E G/D
There is none like You.
주 님 과 같 – – 이 –
C G/B Am D7
No one else can touch my heart like You do
내 마 음 – 만 지 는 분 은 없 네 –
G D/F♯ G/F C/E
I could search for all e - ter - ni - ty long and find
오 랜 세 – 월 찾 아 난 알 았 네 – 내 겐
G/D C/D G
there is none like You.
– 주 밖 에 없 – – – 네 –
Fine
C M7 C/D G Em
Your mer - cy flows like a riv - er wide, and
주 자 비 강 – 같 이 – 흐 – 르 – 고 주
Am D/F♯ G
heal - ing comes from Your hands.
손 길 치 – 료 – 하 – 네
C M7 C/D G Em
Suf - fer - ing chil - dren are safe in Your arms;
고 통 받 는 – 자 녀 품 – 으 – 시 – 니
Am C/G D/F♯ C/E D
There is none like You
주 밖 에 없 네
D.C.

The Spirit Of The Lord

(주님의 성령이)

319

Chris Bowater

The River Is Here

(주 보좌로부터)

Andy Park

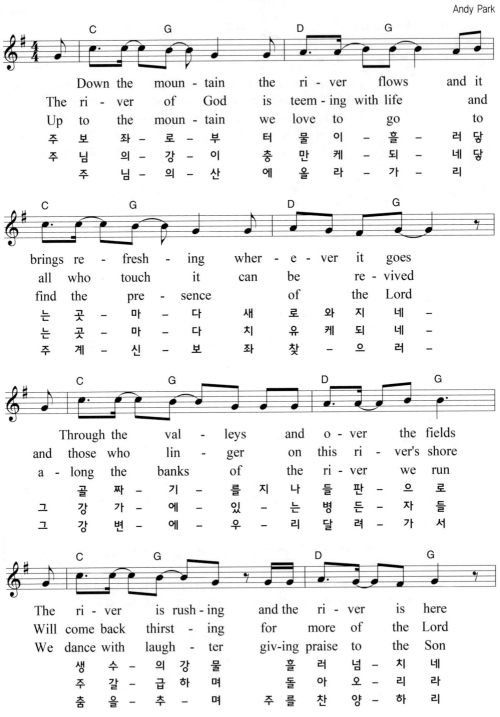

320

Down the moun - tain the ri - ver flows and it
The ri - ver of God is teem - ing with life and
Up to the moun - tain we love to go to
주 보 좌 — 로 — 부 터 물 이 — 흘 — 러 닿
주 님 의 — 강 — 이 충 만 케 — 되 — 네 닿
주 님 의 — 산 에 올 라 — 가 — 리

brings re - fresh - ing wher - e - ver it goes
all who touch it can be re - vived
find the pre - sence of the Lord
는 곳 — 마 — 다 새 로 와 지 네 —
는 곳 — 마 — 다 치 유 케 되 네 —
주 계 — 신 — 보 좌 찾 — 으 러 —

Through the val - leys and o - ver the fields
and those who lin - ger on this ri - ver's shore
a - long the banks of the ri - ver we run
골 짜 — 기 — 를 지 나 들 판 — 으 로
그 강 가 에 — 있 — 는 병 든 — 자 들
그 강 변 — 에 — 우 — 리 달 려 — 가 서

The ri - ver is rush - ing and the ri - ver is here
Will come back thirst - ing for more of the Lord
We dance with laugh - ter giv - ing praise to the Son
생 수 — 의 강 물 흘 러 넘 — 치 네
주 갈 — 급 하 며 돌 아 오 리 라
춤 을 — 추 — 며 주 를 찬 양 — 하 리

The River Is Here

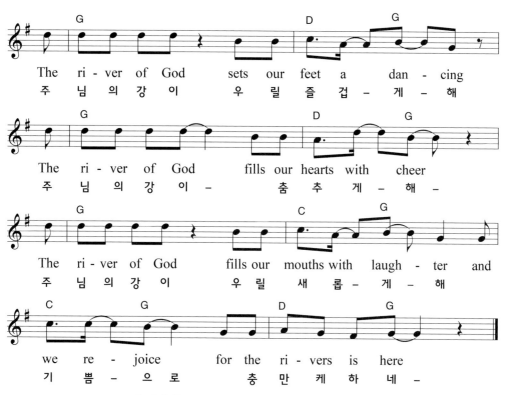

The ri - ver of God sets our feet a dan - cing
주 님 의 강 이 우 릴 즐 겁 – 게 – 해

The ri - ver of God fills our hearts with cheer
주 님 의 강 이 – 춤 추 게 – 해 –

The ri - ver of God fills our mouths with laugh - ter and
주 님 의 강 이 우 릴 새 롭 – 게 – 해

we re - joice for the ri - vers is here
기 쁨 – 으 로 충 만 케 하 네 –

G

Through It All

(영원한 생명의 주님)

Reuben Morgan

Through It All

Words and Music by Reuben Morgan
© 2001 Hillsong Music Publishing Australia (admin in Korea by Universal Music Publishing/ CAIOS)

G

322 To Be Pleasing You

(나 주님의 기쁨되기 원하네)

Teresa E. Muller

Lord I want to live my life to please You.
Lord I lift my heart in full sur - ren - der
나 주 님 의 기 쁨 되 - 기 원 하 - 네 -
겸 손 히 내 마 음 드 - 립 니 - - 다 -

I bring my heart be - fore to re - mold, --
all that I hold dear give to - You. --
내 마 음 을 - 새 롭 - 게 하 소 - 서 - -
나 의 모 - 든 것 - 받 으 소 - 서 - -

make of me a ves - sel fit for - hon - or,
pu - li - fy my heart and make me - ho - ly
새 부 대 - 가 되 - 게 하 - 여 - 주 사 -
나 의 맘 - 깨 끗 - 케 씻 - 어 - 주 사 -

that I might shine for You as spark - ling- gold.
so I might walk the way that's pleas - ing You.
주 님 의 빛 - 비 추 - 게 하 소 - 서 - -
주 의 길 로 - 행 하 - 게 하 소 - 서 - -

To be Pleas - ing You, pleas - ing You, this is all I real-ly want to do.
내 가 원 - - 하 는 - 한 - - 가 지 - 주 님 의 - 기 쁨 이 되 는 것 -

To be pleas - ing You, pleas - ing You, this is all I real-ly want to do.
내 가 원 - - 하 는 - 한 가 지 - - - 주 님 의 - 기 쁨 이 되 는 것 - - -

Together

(우리 함께)

323

Rodger Strader

The Lord our God had plan-ned long a-go
하 나 님 께 서 는   우 리 의 만 남 을

for us to meet and be one in the Lord
계 획 해 놓 셨 네   우 린 하 나 되 어

I will go a-ny-where if it is for the Lord
어 디 든 가 리 라   주 위 해 서 라 면

I will do a-ny-thing to-geth-er with you
무 엇 이 든 하 리 라   당 신 과 함 께

To-geth-er as one bo-dy walk to-geth-er with the love
우 리 는 하 나 되 어 함 께 걷 네 하 늘 아

of our Fa-ther in hea-ven and we will pray to-
버 지 사 랑 안 에 서 우 리 는 기 다

ge-ther Wait with one heart to see our lives o-
리 며 기 도 하 네 우 리 의 삶 에

ver-flow with God's love
사 랑 넘 치 도 록

324 Touching Heaven Changing Earth

(전능의 주 얼굴 구하며)

Reuben Morgan

We will seek Your face, al - migh - ty God,
Ne - ver look - ing back we'll run the race,
전 능 의 – 주 얼 – 굴 구 – – 하 며 –
우 리 생 – 명 다 – 할 때 – – 까 지 –

turn and pray for You to heal our land.
giv - ing You our lives we'll gain the prize
이 땅 위 – 해 주 – 께 기 – 도 할 때 –
주 만 바 – 라 보 – 며 달 – 려 가 리 –

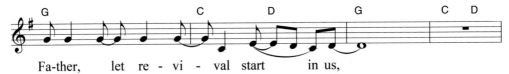

Fa - ther, let re - vi - val start in us,
We will take the har - vest giv - en us,
부 흥 의 – 불 을 – 주 소 – – – 서 –
눈 물 로 – 씨 뿌 – 린 후 – – – 에 –

then ev - 'ry heart will know Your king - dom come.
though we sow in tears, we'll reap in joy.
모 든 영 – 혼 주 – 를 알 – 게 되 리 –
기 쁨 으 – 로 단 – 을 거 – 두 리 라 –

Lift-ing up - the name of the Lord, in pow-er and in u - ni - ty.
능 력 의 – 이 름 – 주 예 수 – 주 의 이 름 높 – – 이 리 –

We will see the na - tion turn. Touch-ing hea-ven, chang - ing earth.
하 늘 향 – 해 기 – 도 할 때 – 이 땅 을 – 고 치 – 소 서 –

Touching Heaven Changing Earth

touch-ing hea - ven, chang - - ing earth.
이 땅 을 – 고 치 – – 소 서 – –

Send re - vi - val,　　　send re - vi - val,
이 땅 위 에 –　　　이 땅 위 에 –

send re - vi - val to us.　　us.
이 땅 위 에 – 부 흥 을　소 – – – 서 –

Words and Music by Reuben Morgan
© 2007 Hillsong Music Publishing (APRA) (admin in Korea by Universal Music Publishing/ CAIOS)

G

325 To You
(나 여기)

Darlene Zshech

Here I stand for-ever in Your migh - ty hand
나 여 기 - 주 의 손 - 안 에 서 - 있 네 -

Li-ving with Your pro - - - mise writ-ten on my heart
내 맘 에 - 새 - 겨 - - - 진 - 그 언 약 - 위 - 에 -

I am yours sur - ren-dered whol - ly to You
내 삶 을 - 주 님 께 - 드 립 니 다 -

You set me in Your fa - mil - y cal-ling me Your own
주 의 자 - 녀 - 삼 으 - - 사 - 구 속 하 - 셨 - 네 -

Now I I be-long to you all I need
이 - 제 - 나 는 주 의 - 것 - 사 - 모 하 네

your spi-rit your word Your truth here my cry my deep de - si - - - re to
- 주 성 령 주 의 - 말 - 씀 - 과 진 리 - 깊 이 알 기 - 원 - 하 - 는

know You more In Your name I will lift my hands to the king
내 소 - 망 - 왕 되 신 - 주 이 름 앞 - 에 두 손 들 고

To You

this on-them of praise   I   bring   hea-ven knows   I long to love
– 주 를 송 축 합 – 니 – 다 – 온 마 음 –   다 하 여 더

you   with   all   I   am   I be-long to You
– 욱 – 주 사 랑 – 해 –   나 는 주 의 것 –

326 To You Alone

(오직 주께)

Reuben Morgan

To You Alone

praise to You a - lone. All praise to You a - lone. All
양 오 직 주 께 찬 양 오 직 주 께 찬

praise to You a - lone. All praise to You a - lone.
양 오 직 주 께 찬 양 오 직 주 께

Words and Music by Reuben Morgan
© 2003 Hillsong Music Publishing Australia (admin in Korea by Universal Music Publishing/ CAIOS)

G

327 Unchanging
(변함없는 완전하신 주님)

Chris Tomlin

Great is Your Faith-ful-ness
Wide is your love and grace
신 실 - 하 신 주 님 -
한 없 - 는 주 사 랑 -

Great is Your Faith-ful-ness
Wide is your love and grace
신 실 - 하 신 주 - 님 -
한 없 - 는 주 은 - 혜 -

You ne-ver change You ne-ver fail, O God - - -
변 함 없 는 - 완 전 하 신 - 주 - 님 - - -

True are your pro-mi - ses
Wide is your love and grace
진 실 - 한 주 약 - 속 -
한 없 - 는 주 사 랑 -

True are your pro - mi - ses
Wide is your love and grace
진 실 - 한 주 약 - 속 -
한 없 - 는 주 은 - 혜 -

You ne-ver change You ne-ver fail, O God - - -
변 함 없 는 - 완 전 하 신 - 주 - 님 - - -

so, we raise up ho-ly hands To praise the ho - ly one
거 룩 - 한 - 손 을 들 - 어 - 찬 양 - 을 드 - 리 네

Who was and is and is to come
- 항 상 - 계 - 신 - 하 나 - 님 께 -

Yeah, we raise up ho-ly hands To praise the ho - ly one
거 룩 한 - 손 을 들 - 어 - 찬 양 - 을 드 - 리 네

who was and is and is to come
- 다 시 - 오 - 실 - 하 나 - 님 께 -

O.T. : Unchanging / O.W. : Chris Tomlin
O.P. : worshiptogether.com Songs, sixsteps Music, Vamos Publishing / S.P. : Universal Music Publishing Korea, CAIOS
Adm. : Capitol CMG Publishing / All rights reserved. Used by permission.

We Declare Your Majesty

(선포하리 주 위엄)

328

Malcom Du Plessis

We de - clare Your maj - es - ty
선 포 하 리 주 위 엄

We pro - claim that Your name - is ex - alt - ed
– 높 으 신 주 의 이 – 름 찬 양 해

for You reign mag - nif - i - cent - ly, rule vic -
– 주 의 크 고 놀 라 우 신 힘 과

tor - i - ous - ly, and Your pow'r is shown through - out the
능 – 력 이 온 땅 위 에 나 타 나 셨

earth. And we ex - claim, "Our God is might - y!"
네 전 능 의 주 – 찬 양 합 니 다

Lift up Your name, for You are ho - ly!
– 거 룩 하 신 – 주 이 름 높 이 며

Sing it a - gain, all hon - our and glo - ry!
– 영 광 의 주 – 그 보 좌 앞 에

In ad - o - ra - tion we bow be - fore Your throne!
– 다 무 릎 꿇 고 주 경 배 합 니 다 –

G

329

We Have Overcome

(승리하였네)

Daniel Gardner

We have o - ver-come By the blo - od of the Lamb
승 리 하 였 네 – 어 린 양 의 보 혈 로 –

By the po - wer of His blood We will stand
우 린 보 혈 의 – 능 력 으 로 서 – 리 라

We have o - ver-come By the blo - od of the Lamb
승 리 하 였 네 – 어 린 양 의 보 혈 로 –

and He will bring the vic - to - ry
주 내 게 승 리 주 – 셨 네 – –

We Want To See Jesus Lifted High

(주 예수의 이름 높이세)

330

Doug Horley

We want to see Je - sus lift - ed high; A ban-ner that files
주 예수의이 이 - 름 높 - 이 세 - 온 땅 을 덮 는

a-cross this land; That all men might see the truth and know,
- 깃 발 - 처 럼 - 모 든 사 람 진 - 리 를 보 며

He is the way to heav - en; We want to see we want to see
- 길 되 신 주 - 를 알 리 주 예 수 여 주 예 수 여

we want to see Je - sus lift - ed high; We want to see we want to see
높 임 을 받 으 - 시 옵 소 서 - 주 예 수 여 주 예 수 여

we want to see Je - sus lift - ed high; Step by
높 임 을 받 으 - 시 옵 - 소 서 - 한 걸

step we're mov-ing for - ward Lit-tle by lit-tle tak - ing ground; Ever - y
음 씩 전 - 진 하 - 며 이 땅 을 정 복 해 - 가 네 - 기 도

prayer a pow-er-ful wea - pon; Strong-holds come tum - bl-ing down
로 무 기 - 삼 으 - 면 원 수 는 무 너 지 리

and down and down and down.
- 무 너 - 지 리 - - 라 - -

O.T. : We Want To See Jesus Lifted High / O.W. : Doug Horley
O.P. : Thankyou Music Ltd / S.P. : Universal Music Publishing Korea, CAIOS
Adm. : Capitol CMG Publishing / All rights reserved. Used by permission.

331 Without Love We Have Nothing

(사랑 없으면)

James Micheal Steven & Joseph M. Martin

If we speak with the tongues of an - gels, and have not
내 가 천 사 의 말 한 다 해 - 도 - 내 맘 에

love, we have noth - ing. If we gain all the world and its
사 랑 없 - 으 - 면 - 내 가 참 지 식 과 믿 음

knowl - edge, and have not love, we have noth - ing. If our
있 어 도 - 아 무 소 용 없 - 으 니 - 산 을

faith is strong to move the moun - tains, and if we give all we have to the
옮 길 믿 음 이 있 어 - 도 나 있 는 모 든 것 줄 지 라

poor, and if we of - fer our-selves, yet our heart nev - er loves, we have
도 나 자 신 다 주 어 도 아 무 소 용 없 네 소 용

noth - ing. With-out love, with-out love, with-out love, we have noth - ing.
없 - 네 사 랑 은 사 랑 은 사 랑 은 - 영 원 하 네 -

Love is pa - tient and kind.
사 랑 은 온 유 하 며

Love is - n't self - ish or boast - ful. Love does - n't seek out its
사 랑 은 자 랑 치 않 으 며 교 만 하 지 아 니

Without Love We Have Nothing

332 Worthy Is The Lamb

(존귀한 어린양)

Darlene Zschech

Thank you for the Cross Lord Thank you for the
love Lord Thank you for the
1.주 님 께 감 사 - - 해 - 생 명 주 신
사 - - 해 - 날 위 해 못

price you paid Bear-ing all my sin and shame In
nail pierced hands Washed me in Your cleans-ing flow Now
그 사 - 랑 - 내 부 끄 러 운 죄 를 - 사
박 힌 - 손 - 주 의 보 혈 로 나 - 를 - 씻

love You came and gave a-maz-ing grace Thank you for this
하 시 - 고 - 놀 라 운 은 - 혜 - 주 - 네 2.주 님 께 감

all I know Your for-give-ness and em-brace
으 시 - 고 - 주 품 - 에 품 으 - 시 네 - 존

Wor-thy is the Lamb Seat-ed on the throne
귀 한 - 어 - 린 양 - - - - 좌 정 - 하 - 신 주 - - - -

Crown You now with man - y crowns You reign vic-to - ri-ous
면 류 관 - 쓰 신 - 주 - 님 - 날 다 스 리 - 시 네 -

Worthy Is The Lamb

G

333

We're Together Again
(우리 함께 모여)

Gordon Jensen & Wayne Hilton

We're to-ge-ther a - gain   Prais - ing the Lord,
우리 함께 모 여   주 의이름 찬 양

We're to-ge-ther a-gain   in one ac - cord
우 리 함께 모 여 –   주 를부르 세 –

Some-thing good is go - na hap-pens Some-thing good is in store
위 대 한 일 행 – 하 셨 네 우 리 소 망 충 만 해 –

We're to-ge-ther a - gain   Prais - ing the Lord.
우 리 함께 모 여   주 의이름 찬 양

You Are Crowned With Many Crowns

(왕의 왕이 되신 주)

John Sellers

334

You are crowned with ma-ny crowns and rule all things in righ-teous-ness
왕 의 왕 이 되 신 주 - 공 의 로 다 스 리 시 네 -

You are crowned with man-y crowns up-hold-ing all things by Your Word
왕 의 왕 이 되 신 주 - 그 말 씀 만 물 붙 드 시 네 -

You rule in pow-er and reign in glo - ry
권 능 - 과 영 광 - 으 로 - 다 스 리 네

You are Lord of hea - ven and earth
주 님 - 온 땅 과 한 - 늘 의 - 주

You are Lord of all
모 든 만 물 을 -

You are Lord of all
주 다 스 리 네 -

G

335 You Are Holy

(거룩하신 전능의 주)

Marc Imboden & Tammi Rhoton

You are ho - ly.
거룩 하 신 -

You are might - y.
전능의 -주 -

You are wor - thy,
찬양받 - 기 -

wor - thy of praise.
합당하 - 신 주

I will fol - low.
나의 평 -생 -

I will lis - ten.
주님 만 -을 -

I will love You,
사 랑 하 - 며 -

all of my days.
따 르 리 라

I will sing – to and wor - ship the
찬양하 – 며 - 경 배 하리 - 귀

You are Lord of lords, You are King of kings, You are
모 든 주 의 -주 - 모 든 왕 의 -왕 - 전 능

King – who is wor - - - thy. And I will love – and a -
하 - 신 -만 왕 의 -왕 주 님 앞 -에 - 엎

might - y God, Lord of ev - 'ry - thing. You're Em - man - u - el, You're the
하 신 -분 - 만 물 의 -주 - 인 주 는 임 마 -누 -엘 위 대

dore – Him, and I will bow – down be - fore – – Him. And I will
드 - 려 - 사 랑 하 -며 - 높 이 - -리 찬 양

Great I am, You're the Prince of Peace who - is - the - Lamb. You're the
하 신 -분 - 어 린 양 되 -신 - 평 - 화 의 -왕 살 아

You Are Holy

336 You Are My Strength
(주 나의 힘)

Reuben Morgan

You Are My Strength

In the full
주 의 - 충 -

Your love, O Lord, rea-ches to the hea-vens
주 의 사 랑 - 하 늘 에 이 르 고 - - -

Your faith-ful-ness rea-ches to - the sky.
주 의 성 실 - 하 늘 두 르 르 네 -

sky. You are my o - ther, rea-ches to me.
- 네 - 주 나 의 않 - 네 내 게 오 네

Words and Music by Reuben Morgan
© 2007 Hillsong Music Publishing Australia (admin in Korea by Universal Music Publishing/ CAIOS)

G

337 You Know Better Than I

(내 길 더 잘 아시니)

David Campbel

I thought I did what's right. I thought I had the an - swers. I
길 을 안 - 다 고 그 렇 게 생 - 각 했 - 죠 다

thought I chose the sur - est road but that road brought me here. So
이 해 할 - 순 없 - 지 만 - 그 길 을 따 랐 죠

I put up a fight and told you how to help me. Now
하 지 만 - 이 곳 - 절 망 의 창 살 안 - 에 주

just when I have giv-en up, the truth is com - ing clear.
내 맘 의 - 문 을 열 때 - 진 실 을 깨 - 닫 죠 -

You know bet - ter than I, you know the way. I've- let
주 는 - 다 - 아 시 죠 - 나 의 - 길 을 - 내 - 삶

go the need to know why, for you know bet - ter than I.
- 을 - 다 맡 - 깁 니 다 - 내 길 - 더 잘 - 아 시 니 -

If this has been a test, I can-not see the rea - son. But
해 답 도 모 르 는 - 시 험 문 - 제 처 - 럼 주

may-be know-ing I don't know is part of get-ting through. I
님 의 뜻 - 을 찾 지 만 - 다 알 수 없 었 죠 - 시

You Know Better Than I

338 You Are My All In All

(주 나의 모든 것)

Dennis Jernigan

You are my strength when I am weak, You are the trea-sure that I
Ta-king my sin my cross my shame, Ri-sing a-gain I bless Your
약 할 때 강 함 되 시 네 나 의 보 배 가 되 신
십 자 가 죄 사 하 셨 네 주 님 의 이 름 찬 양

seek, You are my all in all
name, You are my all in all;
주 주 나 의 모 든 것 - - - -
해 주 나 의 모 든 것 - - - -

Seek-ing You as a pre-cious jewel, Lord to give up I'd be a
When I fall down You pick me up, When I am dry You fill my
주 안 에 있 는 보 물 을 나 는 포 기 할 수 없
쓰 러 진 나 를 세 우 고 나 의 빈 잔 을 채 우

fool, You are my all in all
cup, You are my all in all
네 주 나 의 모 든 것
네 주 나 의 모 든 것

Je - sus Lamb of God, wor - thy is Your name;
예 수 어 린 양 존 귀 한 이 름 - - - -

Je - sus Lamb of God, wor - thy is Your name.
예 수 어 린 양 존 귀 한 이 름

You're Worthy Of My Praise

(경배하리 내 온 맘 다해)

David Ruis

339

G

I will wor-ship with all of my heart
I will bow down and hail You as King
경 배 하 리 — 내 온 맘 다 해 —
무 릎 꿇 고 — 주 맞 이 하 리 —

C / G / Am7

I will praise You with all of my strength
I will serve You, give You ev-'ry-thing
찬 양 하 리 — 내 온 힘 다 해 —
내 모 든 것 — 다 드 리 리 —

G / F

I will seek You, all of my days
I will lift up my eyes to your throne
주 찾 으 리 — 나 사 는 동 안 — 주
주 를 향 해 — 내 눈 을 들 고 — 주

C / G / Am7

I will fol-low all of your ways.
I will trust You, trust You a-lone.
님 의 길 을 — 나 따 라 가 리 —
의 지 하 리 — 주 만 의 지 하 리 —

G / D/F♯ / C/E / C

I will give You all my wor-ship I will give You
주 님 만 을 경 배 하 리 주 님 만 을

Am7 / Dsus4 / D/F♯ / G / D/F♯

all my prai-se You a-lone I long to wor-ship
찬 양 하 리 — 찬 양 받 기 합 당 하 신

C/E / C / Am7 / Dsus4 / D / G

You a-lone are wor-thy of — my — praise
존 귀 하 신 주 만 높 이 리

G

340 Awesome God

(나의 주 크고 놀라운 하나님)

Rich Mullins

O - ur God is an awe-some God, He reigns from hea-ven a - bove with
나의 주 크고 놀라운 하나 님 하늘 위에서 지 혜 –

wis - dom power and love our God is an awe-some God O - ur
와 권 능 과 사 랑 으 로 우 릴 다 스 리 – 네 나의

God is an awe-some God, He reigen from hea-ven a - bove with
주 크고 놀라 운 하나 님 하늘 위에서 지 혜 –

wis - dom power and love our God is an awe-some God
와 권 능 과 사 랑 으 로 우 릴 다 스 리 – 네

He Is Jehovah

(창조의 하나님)

341

Betty Jean Robinson

He is Je - ho - vah, God of cre - a - tion. He is Je - ho - vah,
He is the great I AM, the God of A - bra - ham Je - ho - vah sha - lom,
He's your Pro - vi - der, Je - ho - vah Ji - reh, God of sal - va - tion,
그 는 여 호 – 와 창 조 의 하 나 님 그 는 여 호 와
지 존 의 하 나 님 아 브 라 함 의 하 나 님 여 호 와 샬 롬
여 호 와 이 – 레 그는 나 의 공 급 자 구 원 의 하 나 님

Lord God al - migh - ty. The Balam of Gil - e - ad, the Rock of A - ges.
the God of peace, I AM The God of Is - ra - el, the ev - er - las - ting One
God of Mes - si - ah. The Son He sent to you, He tes - ti - fied of Him
전 능 의 하 나 님 길 르 앗 의 향 료 요 반 석 의 하 나 님
평 강 의 하 나 님 이 스 라 엘 의 하 나 님 영 원 한 하 나 님
구 주 의 하 나 님 아 들 을 보 내 어 그를 증 거 하 셨 네

He is Je - ho - vah the God that heal - eth thee.
그 는 여 호 와 치 료 의 하 나 – 님

Sing Hal - le - lu - jah, Sing Hal - le - lu - jah. Sing Hal - le -
찬 양 – 하 세 할 렐 – 루 야 찬 양 –

lu - jah, Sing Hal - le - lu - jah! He is Je - ho - vah, Lord God al -
하 세 오 – 할 렐 루 야 그 는 여 호 – 와 전 능 의

migh - ty. He is Je - ho - vah the God that heal - eth thee.
하 나 님 그 는 여 호 와 치 료 의 하 – 나 님

G

342

Can't Stop Praising
(내 찬양 멈출 수 없어)

Tule Faletolu & Marty Sampson

I try to find the words   to ex-press the way You are
Lord You're so ama-zing   eve-ry word You say is true

주 님 의 - 길 을 - - 표 현 하 려 하 - 지 만 -
놀 라 우 신 - 주 님 - - 주 의 말 씀 은 - 진 리 -

But the beau-ty of   the Lord   cna - not be de-
Bet-ter than the fi-nest trea-sure   so glad that I found

아 름 다 우 신 - 주 님 - 형 언 할 길 이 - 없
가 장 귀 한 보 - 물 보 다 주 님 알 기 를 - 원

- scribed   in just one life time   Look at the sun o - ver the seas
You   You held me close when I   was down

- 어   내 - 평 생 - 에 -   바 다 덮 은 태 - 양 - 처 럼
- 해   쓰 러 진 날 붙 드 - 셨 네

Look at Your grace that   co - vers me   Now I know
Your world has turned my world a-round   Now I know

- 주 은 혜 날 덮 - 으 - 시 네 -   나 이 제
- 주 님 내 삶 바 - 꾸 - 시 네 -   나 이 제

yes, I know   now   Now I know   I know Your
yes, I know   Now I know   I know how

- 깨 달 았 - - 네   그 사 랑 - 나 를 구
- 깨 달 았 - - 네   주 님 을 - 향 한 내

love has sav - ed me   In the mor-ning   I can't stop   prai-sing Your Name
much I love   You

원 - 하 - 셨 네   아 침 에 는   나 주 이 름 찬 양 하 리
깊 은 사 - 랑 을

Can't Stop Praising

Words and Music by Marty Sampson, Tulele Faletolu
© 2003 Hillsong Music Publishing Australia (admin in Korea by Universal Music Publishing/ CAIOS)

343 Consuming Fire There Must Be More
(성령의 불)

Tim Hughes

Consuming Fire There Must Be More

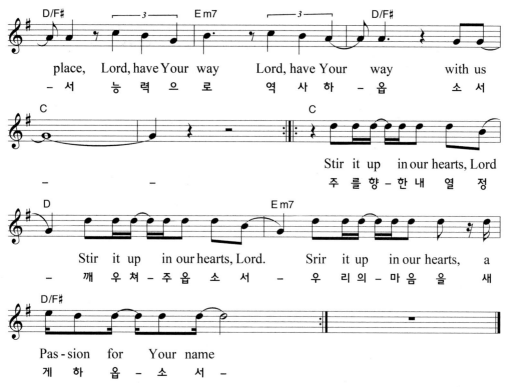

place, Lord, have Your way   Lord, have Your way   with us
- 서   능 력 으 로   역 사 하 - 옵   소 서

\-   \-   Stir it up in our hearts, Lord
         주 를 향 - 한 내 열 정

Stir it up in our hearts, Lord.   Srir it up in our hearts, a
- 깨 우 쳐 - 주 옵 소 서 -   우 리 의 - 마 음 을   새

Pas - sion for Your name
게 하 옵 - 소 서 -

O.T. : Consuming Fire There Must Be More / O.W. : Tim Hughes
O.P. : Thankyou Music Ltd / S.P. : Universal Music Publishing Korea, CAIOS
Adm. : Capitol CMG Publishing / All rights reserved, Used by permission,

G

344 Joshua's Army
(여호수아의 군대)

Scott Brenner

When we hear the word of the Lord our God
우리가 주님-의- - 음성을 들을-때- -

We pre-pare our-sel-ves for the bat-tle cry
우리가 나간-다- - 승리의 함성-을-위해-

When we hear the sound of the trum-pet blast
우리의 나팔-소-리가 - -울-려 퍼질-때- -

All the peo-ple shout And the wall-s co-me tumb-ing down
백성 들이-외-치고 성벽이무너져내 -린다- -

He - y He - y He - y
He---y- He---y- He---y-

He - y He - y He - y Like
He---y- He---y- He---y- 여

Jo-sh-ua's ar-my We en-cir-cle the ci-ty
호수아군-대-처-럼- -우리가 도시를둘-러-싼-다-

Who can stand be-fore the po-wer of our God Like
누가-주-님-앞-에-설-수있는-가- - 여-

When The Spirit Of The Lord Is Within My Heart

345

(우리 주의 성령이)

Margaret Evans

when the Spi-rit of the Lord comes up-on my heart I will dance like Da - vid danced
pray like Da - vid prayed
sing like Da - vid sang

우리 주의 성령이 내게 임 하 여 주를 찬 양 합 - 니 - 다

when the Spi-rit of theLord comes up-on my heart I will dance like Da - vid danced
pray like Da - vid prayed
sing like Da - vid sang

우리 주의 성령이 내게 임 하 여주를 찬 양 합 - 니 - 다

I will dac - ce I will dan - ce dance like Da-vid danced
I will pra - y I will pra - y pray like Da-vid prayed
I will si - ng I will si - ng sing like Da-vid sang

찬양 합 니 다 찬양 합 니 다 주를 찬 양 합 니 다

I will da - nce I will da - nce dance like Da-vid danced
I will pra - y I will pra - y pray like Da-vid prayed
I will si - ng I will si - ng sing like Da-vid sang

찬양 합 니 다 찬양 합 니 다 주를 찬 양 합 니 다

G

346 The Battle Is The Lord's

(모든 전쟁은 주께 속했네)

Tom Brooks/Don Moen & Martin J. Nystrom

When the might-y men of the tribe of Ju-dah faced the en-e-my
When the e-vil one comes a-gainst you to fill your heart with fear

유 다 지 파 의 - 강 한 용 사 들 - 이 원 수 와 맞 - 설 때 -
원 수 마 귀 가 - 너 를 대 적 하 - 여 두 려 움 줄 - 때 에 -

they were told by God not to be a-fraid He would give the vic-to-ry
you can trust in God He will nev-er leave you He prom-ised to be near

두 려 워 말 라 - 승 리 주 리 라 - - 주 님 말 씀 하 - 셨 네 -
주 를 믿 으 라 - 그 가 언 제 나 - - 너 와 함 께 하 - 시 리 -

He said.Lift up a song and lay down the sword
You can lift up a song in the midst of the war

검 을 내 려 놓 고 - 소 리 높 - 여 라 - - - - -
전 쟁 - 중 에 는 - 소 리 높 - 여 라 - - - - -

For the bat-tle is mine says the Lord

전 쟁 은 나 에 게 - 속 했 으 니 - - - - -

Sing un-to the Lord make a joy-ful sound lift your voic-es

기 뻐 춤 추 며 - 소 리 높 여 서 - 주 를 찬 양

let your praise re-sound Sing a vic-tory song in the time of war

승 리 의 노 래 - 시 험 당 할 때 - 기 뻐 노 래 해

trust in Je-sus the bat-tle is the Lord's sing un-to the Lord

- 모 든 전 쟁 은 주 께 속 했 네 - 기 뻐 춤 추 며

The Battle Is The Lord's

make a joy-ful sound   Lift your voi-ces and let your praise re-sound
소 리 높 여 서 - 주 를 찬 양 승 리 의 노 래

sing a vic-tory song   in the time of war   trust in Je-sus the
시 험 당 할 때 - 기 뻐 노 래 해 - 모 든 전 쟁 은

bat - tle is the Lord's
주 께 속 했 네 -

Fine

For the Lord   is good   and His mer
선 하 신 - - - 주 님 - 주 의 자

- cy en-dur-eth for-ev - er   For the Lord   is good   and His mer
- 비 는 영 - 원 하 시 도 다   선 하 신 - - -주 님 - 주 의 자

- cy en-dur - eth for-ev - er   for-ev-er and ev - er
- 비 는 영 - 원 하 시 도 다   영 원 하 시 - 도 다 -

D.S. al Fine

347 To The Ends Of The Earth

(이 세상 끝까지)

Joel Houston & Marty Sampson

Love un-fai - ling, o-ver-ta - king my heart. You
신 실 하 - 신 - -주 님 의 - 그 사 랑 - - 날

take me in. Find-ing peace a-gain, fear is lost in all You
붙 드 네 - 그 평 화 - 안 에 - 모 든 두 - 려 움 없

are. And I would give the world to tell Your sto-
- 네 - - 나 세 상 에 - 외 치 리 주 사 랑

- ry, 'cause I know that You've called me, I know that You've called me. I've
- 을 - 이 것 이 나 의 소 - 명 - 주 님 주 신 소 - 명 - 그

lost my-self for good with-in Your pro - mise, and I won't hide
의 신 실 - 한 약 속 위 해 살 - 리 - - 내 생 명 다

it. I won't hide - - it. Je-sus I be-lieve in You. and
- 해 - - 생 명 다 - - 해 - - 내 안 에 - 살 아 계 신 - -

I would go to the ends of the earth, to the ends of the earth. For You
주 위 - 해 - 나 는 달 려 가 리 - 이 세 상 끝 까 지 - 그 는

To The Ends Of The Earth

a-lone are the Son of God,   and all the world will see   that You are
－ 하 나 님 의 독 생 자－ 온 땅 알 게 － 되 리 － 예 수 는

God,   that You are   God.
－ 주 － － 예 수 는 － 주 － 　　 －

Words and Music by Joel Houston, Marty Sampson
© 2002 Hillsong Music Publishing Australia (admin in Korea by Universal Music Publishing/ CAIOS)

Gloria
(글로리아)

348

Stephen Hah

G

Glo - ri － a   Glo - ri － a,
글로 리 － 아   글로 리 － 아

Ab - ba,   Ab - ba,   Fa － ther
아 바   아 바   아 버 지 － －

Ab - ba,   Ab - ba,   Fa － ther
아 바   아 바   아 버 지

349 Above All

(모든 능력과 모든 권세)

Lenny LeBlanc & Paul Baloche

A-bove all - pow - ers, a-bove all - - king, a-bove all -
모 든 능 - 력 - 과 모 든 권 - - 세 - 모 든 것 -

na - ture and all cre - a - ed things; a - bove all
위 - 에 뛰 어 - 나 신 - 주 님 세 상 이

wis - dom and all the ways of man,
측 량 - 할 수 - 없 는 - 지 혜 - - - 로

You were here be - fore the world be - gan A - bove all -
모 든 만 - 물 창 - 조 하 - 셨 네 - 모 든 나 -

king - doms, a - bove all - - thrones, a - bove all -
라 - 와 모 든 보 - - 좌 - 이 세 상 -

won - ders the world has ev - er known; a - bove all
모 든 - 경 이 - 로 움 - 보 다 - 이 세 상

wealth and treas - ures of the earth,
모 든 - 값 진 - 보 물 - 보 다 - - -

there's no way to meas - ure what You're worth.
더 욱 귀 - 하 신 - 나 의 - 주 님 -

Above All

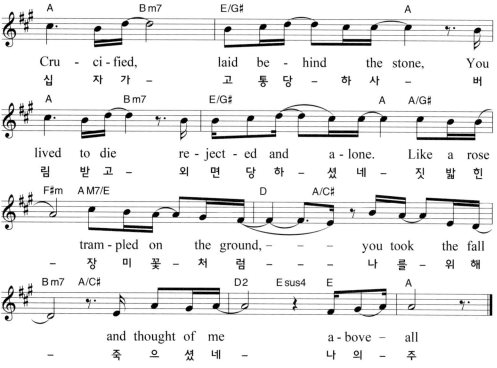

Cru - ci - fied,   laid be - hind   the stone,   You
십 자 가 –   고 통 당 – 하 사 –   버

lived   to   die   re - ject - ed and   a - lone.   Like a   rose
림 받 고 –   외 면 당 하 – 셨 네 –   짓 밟 힌

tram - pled   on   the ground, – – –   you took   the fall
– 장 미 꽃 – 처 럼 – – –   나 를 – 위 해

and thought of   me   a - bove – all
– 죽 으 셨 네 –   나 의 – 주

A

350

Agnus Dei

(하나님의 어린 양)

Michael W. Smith

Al - le-lu - jah   al - le-lu - jah
알 - - 렐루 - 야 -   알 - - 렐루 - - 야

for the Lord God Al-might - y   reigns
- 전 능 하 신 주 다 스 리 네   -

Al - le-lu - jah   Ho - - ly   Ho -
알 - - 렐루 - - 야 -   거 - - 룩   거 -

ly   are You, Lord God   Al - might - y   Wor-thy is the
룩   전 능 하 신 - - 주 - 하 나 님   존 귀 하 신

Lamb wor-thy is the Lamb for You are ho-ly Lamb A - men!
주   존 귀 하 신 주 오 주 는 거 -   주 아 - - 멘

All Heaven Declares

(선포하라)

351

Noel Richards & Tricia Richards

All heav'n de-clares the glo-ry of the ris - en Lord
I will pro-claim the glo-ry of the ris - en Lord
선 포 하 라 부 활 하 신 영 광 의 주
선 포 하 라 부 활 하 신 영 광 의 주

who can com - pare with the beau-ty of the Lord
who once was slain to re-con-clie man to God
아 름 다 운 영 광 의 주 를 보 라
하 나 님 과 화 목 하 게 하 신 주

For-ev-er He will be the Lamb up-on the throne.
For-ev-er You will be the Lamb up-on the throne
보 좌 에 앉 으 신 그 어 린 양 예 수
찬 송 과 존 귀 와 영 광 과 능 력 을

I glad-ly bow my knee and wor-ship Him a - lone.
I glad-ly bow my knee and wor-ship You a - lone
다 무 릎 꿇 고 서 주 경 배 하 리 라
영 원 영 원 토 록 받 아 주 옵 소 서

A

352 Ascribe Greatness To Our God
(나의 반석이신 하나님)

Mary Lou King & Mary Kirkbride Barthow

As - cribe great-ness to our God the rock, His work is
나 의 반 석 이 신 하 나 님 행 하 신

per-fect and all His ways are just. As - cribe
모 든 것 완 전 하 시 니 - 나 의

great-ness to our God the rock, His work is per-fect and
생 명 되 신 하 나 님 내 게 행 하 신 일

all His ways are just. A God of faith-ful-ness and
찬 양 합 니 다 - 신 실 하 신 하 나 - 님

with-out in just - ice, Good and up - right is
실 수 - 가 없 으 - 신 - 좋 으 신 나 의

He. A God of faith-ful-ness and with-out in
주 - - - - - 신 실 하 신 하 나 - 님 실 수 - 가

just - ice, good and up - right is He.
없 으 - 신 - 좋 으 신 나 의 주 -

Be Exalted, O God

(내가 만민 중에)

353

Brent Sinclair Chambers

I will give thanks to thee, O Lord, a-mong the peo - ples
내 가 만 민 중 에 오 - 주 께 감 사 하 - 며

I will sing prais - es to Thee a-mong the na - tions.
주 님 을 찬 양 하 리 열 방 중 에 서 　 －

For thy stead-fast love is great, is - great to the heav - ens
주 의 인 자 는 커 서 커 서 하 늘 에 미 치 － 고

and Thy faith - ful - ness, Thy faith - ful - ness to the clouds.
주 의 진 리 는 넓 은 궁 창 에 이 르 나 니

Be ex - alt - ed, O God a-bove the heav - ens, let thy
－ 하 늘 위 에 주 － 는 높 이 들 리 며 주 의

glo - ry be o - ver all the earth. Be ex -
영 광 은 온 세 계 위 － － 에 － 하 늘

glo - ry be o - ver all the earth. I will glo - ry
영 광 은 온 세 계 위 － － 에 － 내 가 영 광 은

let thy glo - - ry let thy glo - ry be o - ver all the earth.
주 의 영 광 － 은 주 의 영 광 은 온 세 계 위 － － 에 －

A

354 Beautiful Saviour

(예수 아름다우신)

Henry Seeley

Beautiful Saviour

I will sing fo - re - ver Je-sus I love You Je-sus I

영 원 히 주 찬 - - - 양 주 사 랑 해 요 - 주 사 랑

lo - ve You Je - sus beau-ti-ful sa - viour

해 - 요 - 예 - - - 수 아 름 다 우 - - - 신 -

O.T. : Beautiful Saviour / O.W. : Henry Seeley
O.P. : Ninetysix Publishing / S.P. : Universal Music Publishing Korea, CAIOS
Adm. : Capitol CMG Publishing / All rights reserved, Used by permission.

355

Because He Lives
(살아계신 주)

Gloria Gaither & William J. Gaither

Because He Lives

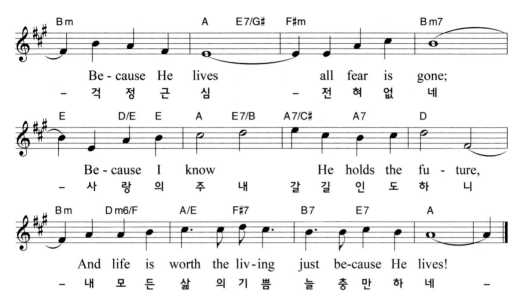

Be - cause He lives　all fear is gone;
－ 걱 정 근 심 － 전 혀 없 네

Be - cause I know　He holds the fu - ture,
－ 사 랑 의 주 내 갈 길 인 도 하 니

And life is worth the liv-ing　just be-cause He lives!
－ 내 모 든 삶 의 기 쁨 늘 충 만 하 네 －

O.T. : Because He Lives / O.W. : Gloria Gaither, William J. Gaither
O.P. : Hanna Street Music / S.P. : Universal Music Publishing Korea, CAIOS
Adm. : Capitol CMG Publishing / All rights reserved, Used by permission.

A

356 Be Strong And Take Courage

(강하고 담대하라)

Basil Chiasson

Be strong and take cour-age do not fear or be dis-mayed;
강하고 - - 담대하라 두려워하 - - 지말라 - -

For the Lord will go be-fore you, and His light! will show the way.
주가네 앞서 가시며 너의길 비추 - - 시리

So, be strong and take cour-age, do not fear or be dis-mayed;
강하고 담대하라 - 두려워하 - - 지말라 - -

For the One who lives with-in You, will be strong in you to day
네안에 계시는 주 - - 님 - 오늘 너를강하 - 게 - 하리

Why don't you give Him all of your fears, why don't you
Noth-ing can take you out of His hand, noth-ing can
너의두려움 너의눈물 주님께
주님품안에 안전하니 아무도

let Him dry all your tears? He knows He's been through pain be
face you that you can't com-mand; I know that al-ways you will
모두다 맡기어라 주님 네고통을아
너를 해치못하리 주의 사랑과능력

Be Strong And Take Courage

fore; And He knows all tha you've been look-ing for. So, be
be in His love, in His pow'r you will be free.
시 _ 며 _ 네 모 든 필 요 를 다 _ 아 시 네 _ _ 강 하
으 _ 로 _ 네 영 혼 언 제 나 자 _ 유 하 리 _ _

day. For the One who lives with - in you,
리 네 안 에 계 시 는 주 _ _ 님 _

will be strong in you to - day.
_ 오 늘 너 를 _ 강 하 게 _ 하 리

A

357

Breathe
(주님은 내 호흡)

Marie Barnett

Close To The Lord

(주께 가까이 날 이끄소서)

Adhemar de Campos

Close to the Lord draw me clos-er to You I des-pe-rate-ly want You a
주 께 가까이 - 날 이 끄 소 서 - - - 간 절 히 주 - 님 만 - 을 원 합 니

- lone Fill me with Your love So that may wor-ship You
- 다 - - 채 워 주 소 서 - 주 의 사 랑 을 - - - 진

more - ful - ly from my heart My soul thirsts for You I
정 한 찬 - 양 드 - 릴 수 있 도 - 록 목 마 - 른 나 의 영 혼 - 주

call out to You Touch my heart deep-ly with - in I des-perate-ly
를 부 르 니 - - 나 의 맘 - 만 져 - - 주 - 소 서 - - 주 님 만 을

long for You I want more of You Touch my soul deep-ly with - in
원 합 니 다 - 더 원 합 니 다 - - 나 의 맘 - 만 져 - - 주 소 - 서 -

A

359

Can't Live A Day
(주 없이 살 수 없네)

Connie Harrington, Joe Beck & Ty Lacy

Can't Live A Day

can't live a day with-out You — Lord there's no night
하 루 도 살 - 수 없 - 네 - 주 - 님 의 사

and there's no mor-ning with-out Your lov - ing arms to hold me You're the
- 랑 의 - 팔 로 - - 날 안 아 주 - 지 않 - 는 다 - 면 - - 난

heart-beat of all I do I can't live a day with-out You
한 순 간 도 - 못 사 네 - 난 주 없 이 살 - 수 없 네 -

Oh Je - sus I live because You live
- 오 - - - 주 님 - - - 내 - 생 명 되 - 시 네 -

You are like the air I breathe Oh Je - sus oh, I have
내 호 흡 과 - 같 네 - 오 - - - 주 - 님 - 내 게 모

be-cause You gave You're ev - er - y-thing to me oh, I could-n't face
- 두 주 - 셨 네 - - - - - 주 나 의 모 - 든 것 - 오 진 실 - 로

I can't live a day with - out You
- 난 주 없 이 살 - 수 없 - - 네 -

360 Come And Fill Me Up

(성령이여 내 영혼에)

Brian Doerksen

I can feel You flow-in' thru me, Ho-ly Spir-it,
성령이여 내 영혼에 충만 하게

come and fill me up come and fill me up
채 워 주 소 서 - 채 워 주 소 서 - -

Love and mer-cy fill my sen-ses. I am thir-sty
주 의 사 랑 주 의 자 비 간 절 하 게

for Your pre-sence, Lord, come and fill me up
기 다 리 오 니 - 채 워 주 소 서 - -

Lord, let Your mer-cy wash a-way all of my sin
크 신 자 비 로 내 죄 를 - 씻 으 소 서 -

Fill me com-plete-ly with Your love once a-gain.
순 전 하 신 - 주 의 사 랑 을 - 새 롭 게 -

I need You, I want You, I love Your pre-sence.
간 절 히 원 하 네 주 임 재 하 심 을

I need You, I want You, I love Your pre- - -sence.
간 절 히 원 하 네 주 님 의 임 재 하 - 심 을 -

Come Into The Holy Of Holies

(거룩하신 주님께 나오라)

361

John Sellers

Come in-to the Ho-ly of Ho — lies,
거룩하신 주 님 께 나 오 라 –

en-ter by the blood of the Lamb,
어 린 양 의 보 혈 로 써 –

Come in-to His pres-ence with sing — — ing,
찬 양 하 며 주 님 앞 에 – 나 와 –

wor-ship at the throne of God
보 좌 앞 에 경 배 하 세 – –

Lift-ing ho-ly hands, to the King of kings
왕 의 왕 – 주 – 께 – 거 룩 한 손 들 고 –

wor — ship Je - sus
경 배 해 – 주 님 께 –

wor — ship Je - sus
경 배 해 – 주 님 께 –

A

362 Come Let Us Sing Come Let Us Sing
(찬양하세)

Danny Reed

Come let us sing
찬 양 하 세 -

Come let us sing
찬 양 하 세 -

Come with
왕 께

praise and a - do - ra - tion to the King
소 리 높 - 여 찬 - 양 드 리 세 -

- tion to the King
- 양 드 리 세

For He is wor-thy of praise for He is Lord
찬 양 받 기 에 합 당 하 신 - 주 님 -

Who was and is and is to come
언 제 나 동 일 하 신 주 -

Ev'-ry knee shall bow and ev'-ry tongue con - fess
무 릎 꿇 고 서 주 이 름 외 치 세

He is Je - sus Christ He is Je - sus Christ
예 수 나 의 왕 예 수 나 의 왕

He is Je - sus Christ the Lord
예 수 나 의 왕 아 멘

Complete

(온전케 되리)

Andrew Ulugla

363

A	E/G#	F#m	D	E	A	E/G#

Here I am O God I bring this sac‑ri‑fice My o‑pen
주 앞 에 나 와 – 제 사 를 드 리 네 – 마 음 열

F#m	D	E	F#m	E/D	D

heart I of‑fer up my life I look to You Lord
어 – 내 삶 을 드 – 리 네 – 주 를 봅 니 다

F#m	E/D D	A/C#	D	Esus4	E

Your love that ne‑ver ends re‑stores me a‑gain So I
– 끝 없 는 사 랑 나 – – 회 복 시 – 키 – 네 – 이 제

A	F#m	D Bm/D A/E E7	A	F#m

lift my eyes to You Lord in Your strength will I break
storm I will hold on Lord and by faith I will walk
눈 들 어 – 주 보 네 – 그 능 력 날 새 롭
속 에 도 주 붙 들 고 – 믿 음 으 로 주 와

D Bm/D A/E Fdim F#m	E/G#

through Lord touch me now let Your love fall
on Lord then I'll see be‑yond my Cal‑va‑ry
게 해 주 님 의 – – 사 랑 날 – 만 –
건 네 갈 보 리 – 언 덕 너 – 머 그 어

A	A/C#	D A/C#	Bm7	Bm7/A

down on me I know Your love dis‑pels all my fears
one day and
지 시 니 – 내 모 든 두 – 려 움 사 라 지
– 느 날 – 주

1. Esus4	E	2. Bm7	D/E	E	A

through the I will be com‑plete in You
네 폭 풍 안 에 온 전 케 되 리

364 Days Of Elijah

(지금은 엘리야 때처럼)

Robin Mark

Days Of Elijah

comes. rid-ing on the clouds. Shin-ing like the sun at the trum pet
님 구름 타 시 고 – 나 팔 불 때 에 – 다 시 오 시

call Lift your voice it's the year of ju-bi-lee, out of Zi-on's
네 모 두 외 치 – 세 이 는 은 혜 의 해 니 – 시 온 에 서

hill sal - va tion comes. And comes.
구 원 이 임 하 네 또 네

A

365 Draw Me Close

(주님 곁으로 날 이끄소서)

Kelly Carpenter

Draw me close to you   nev-er let me go.
You are my de-sire,   No one else will do.
주 님 곁 - 으 로 -   날 이 끄 소 서 -
나 의 참 - 소 망 -   그 무 엇 - 과 도 -

I lay it all down a-gain   to hear You say that I'm Your friend.
'Cause noth-ing else could take Your place   to feel the warmth of Your em-brace
내 모 든 것 - 다 드 - 리 며 -   주 음 성 듣 - 기 원 - 하 네 -
바 꿀 수 없 - 는 주 - 사 랑 -   그 품 안 에 - 나 안 - 기 리 -

Help me find the way. bring me back to You.
주 님 의 - 길 로 - 인 도 하 - 소 서 -

You're all I want,   You're all I've ev - er need-ed
주 님 - 만 이 -   내 모 - 든 것 - 되 시 - 니 -

You're all I want,   Help me know You are near.
주 님 - 만 을 -   더 알 게 하 소 서 -

Dwell In Your House

(주의 집에 나 살리라)

Paul Ewing

366

367 Enough

(주님의 그 모든 것이)

Louie Giglio & Chris Tomlin

You're my sup - ply, my breath of life still more awe-some than I know
You're my sa - cri - fice of great set price still more awe-some than I know
나의 공 - 급 자 - 또 내 - 생 명 - 놀 라 우 - 신 하 나 님 -
내 죄 위 - 하 여 - 대 속 - 하 신 - 놀 라 우 - 신 하 나 님 -

You are my re - ward, worth liv - ing for still more awe-some than I know
You are com-ing King You are ev - 'ry - thing
주 나 의 - 상 급 - 삶 의 - 이 유 - 놀 라 우 - 신 하 나 님 - -
다 시 오 - 실 왕 - 나 의 모 - 든 것

and all of You is more than e-nough for all of me for ev-'ry
주 님 의 - 그 모 - 든 것 - 이 내 삶 을 - 가 득 채 우

thirst and ev - 'ry need You sa - tis - fy me with Your
- 네 내 모 든 - 갈 - 증 과 필 - 요 주 사 랑

love and all I have in You is more than e - nough

Fine

- 으 로 만 족 - 시 키 니 부 족 함 없 네 -

More than all I want more than all I need You are
내 가 원 - 하 는 모 든 것 - 보 다 - 부 족 함

Enough

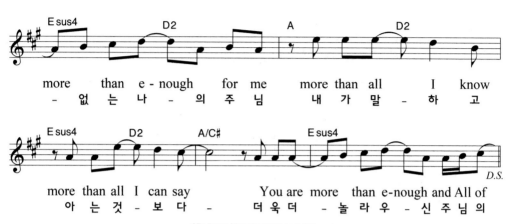

more   than   e - nough   for   me   more than   all   I   know
- 없 는 나 - 의 주 님   내 가 말 - 하   고

more than all I can say   You are more   than e-nough and All of
아 는 것 - 보 다 -   더 욱 더 - 놀 라 우 - 신 주 님 의

D.S.

O.T. : Enough / O.W. : Chris Tomlin, Louie Giglio
O.P. : worshiptogether.com Songs, sixsteps Music, Vamos Publishing / S.P. : Universal Music Publishing Korea, CAIOS
Adm. : Capitol CMG Publishing / All rights reserved, Used by permission.

A

368

Eternity
(나 주의 것 주 내 안에)

Brian Doerksen

I will be Yours   You will be mine   To-ge - ther in e-ter-ni-ty
나 주의 것 - 주 내안에 - 영원 - 히함께하리라

Our hearts of love   will be ent-wined   To-ge - ther in e-ter-ni-ty
우 리맘에 - 주의사랑 - 영원 - 히함께하리라

For-e - ver in e-ter - ni-ty
영원 - 히함께하 리라 -

No   more tears of pain   in you eyes
더 - 눈물없네 - - 우리눈에

No   more fear or shame   for we   will be   with You
더 - 두렴없네 - 주님 - 과함 - 께해

for we   will be   with You
- 주님 - 과함 - 께해 -

We will wor-ship   We will wor-ship You   for-e - ver
주 경배 - 해   주를경 - 배 - 해 - 영원 - 히 -

Everlasting God

(새 힘 얻으리)

369

Ken Riley & Brenton Brown

A

O.T. : Everlasting God / O.W. : Brenton Brown, Ken Riley
O.P. : Thankyou Music Ltd / S.P. : Universal Music Publishing Korea, CAIOS
Adm. : Capitol CMG Publishing / All rights reserved, Used by permission.

370 Falling
(나의 사랑이)

Brenton Brown & Paul Baloche

I would like to walk this would with You al-ways
Would You stay and lis-ten for a while please stay
나 – 주와함 – 께걷 – 기원 – 해요 –
주 님 내곁에 – 머물 – 러 주 – 세요 –

Nev-er want to be a-part from You O Lord
And let me talk of howYoumakeme smile Oh
주 님곁에날품 – 어주 – 세요 –
주 얼굴볼때커 – 지는 – 사랑 –

I am some-times O-ver-whelmed by Truth and Your ways;
I would like to leave it all be-hind my ways;
언 제 나주의 진 – 리날 – 감동 –해 –
주 앞 에나의 모 – 든것 – 버리 –고 –

like Could it be that I was made for You? I'm blown a-way
But I getcaught up in my-self some-times, all I can say
내 영혼오 – 직주 – 님만 – 갈 망 하 네 –
내 사랑주 – 님따 – 르기 – 갈 망 하 네 –

I am fal-ling I am fal-ling in love
나의 – 사 랑이 – 더욱 – 커 – 져가 네

I am fal-ling in love I am fall-ing in love withYou
– 주를 – 향한내 – 사 – 랑 – 더욱 – 깊 어 져

Falling

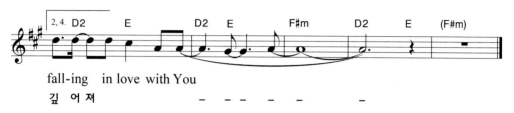

fall-ing   in love with You

깊 어 져   —   —   —   —   —

O.T. : Falling / O.W. : Brenton Brown, Paul Baloche
O.P. : Universal Music – Brentwood Benson Publ./ S.P. : Universal Music Publishing Korea, CAIOS
Adm. : Capitol CMG Publishing / All rights reserved. Used by permission.

A

371

Forever
(왕 되신 주께 감사하세)

Chris Tomlin

Give thanks to the Lord our God and King His
왕 되신 주 께 — 감 사 하 세 — 그

love en-dures for-ev-er For He is good He is a-bove all things
사 랑 영 원 하 리 — 라 — 모 든 것 위 — 에 뛰 어 나 신 — 주 — 그

love en-dures for-ev-er. Sing praise, sing praise.
사 랑 영 원 하 리 — 라 — 찬 양 — 찬 — 양

With a might-y hand and out-stretched arm His
— 능 력 의 손 과 펴 신 팔 — 로 — 그

love en-dures for-ev-er For the life that's been re-born His
사 랑 형 원 하 리 — 라 — 거 듭 난 영 혼 들 을 위 하 여 그

love en-dures for-ev-er. Sing praise sing praise
사 랑 영 원 하 리 — 라 찬 양 — 찬 — 양 —

for-ev-ver God is faith-ful for-ev-er God is strong
영 원 — 히 신 — 실 하 — 신 — 능 력 — 의 하 — 나 님

For-ev-er God is with us, for-ev-
— 영 원 — 히 함 — 께 하 리 — 영 원

Forever

Fine

- - er   for - ev - er   for - ev - er.
- 히 -   영 원 - 히 -   영 원 - 히 -

From the ris - ing to the set-ting sun   His love en-dures for-ev - er   By the
해 뜨 는데서 지 는 데 까 지   그 사 랑 영원하리 – 라

D.S. al Fine

grace of God we will car - ry on   His love en-dures for-ev - er.   Sing
주 은혜로 – 우 리 걸 어가 리   그 사 랑 영원하리 – 라   찬

O.T. : Forever / O.W. : Chris Tomlin
O.P. : worshiptogether.com Songs, sixsteps Music, Vamos Publishing / S.P. : Universal Music Publishing Korea, CAIOS
Adm. : Capitol CMG Publishing / All rights reserved. Used by permission.

A

372

Fill My Cup Lord
(우물가의 여인처럼)

Richard Blanchard

Like the wom-an at the well I was seek-ing for
There are mil-lions in this world who are crav-ing the
So, my broth-er, if the things this world gave you leave

우 물 가 의 여 인 처 럼 난 구 했 네 – 헛
많 고 많 은 사 람 들 이 찾 았 었 네 – 헛
내 친 구 여 거 기 서 – 돌 아 오 라 – 내

things that could not sat-is-fy. And then I heard my Sav-ior
pleas-ure earth-ly things af-ford. But none can match the won-drous
hun-gers that won't pass a-way. My bless-ed Lord will come and

되 고 헛 된 것 들 을 그 때 주 님 – 하 신
되 고 헛 된 것 들 을 주 안 에 감 – 추 인
주 의 넓 은 품 으 로 우 리 주 님 – 너 를

speak-ing 'Draw from my well that nev-er shall run dry.'
trea-sure That I find in Je-sus Christ, my Lord. Fill my
save you If you kneel to Him and hum-bly pray.

말 씀 – 내 샘 에 와 생 수 를 마 셔 라
보 배 – 세 상 것 과 난 비 길 수 없 네 오 –
반 겨 – 그 넓 은 품 에 안 아 주 시 리

cup, Lord, I lift it up Lord. Come and quench this thirst-ing of my
주 님 – 채 우 소 서 – 나 의 잔 을 높 이 듭 니

soul. Bread of heav-en, feed me till I want no more; Fill my
다 하 늘 양 식 내 게 채 워 주 소 서 넘 치

cup, fill it up and make me whole.
도 록 – 채 워 주 소 서

God Is The Strength Of My Heart

(하늘 위에 주님밖에)

Eugene Greco

373

374

God Of Wonders
(온 세계 지으신 창조의 하나님)

Marc Byrd & Steve Hindalong

Lord of all cre-a-tion,　of wa-ter earth, and sky;
Ear-ly in the morn-ing,　I will cel-e-brate the light.
온 세계 - 지으 - 신 -　창조의하 - 나 - 님 -
이른아 - 침에 - 도 -　빛을기뻐하 - 리 - 라 -

The heav-ens are Your tab-er-na-cle.　Glo-ry to the Lord on high!
When I stum-ble in the dark-ness　I will call Your name by night.
저 하늘주의장막되 - 니 -　주 께영광돌 - 리 - 리 -
어둠속에 헤매일때 - 도 -　주 의이름부 - 르 - 리 -

God of won-ders be-yond our gal-ax-y,　You are ho - ly,
우 주위 - 에주의경이로움　주는 거 - 룩 -

ho - ly. The un-i-verse de-clares Your maj-es-ty, You are ho - ly,
거 - 룩 열 방이주 - 의위 - 엄선포해 주는 거 - 룩 -

ho - ly. Lord of heaven and earth,　Lord of heaven and earth.
거 - 룩 - 하늘 과땅 - 의주 -　하 늘 과땅의 - 주 -

1.

2.

Hal-le-lu - jah, to the Lord of heav-en and earth.
할렐루 - 야 온 - 땅과 - 하늘위 - 에

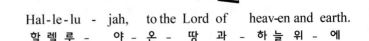

God Of Wonders

O.T. : God Of Wonders / O.W. : Marc Byrd, Steve Hindalong
O.P. : Storm Boy Music, Meaux Mercy, Never Say Never Songs, New Spring Publishing Inc. / S.P. : Universal Music Publishing Korea, CAIOS
Adm. : Capitol CMG Publishing / All rights reserved. Used by permission.

375

Great Are You Lord
(거룩한 나의 주님)

Stephen R. Cook & Vikki Anne Cook

Ho - ly Lord Most Ho - ly Lord You a - lone are
거 룩 한 나 의 주 님 당 신 만 을

wor - thy of my praise O Ho - ly Lord Most
찬 양 합 니 다 - 오 거 룩 한 나

Ho - ly Lord with all of my heart I sing
의 주 님 은 맘 다 해 찬 양 해 -

Great are You, Lord
크 신 주 께

Wor - thy of praise; Ho - ly and
찬 양 하 네 - - - 거 룩 하

true Great are You, Lord, Most Ho - ly Lord
고 진 실 하 신 우 리 주 님 -

Great Is The Lord

(주 여호와는 광대하시도다)

376

Steve McEwan

Great is the Lord and most wor-thy of praise in the
주 — 여호와는광 대 하 시 도 다 그

ci-ty of our God the ho-ly place The joy of the whole earth
거룩한 — 하 나 — 님 성 에 서 찬 양 할 지 — 어 다 —

Great is the Lord in whom we have the vic-to-ry He
주 — 승 리 우 리 에 — 게 주 셨 도 — 다 모

aids us a-gainst the en-e-my We bow down on our knees
든 원 — 수 물 — 리 치 — 셨 네 — 엎 드 려 절 — 하 세 —

And Lord we want to lift Your name on high And
다 주의 크 신 이 — 름 높 이 며 우

Lord we want to thank You for the works You've done in our lives and
리 에 게 행 하 — 신 위 대 한 일 감 사 하 — 세 오

Lord we trust in Your un-fail-ing love For
주 의 신 실 하 — 신 그 사 랑 온

You a-lone are God e-ter-nal through-out earth and hea-ven a-bove
땅 과 하 — 늘 위 에 계 — 셔 홀 로 영 — 원 하 신 이 름 — —

377 Healer

(치료자)

Mike Guglielmucci

You hold my ev-ery mo-ment. You calm my ra-ging seas. You
주 모 든삶－붙드－사－ 날 잠 잠케－하네 － 주

walk with me through fi - re, and heal all my dis-ease. I
나 와 함－께하－며－ 내 상 처치－유해 － 주

trust in You. I trust in - You.
신 뢰 해 주 신 뢰 － 해

I be-lieve, You're my Hea-ler. I be-lieve, You are all I
난 믿 네 내 치 료 자 난 믿 네 주 내 모 든

need. I be-lieve, You're my por-tion.
것 난 믿 네 주 내 기 업

I be-lieve, You're more than e-nough for me.
난 믿 네 내 게 부 족 함－없 는 －

Je-sus, You're all I - need.
예 수 내 모 든 － 것 －

Healer

No-thing is im-pos-si-ble for You. No-thing is im-pos-
능 치 못 – 함 없 – 으 리 – 주 께 능 치 못 – 함 없

- si - ble. No-thing is im-pos - si - ble. for You.
– 으 리 – 능 치 못 – 함 없 – 으 리 – 주 께

You hold my world in Your – hands.
– 주 의 손 날 – 붙 드 – 네 –

in Your – hands.
–붙 드 – 네 – –

A

378 Heal Our Land

(나의 백성이)

Tom Brooks & Robin Brooks

Heal Our Land

Lord, heal our land Fa - ther, heal our land
아 버 지 여 – 고 쳐 주 소 서 –

Hear our cry and turn our na - tion back to - You,
이 나 라 주 의 것 되 게 하 소 – 서

Lord, heal our land, Hear us, O Lord, and heal our land
주 하 나 님 간 절 히 기 도 하 오 니 –

For - give our sin and heal our bro - ken - land
상 한 이 땅 새 롭 게 하 – 소 – 서 –

A

379

Holy Is The Lord

(거룩하신 주)

Chris Tomlin & Louie Giglio

We stand and life up our hands　　　for the joy
일 어 나 두 손 들 고 —　　　나 의 힘

of the Lord　　is our strength
— 이 되 신 — 주 님 께 —

We bow down　　and wor - ship Him now　How great
엎 드 려 — 경 배 — 드 리 세 — 크 고

how awe - some is He　　And to - geth - er we sing
— 위 대 하 신 주 —　우 리 모 두 함 — 께 —

ev - ry - one　sing　　ho - ly is　the Lord
찬 양 — 하 — 세 —　　거 룩 하 — 신 주

God　Al - might - y　The earth　is filled with His glo-
— 전 — 능 — 의 — — 주 —　영 광 온 땅 — 에 가 득

- ry　Ho - ly is　the Lord　God　Al - might - y　The earth
— 해 거 룩 하 — 신 주 —　전 — — 능 — 의 — — 주 —　영 광

is filled with His glo - ry　the earth　is filled with His glo-
— 온 땅 — 에 가 득 — 해 —　영 광 — 온 땅 — 에 가 득

Holy Is The Lord

O.T. : Holy Is The Lord / O.W. : Chris Tomlin, Louie Giglio
O.P. : worshiptogether.com Songs, sixsteps Music, Vamos Publishing / S.P. : Universal Music Publishing Korea, CAIOS
Adm. : Capitol CMG Publishing / All rights reserved, Used by permission.

380 Hope Of The Nations

(예수 열방의 소망)

Brian Doerksen

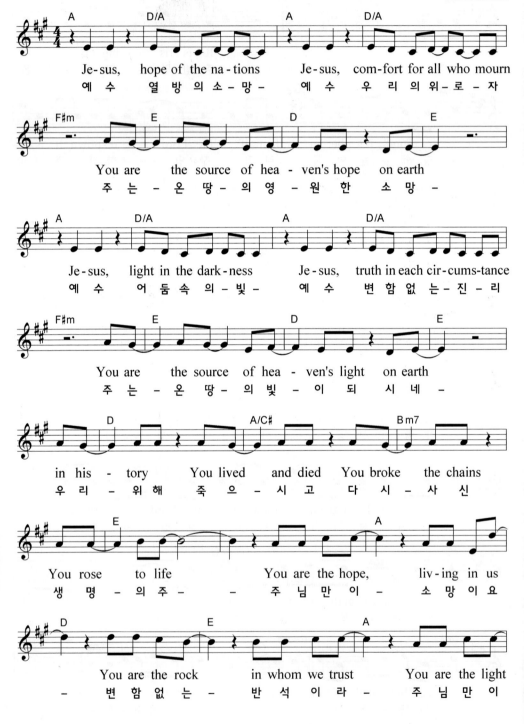

Je-sus, hope of the na-tions Je-sus, com-fort for all who mourn
예 수 열 방 의 소 - 망 - 예 수 우 리 의 위 - 로 - 자

You are the source of hea - ven's hope on earth
주 는 - 온 땅 - 의 영 - 원 한 소 망 -

Je-sus, light in the dark-ness Je-sus, truth in each cir-cums-tance
예 수 어 둠 속 의 빛 - 예 수 변 함 없 는 - 진 - 리

You are the source of hea - ven's light on earth
주 는 - 온 땅 - 의 빛 - 이 되 시 네 -

in his - tory You lived and died You broke the chains
우 리 - 위 해 죽 으 - 시 고 다 시 - 사 신

You rose to life You are the hope, liv-ing in us
생 명 - 의 주 - - 주 님 만 이 - 소 망 이 요

You are the rock in whom we trust You are the light
- 변 함 없 는 - 반 석 이 라 - 주 님 만 이

Hope Of The Nations

shin - ing for all the world   to see
－ 온 세 상 을 비 추 － － 시 네 －

You rose from the dead   con-quer-ing fear   Our prince of Peace
－ 또 죽 음 에 서 － 부 활 하 신 － 우 리 구 주

draw-ing us near   Je - sus our hope   Liv - ing for all
－ 평 강 의 왕 － 주 를 믿 는 － 모 든 자 의

who will   recei-ve   Lord we   be-lieve
－ 소 망 － 되 신 － 주 를 － － 믿 네 －

A

381 How Can I keep From Singing
(나의 찬양 멈출 수 없네)

Chris Tomlin, Matt Redman, Ed Cash

There is an end-less song ech-oes in my soul   I hear the mu-sic
lift my eyes in the dark-est night   for I know my Sav-ior
끝 없 이 울 리 는 나 의 영 혼 의 - -   노 래 가 들 리
가 운 데 바 라 보 리 라 - -   살 아 계 신 내 구

ring   And thought the storms may come, I am hold-ing on
lives   And I will walk with You know-ing You'll see me   through and
네   폭 풍 이 일 어 도   내 반 석 되 - -신 - -
주   날 감 찰 하 시 는   주 를 찬 양 하 -며 - -   주

to   the rock I   cling   How can I keep from sing-ing Your
sing the songs You give
주 님 붙 드 네   나 의 찬 양 멈 출 수 없
님 과 걸 으 리

praise? How can I ev - er say e-nough how a-maz-ing is Your love?
- 네 - 놀 라 운 주 의 사 랑 을   말 로 다 할 -수 없 - -네 -

How can I keep from shout-ing Your name?   I know I am loved by the King and it
주 를 향 한 끝 - 없 는 외 - -침 - 주 님 날 사 랑 하 시 네   내 마

Last time
to coda ⊕ | 1. A

makes my heart   want to sing   I will
음 주 를 - - 노 래 해   어 둠

How Can I keep From Singing

sing   I can sing in the trou-bled times sing when I win I can
해   찬양 해 고난가운데-- 난 승리해 찬양

sing when I lose my step and fall down a - gain I can
- 해 갈길을잃고- 또 넘 - 어 져 도 찬 양

sing 'cause You pick me up sing 'cause You're there I can
해 주 향 상 계 셔 날 붙 드 네 찬 양

sing 'cause You hear me Lord when I call to You in pray - er I can
해 - 나 의 기 도 에 항 상 응 답 하 시 네 - - 찬 양

sing with my last breath sing for I know that I'll
- 해 생 명 다 해 주 - 보 좌 앞 - - 천 사

sing with the an - gels, and the saint a-round the throne. sing
- 들 성 도 들 - 도 - 함 께 찬 양 하 리 라 - 해

O.T. : How Can I Keep From Singing / O.W. : Matt Redman, Chris Tomlin, Ed Cash
O.P. : worshiptogether.com Songs, sixsteps Music, Vamos Publishing, Thankyou Music Ltd / S.P. : Universal Music Publishing Korea, CAIOS
Adm. : Capitol CMG Publishing / All rights reserved. Used by permission.

A

382

Hosanna

(호산나)

Todd Pettygrove

Ho - san - na, Ho - san - na Ho - san - na to the King Ho -
호 산 - 나 호 산 - 나 왕 되 신 주 님 께 호

san - na Ho - san - na Ho - san - na to the King
산 - 나 호 산 - 나 왕 되 신 주 님 께

mag - ni - fy the Lord and sing sing prais - es to the ri - sen
광 대 하 신 주 - 찬 양 다 시 사 신 왕 께 - 찬

King oh mag - ni - fy the Lord most high He is
양 지 존 하 신 - 주 를 찬 양 경

wor - thy to be praised oh mag - ni - fy the
배 를 드 리 세 지 존 하 신 - 주

Lord most high He is wor - thy to be praised Ho -
를 찬 양 경 배 를 드 리 세 호

san - na Ho - san - na Ho - san - na to the King
산 - 나 호 산 - 나 왕 되 신 주 님 께

I Extol You

(평강의 왕이요)

383

Jennifer Randolph

A

384 How Great Is Our God
(위대하신 주)

Chris Tomlin, Jesse Reeves & Ed Cash

The splen-dor of the King　clothed in ma-je-sty
And age to age He stands　and time is in His hands
빛 나 는 왕 의 왕　영 광 의 주 님
영 원 한 주 의 주　시 간 의 주 관 자

Let all the earth re-joice　all the earth re-joice　He wraps
Be-gin-ning and the End　Be-gin-ning and the End　The God
온 땅 기 뻐 하 라　온 땅 기 뻐 하 라　광 채
알 파 와 오 메 가　알 파 와 오 메 가　삼 위

Him-self in light　and dark-ness tries to hide
Head Three in One　Fa-ther Spir-it Son
의 옷 입 고　어 두 움 물 리 쳐
의 하 나 님　아 바 성 령 예 수

and tem-bles at His voice　and trem-bles at his voice　How great
The Li-on and the Lamb　The Li-on and the Lamb
저 원 수 는 떠 네　저 원 수 는 떠 네　위 대
사 자 와 어 린 양　사 자 와 어 린 양

is our God　Sing with me How great　is our God
하 신 주　찬 양 해 위 대　하 신 주

And all will see how great　How great　is our God
모 두 알 게 되 리 라　위 대　하 신 주

Name a-bove all names　wor-thy of all praise　My
모 든 이 름 위 에　뛰 어 나 신 이 름　다

How Great Is Our God

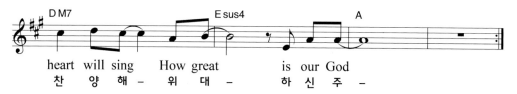

heart will sing   How great   is our God
찬 양 해 – 위 대 – 하 신 주 –

In Christ Alone

(오직 예수)

385

Don Koch & Shawn Craig

In christ a - lone   I place my trust   and find my
나 의 믿 음   주 께 있 네   십 자 가

glo - ry in   the po - wer of   the   cross   In ev' - ry
능 력 이 – 내 영 광 되 – 었 – 네   주 께 – 서

vic - to - ry   let it be said   of me   my
우 리 를 – 승 리 케 하   시 니 –   나

source of strength   my source of hope   is Christ a - lone
의 능 력   나 의 소 망   주 께 있 네

A

386

I Know Who I am

(예수 나의 주)

Chris Tomlin & Israel Houghton

I Know Who I am

387 I Sing Praises To Your Name O Lord

(나는 찬양하리라)

Terry MacAlmon

I sing Prais-es to Your name, Oh Lord Prais-es to your name
I give glo-ry to Your name, Oh Lord Glo-ry to Your name
나 는 찬 양 하 리 라 주 — 님 그 이 름 찬 양
나 는 영 광 돌 리 리 주 — 님 영 광 의 이 름

Oh Lord For Your name is great, and great-ly to be praised
Oh Lord For Your name is great, and great-ly to be praised
예 — 수 크 신 주 이 름 나 찬 양 하 리 라
예 — 수 크 신 주 이 름 나 찬 양 하 리 라

I sing Prais-es to Your name, Oh Lord Prais-es to Your name Oh Lord
I give glo-ry to Your name, Oh Lord Glo-ry to Your name Oh Lord
나 는 찬 양 하 리 라 주 — 님 그 이 름 찬 양 예 — 수
나 는 영 광 돌 리 리 주 — 님 영 광 의 이 름 예 — 수

For Your name is great, and great-ly to be praised
For Your name is great, and great-ly to be praised
크 신 주 이 름 나 찬 양 하 리 라 —
크 신 주 이 름 나 찬 양 하 리 라 —

I Stand In Awe

(아름답고 놀라운 주 예수)

388

Mark Altrogge

You are beau-ti-ful be-yond de-scrip-tion. too
아 름 답 고 놀 – 라 운 주 예 수 말

mar-vel-ous for words. too won-der-ful for com-pre-hen-
로 할 수 – 없 네 – 그 측 량 할 수 없 는 위

- sion like noth-ing ev-er seen or heard. Who can
– 엄 – 주 님 과 같 은 분 없 네 – 한 없

grasp Your in-fi-nite wis-dom? who can faith-om the depth of Your love?
는 그 지 혜 와 사 랑 그 누 구 도 다 알 수 없 네

You are beau-ti-ful be-yond de-scrip-tion. maj-es-
– 아 름 답 고 놀 – 라 운 주 예 수 보 좌

ty en-throned a-bove And I stand, I stand in
에 앉 으 – 셨 네 – 주 님 앞 에 – 내 가

awe of You. I stand, I stand in awe of You. Ho-ly
서 있 네 – 주 앞 에 – 내 가 서 있 네 – 주 는

God, to whom all praise is due, I stand in awe of You.
거 룩 – 하 신 하 나 님 그 앞 에 서 있 네

389

It's Your Blood
(주 보혈 날 씻었네)

Michael Christ

It's Your blood that cleans - es me, it's Your
It's the blood of the Lamb, it's the
주 보 혈 날 씻 었 네 내 게

blood that gives me life, it's Your blood that took my
blood of the Lamb, it's the blood of the
생 명 을 주 셨 네 주 보 혈 나 의 죄

place in re - deem - ing sac - ri - fice, wash - es me
Lamb that can cleanse the deep - est stain, wash - es me
를 구 속 하 신 어 린 양 - - - 날 씻 었 네 -

whit - er than the snow, than the snow,
흰 눈 보 다 더 희 - 게 하 셨 네 - - -

my Je - sus, God's pre - cious sac - ri - fice.
예 수 님 - 귀 하 신 어 린 양

I Walk By Faith

(믿음따라)

Christopher John Falson

I walk by faith Each step by faith
믿 음 따 라 걸 음 마 다

To live by faith I put my trust in You I
말 씀 따 라 주 님 만 따 르 리 – 믿

Ev - 'ry step I take is a step of faith
나 의 가 – 는 길 – – 믿 음 따 – 라 갈 – 때

No wea-pon formed a-gain - st me shall pro - sper
군 대 가 날 에 워 싸 – 도 겁 없 네 –

and ev - 'ry prayer I make Is a prayer of faith
또 내 입 술 – 의 기 – 도 믿 음 의 선 포 –

If my God is for me who can be a-gainst me I
주 님 날 위 하 시 – 면 누 가 날 대 적 하 – 리 믿

391
Jesus, We Enthrone You
(예수 우리 왕이여)

Paul Kyle

Je - sus   we en - throne You
예 수 - 우 리 왕 이 여 -

we pro - claim You are King
이 곳 에 오 소 서 -

stand - ing here   in the midst of us
보 좌 로 - 주 여 임 하 사 -

We raise You up with our paise
찬 양 을 받 아 주 소 서 -

And as we wor - ship build a throne
주 님 을 찬 양 하 오 니

and as we wor - ship build a throne
주 님 을 경 - 배 하 오 니

and as we wor - ship build a throne Come Lord
왕 이 신 예 수 여 오 셔 서 좌 정

Je - sus and take Your place
하 사 다 스 리 소 서 -

Jesus You Alone

(예수 나의 첫사랑 되시네)

392

Tim Hughes

Je - sus You a - lone shall be my first love　　my first love The
Day and night I'll lift my eyes to seek You　　to seek You
예 수 나의 첫 사 랑 되 시 네 – 　　내 첫 – 사랑 – 지
내 눈 들어 항 상 주 를 찾 – 네 – 　　나 의 – 주님 –

se - cret place and high - est praise shall be Yours　　shall be Yours
Hun - gry for a glimpse of You in glo - ry　　in glo - ry
존 자 되신 그 리 스 도 예 – 수 – 　　찬 양 – 하리 –
영 광 중의 주 님 보 길 원 – 해 – 　　보 길 – 원해 –

To Your throne I'll bring de - vo - tion May it be the sweet - est sound
보 좌 앞 에 나의 삶 이 향 기 로 운 제 사 로

Lord this heart is reach - ing for You now
주 께 드 려 지 기 원 하 네 –

So I'll set my sight up - on You　　Set my life up - on
You a - lone will be my pas - sion　　Je - sus, You will be
오 직 주 만 바 – 라 보 – 며　　나 의 삶 을 드
나 의 온 전 한 – 열 정 – 과　　나 의 찬 양 되

Your praise Nev - er look - ing to a - no - ther way
my song You will find me long
– 리 네 – 다 른 길은 찾 – 지 않 – 으 리
– 시 네 – 주 의 길을 따

ing af - ter You
– 라 가 – 리 라 –

393 Jesus Shall Take The Highest Honour

(주님 큰 영광 받으소서)

Chris Bowater

Je-sus shall take the high – est ho-nour,
주 님 큰 영 광 받 – 으 소 서 –

Je – sus shall take the high – est praise. Let all
홀 로 찬 양 받 으 – 소 서 모 든

earth join hea-ven in ex-al-ting the
이 름 위 에 – 뛰 어 난 그 이 름 – 온

name which is a-bove all o – ther names.
땅 과 하 – 늘 이 다 찬 – 양 해

Let's bow our knees in hum-ble ado-ra-tion For
겸 손 하 – 게 우 리 무 – 릎 꿇 고 – 주

at His name eve-ry knee must bow. Let
이 름 앞 – 에 영 광 돌 – 리 세 모

every tongue con-fess He is Christ God's only Son.
두 절 하 세 – 독 생 자 예 – 수 –

Jesus Shall Take The Highest Honour

Sovereign Lord we give You glo - ry now, for all
주 님 께 – 찬 양 드 – 리 리 모 든

ho - nour and ble - ssing and po - wer be - longs to You
영 광 과 존 귀 와 능 력 – 받 으 소 서 –

be - longs to You ho - nour and ble - ssing and po - wer
받 으 소 서 – 영 광 과 존 귀 와 능 력 –

be - longs to You be - longs to You Lord, Je - sus Christ,
받 으 소 서 – 받 으 소 서 – 그 리 스 도

Son of the Li - v - ing God.
살 아 계 신 – 하 나 님 –

A

394

King Of Majesty
(주님은 아시네)

Marty Sampson

Lord Over All

(예수 만물의 주)

Gary Sadler

395

396

Lamb Of God

(하나님 어린 양)

Chris Bowater

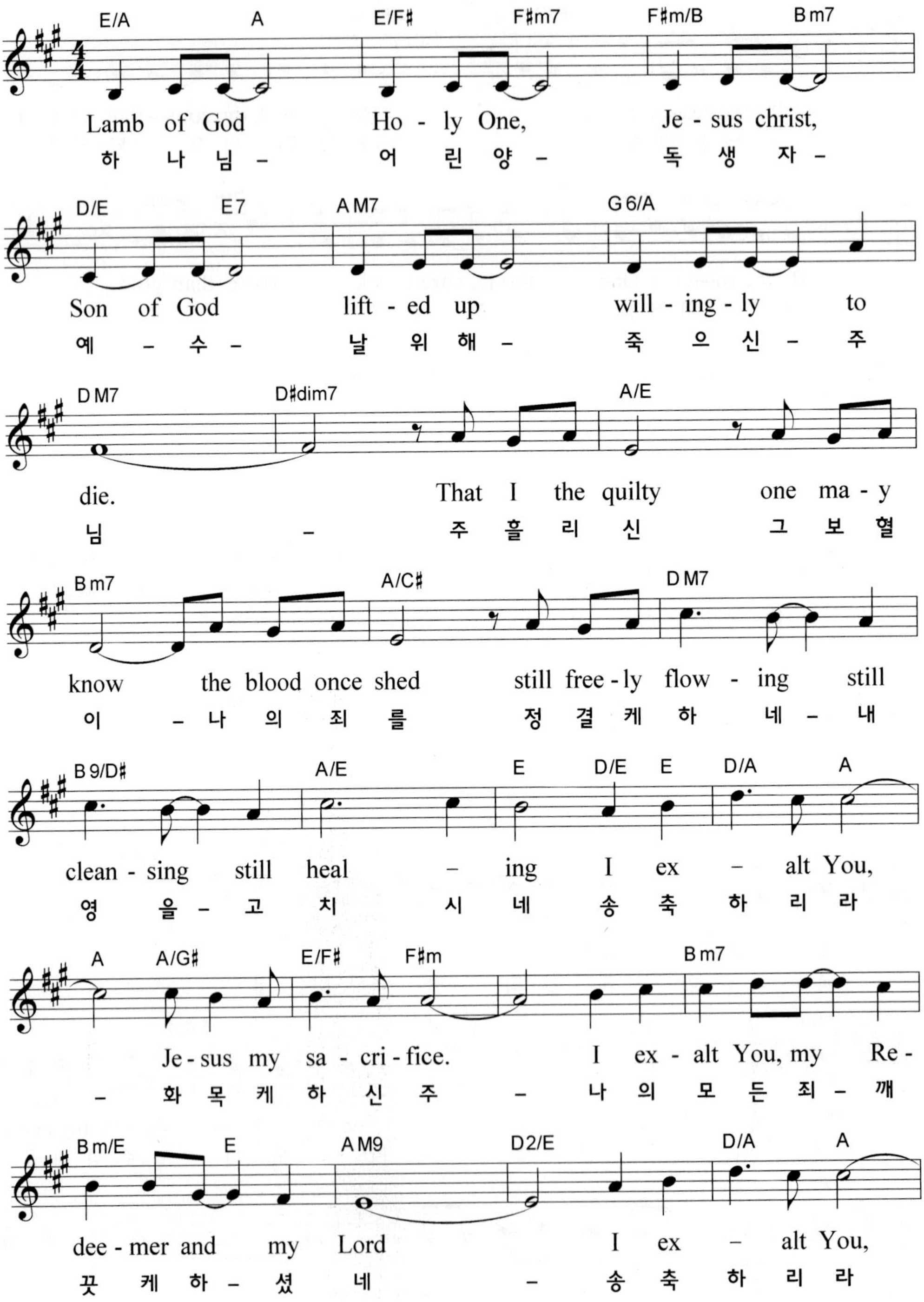

E/A A E/F♯ F♯m7 F♯m/B Bm7
Lamb of God Ho - ly One, Je - sus christ,
하 나 님 – 어 린 양 – 독 생 자 –
D/E E7 AM7 G6/A
Son of God lift - ed up will - ing - ly to
예 – 수 – 날 위 해 – 죽 으 신 – 주
DM7 D♯dim7 A/E
die. That I the quilty one ma - y
님 – 주 흘 리 신 그 보 혈
Bm7 A/C♯ DM7
know the blood once shed still free - ly flow - ing still
이 – 나 의 죄 를 정 결 케 하 네 – 내
B9/D♯ A/E E D/E E D/A A
clean - sing still heal – ing I ex – alt You,
영 을 – 고 치 시 네 송 축 하 리 라
A A/G♯ E/F♯ F♯m Bm7
Je - sus my sa - cri - fice. I ex - alt You, my Re -
– 화 목 케 하 신 주 – 나 의 모 든 죄 – 깨
Bm/E E AM9 D2/E D/A A
dee - mer and my Lord I ex – alt You,
끗 케 하 – 셨 네 – 송 축 하 리 라

Lamb Of God

wor - thy ` the Lamb of God and in
귀 하 신 어 린 양 - 모 두

ho - nour I bow down be - fore Your throne.
절 하 고 - 모 두 외 치 리 라 -

Lift Up Your Heads
(고개 들어)

397

Steve Fry

Lift up your heads to the com - ing King
고 개 들 어 주 를 맞 이 해

Bow be - fore Him and a - dore Him, sing.
엎 드 리 어 경 배 하 며 찬 양

To His ma - jes - ty let your prais - es be
왕 의 위 엄 을 신 령 과 진 정 한

pure and ho - ly Give - ing glo - ry to the King of Kings.
찬 양 으 로 영 광 돌 려 만 왕 의 왕 께

A

398 Lord I Come Before Your Throne Of Grace

(주님 보좌 앞에 나아가)

Robert Critchley & Dawn Critchley

Lord I come be-fore Your throne of grace I find
Lord of mer-cy You have heard my cry through the
주 님 보 좌 앞 에 나 아 가 참 된
기 도 들 으 시 는 하 나 님 폭 풍

rest in Your pre-sence and ful-ness of Joy in
storm You're the bea-con my song in the night in the
안 식 과 기 쁨 나 누 리 겠 네 경
속 에 내 등 불 내 노 래 시 라 주 의

wor-ship and won-der I be-hold Your face sing-ing
shel-ter of Your wings hear my heart's re-ply sing-ing
배 하 며 주 의 얼 굴 구 할 때 신 실
날 개 아 래 서 내 맘 쉬 리 니

what a faith-ful God have I What a faith-ful
하 신 주 님 찬 양 해 신 실 하 신

God have I what a faith-ful God
하 나 님 신 실 하 신 주

What a faith-ful God have I faith-ful in eve-ry
나 의 주 하 나 님 은 신 실 하 신 주

Lord I Come Before Your Throne Of Grace

way
님

Lord all sover-eign grant-ing peace from heaven let me
평 화 내 려 주 신 하 나 님 나 로

com-fort those who suf-fer with the com-fort You have given I will
고 통 받 – 는 자 – 를 위 로 하 게 하 – 소 서 나 의

tell of Your great love for as long as I live sing-ing
평 생 에 – 주 의 사 랑 을 전 하 리 – 신 실

what a faith-ful God have I What a faith-ful
하 신 주 – 님 찬 양 해 신 실 하 – 신

O.T. : What A Faithful God Lord I Come Before Your., / O.W. : Robert Critchley, Dawn Critchley
O.P. : Thankyou Music Ltd / S.P. : Universal Music Publishing Korea, CAIOS
Adm. : Capitol CMG Publishing / All rights reserved. Used by permission.

A

399 Love Came Down

(그 사랑이 내려와)

Brian Johnson, Jeremy Edwardson, Ian Mcintosh

If my heart is ov - er - whelmed and I can - not hear Your voice,
heart is filled with hope and ev - 'ry prom - ise comes my way,
고 난 중 에 주 - 음 성 - 들 을 수 없 다 - 해 도 -
약 속 이 - 뤄 져 - 소 망 이 넘 칠 - 때 도 -

I'll hold on to what is true though I can - not see.
when I feel Your hands of grace rest u - pon me
참 된 진 리 되 - 신 주 - 나 는 붙 드 네 -
은 혜 로 운 주 - 손 길 - 느 - 낄 때 도 -

If the storms of life they come and the road a - head gets steep,
stay - ing des - p'rate for You God, stay - ing hum - ble at Your feet,
폭 풍 이 몰 려 - 와 도 - 험 한 길 을 간 - 대 도 -
주 를 향 한 갈 - 망 과 - 겸 손 한 마 음 - 으 로 -

I will lift these hands in faith. I will be - lieve.
I will lift these hands and praise. I will be - lieve.
믿 음 의 두 손 - 들 고 - 주 신 뢰 해 -
믿 음 의 두 손 - 들 고 - 주 신 뢰 해 -

I'll re - mind my - self of all that You've done, and the
내 게 행 하 신 그 놀 라 운 일 - 생 명

life I have be - cause of Your Son.
주 신 주 를 기 억 하 네 -

Love Came Down

Love came down and res-cued me, Love came down and set me free. and
그 사 랑 이 내 려 와 날 자 유 케 하 셨 네

I am Yours, I am for-ev-er Yours. Moun-tain high or val-ley low,
영 원 히 나 는 주 님 의 것 - 산 과 골 짜 기 에 서

I sing out, re-mind my soul that I am Yours, I am for-ev-er
내 영 혼 노 래 하 네 영 원 히 나 는 주 님 의 것 -

when my I am Yours. I am Yours. All my days,
주 의 나 의 - 삶 - 주 의 - 것 - 내 모 든 - 삶

Je-sus, I am Yours. I am Yours.
- 오 직 주 의 - 것 - 나 의 - 삶 -

A

400 Majesty
(영광의 주)

Jack Hayford

Ma - jes - ty　　worship His ma - jes - ty
영 광 의 　－　주 님 찬 양 하 세 　－

Un - to Je - sus be all glo - ry, pow-er and praise
모 든 영 광 능 력 찬 송 예 수 님 께 　－

ma - jes - ty　　king-dom au - thor - i - ty
영 광 의 　－　주 님 찬 양 하 세 　－

flow from His throne un - to His own His an - them raise
주 의 백 성 모 두 함 께 찬 양 하 세 　－　－

So ex - alt, lift up on high the name of Je - sus
두 손 을 높 이 들 고 주 이 름 찬 양 　－

mag - ni - fy, come glo - ri - fy Christ Je-sus the King
존 귀 와 영 광 모 두 주 예 수 님 께

Ma - jes - ty　　worship His ma - jes - ty
영 광 의 　－　주 님 찬 양 하 세 　－

Je - sus who died, now glo - ri - fied, King of all kings.
죽 으 시 고 부 활 하 신 만 왕 의 왕 　－

My Heart Sings Praises

(내 마음 다해)

Russell Fragar

401

My heart sings prai-ses   Each time I say Your name
내 마음 다 해 - -   주 이름 찬 양 - 해 -

This love is deep-er   than sim-ple words can say
주 사 랑 깊 어 - - -   말 로 다 못 하 네

You go be-fore me   You make a per-fect way
주 앞 서 가 며 - -   길 을 만 드 시 네 -

My one de-si-re   is to give You per-fect praise
오 직 내 갈 망 - - -   영 원 히 주 찬 양

In my heart You are the po-wer   In my night Ne-ver fail-ing light
내 맘 에 힘 이 되 신 - 주   영 원 한 - 빛 이 되 - 신 주

with ev-ery breath that I take I'll de-clare   the thing You've done
- 내 모 든 호 흡 이 주 의 행 하 - 심 찬 - 양 해 -

In my mind, migh-ty over-come - - er   In my soul, the rea-son why
주 는 위 대 한 통 치 - - 자   내 모 든 것 주 께 순 복 해

In my life, You are the fire   that calls me on
- 내 삶 을 주 의 불 로 - 채 우 - 소 서 -

402 Mighty To Save
(내 주는 구원의 주)

Reuben Morgan & Ben Fielding

Mighty To Save

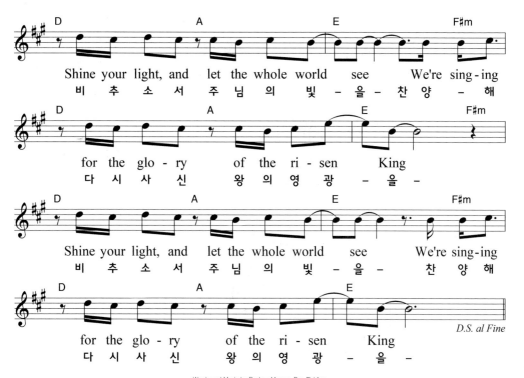

Shine your light, and let the whole world see We're sing-ing
비 추 소 서 주 님 의 빛 — 을 — 찬 양 — 해

for the glo - ry of the ri - sen King
다 시 사 신 왕 의 영 광 — 을 —

Shine your light, and let the whole world see We're sing-ing
비 추 소 서 주 님 의 빛 — 을 — 찬 양 해

D.S. al Fine

for the glo - ry of the ri - sen King
다 시 사 신 왕 의 영 광 — 을 —

A

403

My Heart Is Yours

(나의 마음을 드립니다)

Daniel Carson, Kristian Stanfill,
Brett Younker & Jason Ingram

My Heart Is Yours

Je - - - sus My heart is Yours my heart is Yours take it
예 - - - 수 - 내 마 음 을 드 립 니 다 - 모 든

all take it all my life in Your hands my heart is Yours Lord, my
것 모 든 것 주 받 으 소 서 - 내 마 음 을 드

heart is Yours take it all take it all my life in Your hands take it
립 니 다 - 모 든 것 모 든 것 주 받 으 소 서 - 모 든

all take it all my life in Your hands And all to Je - sus
것 모 든 것 주 받 으 소 서 - 또 내 게 있 는

I sur - ren - der All to You, I free - ly give Oh, I will ev - er
모 든 것 을 아 낌 없 이 바 치 네 오 사 랑 하 고

love and trust You In Your pres - ence I will live And
의 지 하 여 주 만 따 라 가 겠 네 또

In Your pres - ence I will live.
주 만 따 라 가 겠 네

A

404 My Redeemer Lives

(내 주님 살아 계시기에)

John Willison

O Lord Our Lord

(오 하나님 온 땅 위에)

Doug Bergsma

O Lord our Lord, how ma-jes-tic is Your name in all the earth!
오 하 나 - 님 - 온 땅 위 에 위 - 대 하 신 주 - 이 름

O Lord, our Lord how ma-jes-tic is Your name in all the earth!
오 하 나 - 님 - 온 땅 위 에 위 - 대 하 신 주 - 이 름

We give You praise, we give You glo-ry and mag-ni-fy your ho-ly na - me
찬 양 과 영 광 을 - 주 님 께 거 룩 하 신 - 주 이 름 찬 양

We ho - nor You, we wor-ship You and glo - ri - fy Your name!
존 귀 와 경 배 주 님 께 영 광 을 돌 리 세

A

406 Need You Here
(나 주님을 구하오니)

Reuben Morgan

I need You here   I need You here
O look to You   I look to You
나 – 주 – 님을 – – – –   구 – 하 – 오 – 니 – – – –
나 – 주 – 님만 – – – –   바 – 라 – 오 – 니 – – – –

You're like the rain that falls   fall on this heart and make me
You're King a-bove the earth   and You have put hea - ven in my
날 – 새 – 롭 게 – 하 실 – –   성 령 – 의 비 – 날 적 – 시
왕 – 되 – 신 주 – 께 서 – –   내 맘 에 – 천 국 – 이 루 – 시

1. new   2. heart
– 네 – –   – 네 –

I on-ly want   to be   where   You are
주 계 신 곳 – – 에 나 – 거 – 하 리 –

Ho - ly   ho - ly   is the Lord   King of
거 – – 룩 –   거 – – 룩 – 하 신 주 –   영 광

Glo - ry   For - e - ver   Sa - viour   of the world
의 – – 왕   영 원 – – 한 –   나 – – 의 – 구 원 자

Though moun-tains may be moved   and
산 – 이 – 요 동 – 하 며 – –   바

Need You Here

Words and Music by Reuben Morgan
© 2001 Hillsong Music Publishing (admin in Korea by Universal Music Publishing/ CAIOS)

A

407 Nothing But The Blood
(예수 피밖에)

Matt Redman

Nothing But The Blood

of God? Noth-ing but Your blood, noth-ing but Your blood, King
– 시 는 – 예 수 피 밖 에 – – 예 수 의 피 밖 – 에

Je – sus. King Je - sus. 3.Your
없 – 네

It's the blood, it's the blood.

It's the blood, it's the blood. It's the blood, it's the blood.

Yeah, what can wash us? Noth-ing but Your blood, King

Je - sus. Oh, King Je sus.

O.T. : Nothing But The Blood / O.W. : Matt Redman
O.P. : Thankyou Music Ltd / S.P. : Universal Music Publishing Korea, CAIOS
Adm. : Capitol CMG Publishing / All rights reserved, Used by permission.

408

One Day
(하루)

Reuben Morgan

More than I could hope or dream of You have poured Your favour on me
주 님께서 주신은혜 넘 치 도 록 채 우 시 네 -

One day in the House of God is bett-er than a thou-sand days in the world
주 의 성 전 의 하 루 가 세 상 에 서 천 - 날 보 다 낫 네

So blessed, I can't con-tain it, so much I've got to
- - 축 - 복 넘 치 는 축 - 복 - 주 내 게 거 저

give it a-way Your love has taught me to live now You are
주 시 었 네 - 사 - 랑 날 가 르 치 - 니 주 의

more than e-nough for me.
은 혜 가 족 하 네 -

Lord You're more than e-nough for me
주 - - 은 혜 내 게 족 하 네 - - -

Lord You're more than e-nough for me
주 - - 은 혜 내 게 족 하 네 - - -

You're more than e-nough for me.
- 은 혜 내 게 족 하 네 - - -

One Thing I Have Desired

(주께 구했던 한가지 소망)

Scott Brenner

409

One thing I have des-ired of the Lord That will I seek
주께 구 - 했던 한 - 가 - 지 - 소 - 망 - 기 도 하 - 니 -

That I may dwell in the house of the Lord All the days of my life
나 의 사 - 는 - 날 - - 동 - - 안 주 의 집 에 - 거 하 며 -

To beh-old the beau-ty of the Lord
주 아 름 - 다 움 - 앙 망 - 하 며 - - 그

And to inq-uire in His temple just let me live in the beau-
전 에 서 - 사 모 - 케 하 - 소 서 - 오 나 의 - 주 - 거 룩 한

- -ty of Your hol - in-ess this one thing I have des-ir-
- 주 의 - 아 름 - 다 움 - 오 직 한 가 - 지 내 소

- -ed To be changed in-to Your pur - it-y From glo-ry to glo-ry for-ev-
- 망 - 주 님 정 - 결 하 - 게 하 - 소 서 - 영 광 에 서 - 영 광 으

1. C#7sus4 C#7 F#m7 Bm7 E AM7 DM7 Bm7 C#7sus4 C#7
- - - er with You
- - - 로 - 영 원 히 -

2. C#7sus4 C#7 D.S. C#7sus4 C#7 DM7 Dm6 C#7sus4 C#7 F#m
er In the beau er with You
- 로 - 거 룩 한 - - 로 - 영 원 히 -

A

410

Praise Be To The Lord

(찬양하리라 이스라엘의 하나님)

Chris Bowater

Praise be to the Lord my God of Is - ra - el
찬 양 하 리 라 -이 스 라 엘 의 하 나 님-

ra - el Great thing He has done for me Praise be to the name of the Lord
하 - 나 님- 위 대 한 일 행 하 셨 네 - 찬 양 하 세 주 의 이 름

Praise be to the name of the Lord The whole earth is
- 찬 양 하 세 주 의 이 름 - 주 의 영 광 온

full of His glory The whole earth is full of His glory The whole earth is
땅 에 가 득 해 주 의 영 광 온 땅 에 가 득 해 주 의 영 광 온

full of His glory A - men A - men A - men
땅 에 가 득 해 아 멘 - 아 멘 - 아 멘 - -

Purify My Heart

(주의 도를)

Eugene Greco

Teach me your ways O Lord my God
주 의 도 를 – 내 게 알 – 리 소 서

And I will walk In your – truth
진 리 의 길 로 행 하 리

Give me a to-tal-ly Un-di-vi-ded heart
주 님 의 이 – 름 을 – 경 외 하 – 리 라 –

That I may fear Your – name
내 마 음 다 하 – 여 –

Pu-ri-fy my heart Cleanse me Lord I pray
나 의 마 – 음 을 – 씻 어 주 – 시 고 –

Re-move from me all that is stan-ding in the –way
내 발 걸 음 을 주 – 의 길 로 인 도 하 – 소 – 서 –

stan-ding in the – way of Your love
인 도 하 – 소 – 서 – 주 께 로 –

A

412 Redeemed

(주의 집에 영광이 가득해)

John Barnett

Let Your house be filled with Your glo — ry Lord
주 의 – 집 – 에 – 영 – 광 – 이 가 – 득 해

Let Your house be filled with Your glo — ry Lord
주 의 – 집 – 에 – 영 – 광 – 이 가 – 득 해

Let Your house be filled with Your prai — ses Lord
주 의 – 집 – 에 – 찬 – 양 – 이 가 – 득 해

Let Your house be filled with Your prai – ses Lord
주 의 – 집 – 에 – 찬 – 양 – 이 가 – 득 해

Let the re-deemed of the Lord give You glo — ry oh
주 나 – 를 구 원 – 했 네 영 광 돌 리 세

let the re-deemed of the Lord sing You prai — ses and
주 나 – 를 구 원 – 했 네 찬 양 드 리 세

let the re-deemed of the Lord fall and wor-ship You
주 나 – 를 구 원 – 했 네 와 서 경 배 해

ev-er – more ev-er – more ev-er – more ev-er – more
영 원 – 히 영 원히 – 영 원 – 히 영 원히 –

Rock Of Ages

(만세 반석)

Rita Baloche

There is no rock, there is no god like our God,
주 님 같 은 - 반 석 은 없 - 도 다 -

No oth-er name wor-thy of all our praise. The
찬 양 받 기 - 합 당 하 신 - 이 름 - - 변

Rock of Sal-va-tion that can-not be moved, He's pro-ven Him-self to be faith-
치 않 으 시 - 는 구 원 의 반 석 - 신 실 하 시 고 - 진 실 하

- ful and true. There is no rock, there is no god like ours.
- 신 주 - 주 님 같 은 - 반 석 은 없 - 도 다 - -

Rock of A - - - ges, Je - sus is the Rock
만 세 반 - - - 석 예 수 내 - 반 - 석

Rock of A - - ges, Je - sus is the Rock
- 만 세 반 - - 석 - 예 수 내 - 반 - 석

Rock of A - - - ges, Je - sus is the Rock
- 만 세 반 - - - 석 예 수 내 - 반 - 석 -

There is no Rock, there is no god like ours.
주 님 같 은 - 반 석 은 없 - 도 다 - -

O.T. : Rock Of Ages / O.W. : Rita Baloche
O.P. : Universal Music - Brentwood Benson Publ. / S.P. : Universal Music Publishing Korea, CAIOS
Adm. : Capitol CMG Publishing / All rights reserved, Used by permission,

414 Salvation Belongs To Our God

(보좌에 계신 하나님)

Adrian Howard & Pat Turner

Sal - va - tion be - longs to our God who sits up - on the
And we the re - deemed shall be strong in pur - pose and
보 좌 에 계 신 - 하 나 님 그 의 어 린 양
주 께 구 속 된 - 우 리 들 한 마 음 과 한

throne, and un - to the Lamb.
u - ni - ty, de - clar - ing a - loud;
예 - 수 구 원 하 - 셨 네 -
뜻 으 로 선 포 하 리 라 -

Praise and glo - ry, wis - dom and thanks,
찬 양 영 광 - 지 혜 감 사

hon - er and pow - er and strength
존 귀 - 와 힘 과 - 능 력 -

be to our God for - ev - er and ev - er be to our God for -
하 나 님 께 영 원 히 - 영 원 - 히 하 나 님 께 영

ev - er and ev - er, be to our God for - ev - er and ev - er, A
원 히 - 영 원 - 히 하 나 님 께 영 원 히 - 영 원 히 아

- men.
- 멘 - - -

Shine Jesus, Shine

(비추소서)

415

Graham Kendrick

416 That's What We Came Here For
(우리 주 안에서 노래하며)

Russell Fragar & Darlene Zschech

We come in-to Your presence with sing-ing   come in-to Your pres-ence with praise
우리 주 안에서 노 래 하 –며– 주 –의 이름 찬 양 – 해

And en - ter Your gates with thank - ful hearts we are going to cel-
– 감 사 로 – 그 – 문 – 에 들 – 어 가 – 주 이 름 송 축

- e-brate   All of heav-en's wait - ing   pow'r is on its way;
–하 네 – – 진 실 한 찬 – 양 안 – 에 – 권 – 능 임 – 하 니

so we shout "Hal-le-lu-jah!" lift - ing to You a might-y roar of praise
– 외 치 세 – 할 렐 루 – 야 손 – 뼉 치 – 며 전 능 하 신 – 주 께 –

You de-serve the high - est praise   that we can give and more
높 이 계 –신 주 – 님 께 – 우 리 여 기 모 인 이 유 –

Lord we give You our praise   that's what we came here   for
우 리 마 음 모 아 – 주 님 을 높 – 이 는 것 –

Eve - ry - thing with-in   me
내 안 에 – 모 든 – 것 –

reach-es out   to you   Your pow - er   And maj - es - ty
주 를 바 – 랄 때 – 주 의 능 력 – 또 영 광 – 은

That's What We Came Here For

grace and mer - cy too   There'll be sing - ing   and danc - ing
혜 와 자 비 도 –   찬 양 하 며 –   춤 추 세 –

hearts and voic - es raised   You have set   Your   peo -
마 음 문 – 열 어 –   주 가 자 유 케

- ple free   now the house is   filled   with praise
– 하 리 –   주 의 이 름 찬 –   양 해 –

that's what we came   here   for
주 님 을 높 – 이 는 것 –

You de-serve the high - est praise You de-serve the high - est praise
높 이 계 – 신 주 – 님 께 – 높 이 계 – 신 주 – 님 께 –

Written by Russell Fragar, Darlene Zschech
© 1997 Hillsong Music Publishing Australia (admin in Korea by Universal Music Publishing/ CAIOS)

A

417 Thank You For The Cross

(우리 죄 위해 죽으신 주)

Mark Altrogge

Thank you for the cross the migh – ty cross that
우 리 죄 위 해 – 죽 으 – 신 주 – 십

God Him - self shoud die for such as us and
자 가 그 사 랑 – 감 – 사 하 네 날

ev - ery day we're changed into Your image more and more yes
마 다 주 의 형 상 대 로 변 화 되 리 라 – – 십

by the cross we've tru - ly been trans - formed and we're
자 가 우 – 릴 새 롭 게 하 리 놀 라

so ama-zed and we give You praise that You would save us at such a co-
운 사 랑 – 찬 양 하 – 리 라 우 리 를 위 해 생 명 주 셨

st we're so ama-zed and we give You praise for the
네 – 놀 라 운 사 랑 – 찬 양 하 – 리 라 십 자

po-wer of the cross for the po-wer of the cross
가 의 그 능 력 십 자 가 의 그 능 력

The Lord's Prayer

(주기도문)

418

Albert Malotte(d.1964) & Peter Henry Mooney

Our Fa - ther, which art in heav - en hal - low - ed
하 늘 에 — 계 신 아 버 지 — 이 름 거

be thy name. Thy King - dom come, Thy will be
룩 하 사 주 님 나 라 임 하 시

done on earth as it is in heav - en.
고 뜻 이 이 루 어 지 이 다

Give us this day our dai - ly bread, and for -
일 용 할 양 식 주 시 고 우 리

give us our debts, as we for - give our debt - ors. And
들 의 큰 죄 — 다 용 — 서 하 옵 시 고 또

lead us not in - to temp - ta - tion, but de - liv - er us from
시 험 에 들 게 마 시 고 악 에 서 구 원 하

e - vil. for thine is the King - dom and the pow - er and the
소 서 대 개 주 의 나 라 — 주 의 권 세 — 주 의

glo - ry for - ev - er. A — — man
영 광 — 영 원 — 히 — 아 — — 멘

A

419 The Power Of Your Love

(주께 가오니)

Geoff Bullock

Lord, I come to You Let my heart be changed, re newed,
Lord, un-veil my eyes Let me see You face to face
주 께 가 오 니 – 날 새 롭 게 하 시 고
나 의 눈 열 어 – 주 를 보 게 하 시 고

flow - ing from the grace, that I've found in You
the knowl-edge of Your love, as You live in me
– 주 의 은 혜 를 부 어 주 – 소 서
– 주 의 사 랑 을 알 게 하 – 소 서

And Lord, I've come to know the weak-ness - es I
And Lord, re - new my mind as Your will un-
내 안 에 발 견 한 – 나 의 연 약
매 일 나 의 삶 에 – 주 뜻 이 뤄

see in me will be stripped a - way
folds in my life, in liv - ing ev - 'ry day
함 모 두 – 벗 어 지 리 라
지 도 록 – 새 롭 게 하 소 서

by the pow - er of Your love.
– 주 의 사 랑 으 로 – – –

Hold me close, let Your love sur-round me,
주 사 랑 – 나 를 붙 드 시 – – 고

The Power Of Your Love

Bring me near, draw me to your side
주 곁에 – 날 이 끄 소 – 서 – –

And as I wait I'll rise up like the ea
독 – – 수 리 – 날 개 쳐 올 라 가 – –

gle And I will soar with You, Your spi - rit leads me
듯 나 주 님 과 함 께 일 어 나 걸 으

on by the pow - er of Your love.
리 주 의 사 랑 안 에 – – – –

A

420 The Stand

(태초부터 계신 주)

Joel Houston

You stood be-fore cre-a-tion, e-ter-ni-ty in Your hand.
태 초 부 터 - 계 신 - 주 - 영 원 히 다 스 - 리 네 -

You spoke the earth in-to mo-tion, my soul now to stand.
말 씀 으 로 - 창 조 하 - 신 주 앞 에 - 서 네 -

You stood be-fore my fail - ure, and car-ried the cross for my shame. My
I'll walk u-pon sal-va - tion, Your Spi-rit a - live in me. This
내 모 든 허 - 물 위 - 해 - 주 십 자 가 를 - 지 셨 네 - 내
구 원 의 길 - 걸 으 - 리 - 주 성 령 이 인 - 도 해 - - 주

sin weighed u-pon Your shoul-ders, my soul now to stand. So what can I say?
life to de-clare Your pro-mise. My soul now to stand.
모 든 죄 짊 - 어 지 - 신 주 앞 에 - 서 - 네 - 그 어 느 것 - 도
약 속 을 선 - 포 하 - 리 주 앞 에 - 서 - 네 -

And what could I do, but of-fer this heart,
- 나 할 수 없 - 네 - 다 만 내 맘 드

O God, com-plete-ly to You. So
- 리 네 온 전 히 - 주 께 - -

1. F#m

2. F#m

to You So what can I say? And what could I do,
주 께 - - 그 어 느 것 - 도 - 나 할 수 없 - 네

The Stand

but of-fer this heart, O God, com-plete-ly
다 만 내 맘 드 -리 네 - 온 전 히

to You.
- 주 께 -

So I'll stand, with arms high and heart a-ban-doned, in awe of the
나 주 께 -손 들 고 내 맘 드 리 네 - 나 의 경 외

One who gave it all. I'll stand, my soul, Lord, to You sur-ren-dered.
하 는 주 님 께 - 주 께 - 나 의 모 든 것 드 립 니

All I am is Yours. All I am is Yours.
다 나 주 - 의 것 - 다 나 주 - 의 것 -

So what can I say? And what could I do,
그 어 느 것 -도 - 나 할 수 없 -네 -

but of -fer this heart, O God, com-plete-ly to You.
다 만 내 맘 드 -리 네 - 온 전 히 -주 께 -

Words and Music by Joel Houston
© 2005 Hillsong Music Publishing Australia (admin in Korea by Universal Music Publishing/ CAIOS)

A

421 The Time Has Come

(주의 때에)

Joel Houston

Found love be-yond all rea-son. You gave Your life, Your all for
주 의 그 크 신 사 랑 주 생 명 내 게 주 셨

me. And called me Yours for-e - ver.
- 네 - 영 원 히 난 - 주 의 - 것 - -

Caught in the mer-cy fall-out. I found hope, found life, found all I
주 의 자 비 안 에 서 소 망 과 생 명 찾 았

need. You're all I - need. The time
- 네 - 주 만 원 해 - 주 의

has come to stand for all we be-lieve in. So I
- 때 에 나 믿 음 으 로 일 어 - 나 - 오 직

for one, am gon-na give my praise to You. (Je-sus.) To-day,
- 주 님 - 께 나 의 찬 양 드 리 네 - (예 수 -) 오 늘

to-day, it's all or no-thing. All the way, praise goes out to You.
- 나 는 - 주 위 - 해 살 리 영 원 히 - 찬 양 을 주 께

Yeah, all the praise goes out to You. To-day,
- 주 님 께 찬 양 드 리 네 - 오 늘

to-day, I live for one thing to give You praise, in ev-ery-thing I do.
나 는 - 주 위 - 해 살 리 주 찬 양 해 내 모 든 삶 으 로

The Time Has Come

Words and Music by Joel Houston © 2004 Hillsong Music Publishing Australia (admin in Korea by Universal Music Publishing/ CAIOS)

422 Thou Art Worth

(오 하나님 영광 존귀)

Though The Fig Tree

(무화과 나뭇잎이 마르고)

Tony Hopkins

Th-ou-gh the fig tree does not blo-ss-om, and there
무 화 과 나 뭇 잎 이 – 마 르 고 – 포 도

be no fru-it on the vine, The pro-du-ce of the olive fa-il and the
열 매 가 없 으 며 – 감 람 나 무 열 매 그 치 고 – 논 밭 에

fie-ld yi-eld no fruit Though the flock be cut off
식 물 이 없 어 도 – 우 리 에 양 때 가

from the fold, and there be no he-rd in the stall Yet will I re-
없 으 며 – 외 양 간 송 아 지 없 어 도 – 난 여 호 와 로

jo-ice in the Lord, Yet will I re-jo-ice in the Lord,
즐 거 워 하 리 난 여 호 와 로 즐 거 워 하 리 난

Joy in the God of my sal-va-tion God the Lord is my strength
구 원 의 하 나 님 을 인 해 – 기 뻐 하 리 라 –

A

424 Under The Blood

(유월절 어린양의 피로)

Martin J. Nystrom & Rhonda Scelsi

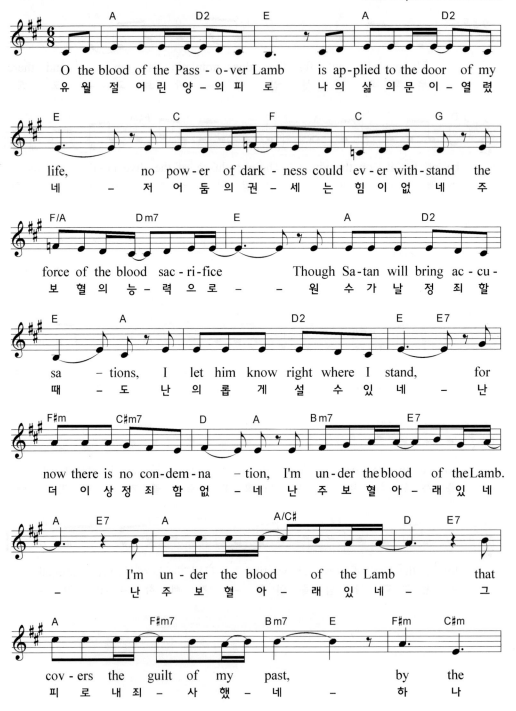

O the blood of the Pass - o - ver Lamb   is ap - plied to the door of my
유 월 절 어린 양 - 의 피 로   나 의 삶 의 문 이 - 열 렸

life,   no pow - er of dark - ness could ev - er with - stand   the
네 - 저 어 둠 의 권 - 세 는 힘 이 없 네 주

force of the blood sac - ri - fice   Though Sa - tan will bring ac - cu -
보 혈 의 능 - 력 으 로 - - 원 수 가 날 정 죄 할

sa - tions, I let him know right where I stand,   for
때 - 도 난 의 롭 게 설 수 있 네 - 난

now there is no con - dem - na - tion, I'm un - der the blood of the Lamb.
더 이 상 정 죄 함 없 - 네 난 주 보 혈 아 - 래 있 네

I'm un - der the blood   of the Lamb   that
- 난 주 보 혈 아 - 래 있 네 - 그

cov - ers the guilt of my past,   by the
피 로 내 죄 - 사 했 - 네 - 하 나

Under The Blood

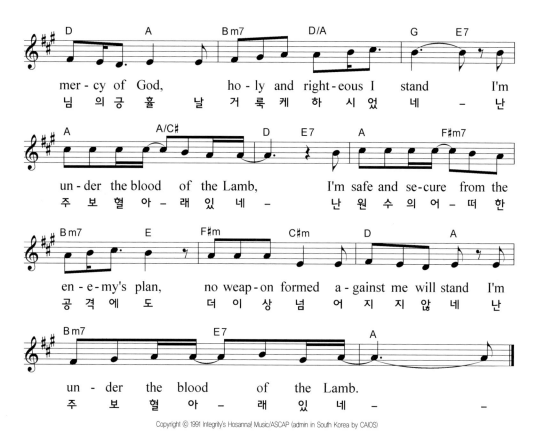

mer - cy of God,   ho - ly and right - eous I   stand   I'm
님 의 긍 휼   날 거 룩 케 하 시 었   네 –   난

un - der the blood   of the Lamb,   I'm safe and se - cure from the
주 보 혈 아 – 래 있 네 –   난 원 수 의 어 – 떠 한

en - e - my's plan,   no weap - on formed a - gainst me will stand   I'm
공 격 에 도   더 이 상 넘 어 지 지 않 네   난

un - der   the   blood   of   the   Lamb.
주 보 혈 아 – 래 있 네 –   –

A

425 We Are The Reason That He Gave His Life

(우리 때문에)

David Meece

As little child-ren we would dream of Christ-mas morn of all the gifts and
years went by we learned more a-bout gift and giv-ing of our

잊을 수 없네 – 하 나 님 의 사 랑 날 살 리 시 려
보 았 네 – 피 묻 은 십 자 가 날 구 하 시 려

toys we knew we'd find But we nev-er real-ized a ba-by born one bless-ed
selves and what that means on a dark and cloudy day a man hung cry-ing in the

고 주 신 생 명 내 – 십 자 가 지 고 오 르 신 갈 보 리 언
고 흘 린 사 랑 나 를 바 라 보 시 며 흘 리 신 용 서 의 눈

night Gave us the greatest gift of our lives
rain be-cause of love be-cause of love

덕 – 날 향 한 사 – 랑 때 문 에
물 – 날 향 한 사 – 랑 때 문 에

We were the reas-on that He gave His life We were the reas-on that He
우 리 때 문 – 에 생 명 – 주 셨 고 – 우 리 때 문 – 에 고 통

suff-red and died To a world that was lost He gave all He could give to
당 하 셨 네 – 우 리 때 문 에 갈 – 보 리 오 – 르 셨 네 – 무

show us the reas-on to live As the I've
지 한 우 리 – 때 문 에 – 나 는 – 내 가

fi-nally found the reas-on for liv – ing It's in giv – ing eve-ry part of my heart
살 아 야 할 – 이 유 찾 았 – 네 – 나 의 삶 – 을 모 두 주 께 드 리

We Are The Reason That He Gave His Life

426 What The World Will Never Take
(세상은 주를 빼앗지 못해)

Matt Crocker, Scott Ligertwood, Marty Sampson

with all I'm hol-ding in-side with all my hopes and de - si - res
나 의 지 하 는 것 들 – 바 라 는 그 모 든 소 망

And all the dreams that I've dreamt with all I'm ho-ping to be
꿈 꿔 왔 던 모 든 것 – 미 래 의 모 든 계 획

and all that the world will bring And all that fails to com-pare
– 세 상 이 주 는 약 속 – 비 할 수 없 는 것 들

You say You want all of me I would-n't
– 주 께 모 두 드 리 리 – 세 상 의

have it a-ny o-ther way I've got a Sa-viour and He's li-ving in me whoa
길 따 르 지 않 으 리 – 나 의 구 원 자 살 아 계 신 주 님 – 워 –

I wan-na know I wan - na know You to - day
– 알 기 원 해 주 님 을 알 기 원 해

And You're the best thing that has hap-pend to me And the
– 그 무 엇 보 다 귀 하 신 주 님 – 세 상

world will ne-ver take the world will ne-ver take You a-way
어 떤 유 혹 도 내 주 님 을 빼 앗 지 못 해 –

What The World Will Never Take

No one could ever take You a - way

－ 예 수 － 세 상 은 뺏 지 못 해

No one could e - ver take You a - way

－ 예 수 － 누 구 도 뺏 지 못 해 －

Words and Music by Marty Sampson, Matt Crocker, Scott Ligertwood
© 2004 Hillsong Music Publishing Australia (admin in Korea by Universal Music Publishing/ CAIOS)

A

427

We Sing Alleluia
(거룩한 성전에 거하시며)

Walter S. Harrah

A   E/A   D/A   A   F#sus4   F#/A#   Bm

The Lord is in His ho-ly tem-ple   The Lord is on His heav'n-ly throne;
We sense the beau-ty of His pres-ence,   We hear the great tri-um-phant shout!
The Lord is in His ho-ly tem-ple   And we are in His pres-ence now

거 룩 한 성 전 에 거 하 시 며   하 늘 보 좌 에 계 신 - 주
오 아 름 다 운 주 의 영 - 광   승 리 의 함 성 들 리 - 네
거 룩 한 성 전 에 계 신 - 주   우 리 주 님 앞 에 서 - 서

C#sus4   C#/F   F#m   Dm6/F   E

We bring our prais-es un-to Je-sus   For all the love that He has shown
The Lamb for sin-ners slain is wor-thy,   How can we keep from cry-ing out?
The ones who've gone be-fore have gath-ered   As one be-fore the Lord we bow.

주 가 베 푸 신 모 든 사 랑   우 리 찬 양 을 주 님 께
죽 임 당 하 신 어 린 양 께   우 리 큰 소 리 외 치 며
이 전 의 성 도 들 과 함 께   주 보 좌 앞 에 엎 드 려

D/F# E/G# A2   A   Em6/G   F#7   B9   D/E E   A

Sing-ing al-le-lu-ia,   al-le-lu-ia,   al-le-lu - ia!
찬 양 할 렐 루 야   할 렐 루 야   할 렐 루 - 야

D/F# E/G# A2   A   Em6/G   F#7   B9   D/E E   A

Sing-ing al-le-lu-ia,   al-le-lu-ia,   al-le-lu - ia!
찬 양 할 렐 루 야   할 렐 루 야   할 렐 루 - 야

With My Whole Heart

(온 맘으로 송축하리)

428

Chris Bowater

With my whole heart I will bless You With my
온 맘 으 로 송 축 하 리 생 명

whole life I will serve You And with all that I am and
다 해 주 섬 기 리 나 의 힘 나 의 맘 내

have and long to be I'll wor - ship, wor - ship You so make my
모 든 것 드 려 – 주 경 배 경 배 해 내 삶 을

whole life li - ving wor - ship, wor-ship un - to You so make my
드 려 주 께 경 배 경 배 드 – 리 리 – 내 삶 을

while life li - ving wor - ship, wor-ship un - to You
드 려 주 께 경 배 경 배 드 – 리 리

A

429 You Are My King
(왕 되신 주)

Brian Doerksen

You are my King and I love You
왕 되신 주 사랑합니다

You are my King and I wor-ship You
왕 되신 주 경배합니다

Kneel-ing be-fore You now, all of my life I
주께 무릎 꿇고 기쁨으로 내

glad - ly give to You You are my
삶을 드리네 왕 되신

You plac-ing my hopes and dreams, in Your hands I
네 내 꿈과 소 망도 주 손에 다

give my heart to You I love You,
맡 겨 드리네 주를 사 랑

love You Je - - sus Yes I love You,
사 랑 예 수 주를 사 랑

love You Je - - sus my King
사 랑 주 나의 왕

Your Name

(그 이름)

Paul Baloche & Glenn Packiam

430

431

Your Grace Is Enough

(주님의 은혜 넘치네)

Matt Mahe

Great is your faith - ful - ness oh God
Great is your love and jus - tice God
주 신 - 실 하 - 심 놀 - 라 워 -
공 의 - 와 사 - 랑 놀 - 라 워 -

You wres - tle with the sin - ner's rest - less heart
You use the weak to lead the strong
죄 인 - 의 마 - 음 흔 - 드 네 -
약 한 - 자 들 - 어 쓰 - 시 네 -

You lead us by still wa - ters and to mer - cy
You lead us in the song of your sal - va - tion
자 비 - 의 물 - 가 로 - 인 도 - 하 시 니
구 원 - 의 노 - 래 로 - 인 도 - 하 시 - 니

And noth - ing can keep us a - part So re -
And all your peo - ple sing a - long
그 무 - 엇 도 - 끊 지 - 못 해 - 주 여
만 백 - 성 함 - 께 찬 - 양 해 -

mem - ber Your peo - ple Re - mem - ber Your chil - dren Re -
기 억 - 하 소 서 - 주 백 성 - 자 녀 들 - 신

mem - ber Your prom - ise oh – God Your
실 한 - 주 님 의 - 약 - 속 - 주

Your Grace Is Enough

grace is e-nough   Your grace is e-nough   (yeh) Your
님 의 은 혜 –   내 게 넘 치 네 –   나

grace is e-nough   for   me
를 향 한 주 – 은 - - 혜 –

O.T. : Your Grace Is Enough / O.W. : Matt Maher
O.P. : Thankyou Music Ltd / S.P. : Universal Music Publishing Korea, CAIOS
Adm. : Capitol CMG Publishing / All rights reserved, Used by permission,

A

432 Better Than Life

(이 세상의 부요함보다)

Marty Sampson

Better Than Life

fall-ing in love with You I'll nev-er stop fall-ing in love with You
영원히사 - 랑해 - 나의사랑 멈추 - 지않 - 으리

I can't stop
- 주 님 만 -

You
붙

hold me now in Your arms, and nev-er let me go
드 - 소 서 - 주 님 나 - - 를 놓 - 지 마 소 서 -

You hold me now in Your arms,
붙 드 - 소 서 - 주 님 나

and ne - ver let me go
- - 를 놓 - 지 마 소 서 -

Words and Music by Marty Sampson
© 2003 Hillsong Music Publishing Australia (admin in Korea by Universal Music Publishing/ CAIOS)

A

433 You're The Glory

(주는 나의 영광이요)

Joshua Mills

You're the glo - ry   You're the lif - ter   You're the
주 는 나 의   영 광 이 요   나 의

glo - ry and   the lif - ter of   my   head   You're the
머 리 를 – 드 시 – 는 하 – 나 님   주 는

head   you ta-ken me high – er   high-er and high - er   You're the
님   날 높 이 드 시 – 네 – 높 이 더 높 – 이 –   나 의

glo - ry and the lif - ter of   my head   you ta-ken me high
머 리 를 – 드 시 – 는 하 – 나 님   날 높 이 드 시 님

For Who You Are

(내 주 되신 주)

434

Marty Sampson

435 Blessed Be Your Name

(주 이름 찬양)

Beth Redman & Matt Redman

Bless-ed be Your name in the land that is plen - ti-ful
Bless-ed be Your name when the sun's shin-ing down on me
주 – 이 름 – 찬 양 – 풍 요 의 강 – 물 흐 – 르 는 –
주 – 이 름 – 찬 양 – 햇 살 이 나 – 를 비 – 추 고 –

where Your streams of a-bun-dance flow Bless-ed be Your name
When the world's "all as it should be" Bless-ed be Your name
부 요 한 땅 – 에 살 – 때 에 – 주 님 – 찬 양 해 –
만 물 이 새 – 롭 게 – 될 때 – 주 님 – 찬 양 해 –

Bless - ed be Your name When I'm found in the de - sert place
Bless - ed be Your name on the road marked with suf - fer - ing
주 – 이 름 – 찬 양 – 거 치 른 광 – 야 와 – 같 은 –
주 – 이 름 – 찬 양 – 가 는 길 험 – 할 지 – 라 도 –

Though I walk through the wil - der-ness Bless-ed be Your name
though there's pain in the of - fer - ing Bless-ed be Your name
인 생 길 걸 – 어 갈 – 때 도 – 주 님 – 찬 양 해 –
고 통 이 따 – 를 지 – 라 도 – 주 님 – 찬 양 해 –

Eve-ry bless-ing You pour out I'll turn back to praise
모 든 축 복 주 신 주 님 찬 양 하 리

when the dark-ness clos-es in, Lord still I will say
어 둔 날 이 다 가 와 도 난 외 치 리

Blessed Be Your Name

Bless-ed be the name of the Lord Blsse-ed be Your name
주의 이름을 찬 – 양 – 해 – 주의 이름 을

Bless - ed be the na - me of the Lord
주의 이름을 찬 – 양 – 해 –

Bless - ed be Your glo – ri - ous name
영 화 로 운 주 이름 – 찬 양 –

You give and ta - ke a-way You give and take a-way
주 님 은 주 시 – 며 주 님 은 찾으 시 네 – –

My heart will choo-se to say Lord, bless-ed be Your name
내 맘 에 하 – 는 말 주 찬 양 합 니 다 – –

O.T. : Blessed Be Your Name / O.W. : Beth Redman, Matt Redman
O.P. : Thankyou Music Ltd / S.P. : Universal Music Publishing Korea, CAIOS
Adm. : Capitol CMG Publishing / All rights reserved, Used by permission.

B

436

Everyday
(날마다)

Joel Houston

Everyday

It's You I live for ev-
나 주 만 – 위 – 해 – 살

- -ery day It's You I live for ev - ery day It's
– 겠 네 – 나 주 만 – 위 – 해 – 살 – 겠 네 – 나

You I live for ev - ery day
주 만 – 위 – 해 – 살 – 겠 네 – – –

Words and Music by Joel Houston
© 1999 Hillsong Music Publishing Australia (admin in Korea by Universal Music Publishing/ CAIOS)

B

437

Go
(주님 안에 자유 있네)

Matt Crocker

B

In the Fa-ther there is free-dom There is hope in the Name that is Je-sus
We are sold out to Your cal-ling Ev-ery-thing that we are for Your glo-ry
주님 안에 자유 있네 예수의 이름에 소망 있네
주님 우릴 부르셨네 모든 것 주님의 영광 위해

B

Lay your life down Give it all now We are found in the love of the Sa-viour
Take our hearts now Have it all now Let our lives shine Your light like the mor-ning
우리 삶을 모두 드려 주 사랑 우리를 구원했네
우리 마음 다 드리니 주의 빛 어둠을 비추소서

E **G#m** **E** **G#m**

We've come a - live in You Set free to show the truth
새 롭 게 되었네 - 자 유 케 되었네 -

E **G#m** **F#**

Our lives will ne - ver be the same We're gi-ving it all
이 전 과 같지 않 - 으리 - 내 모든 것 다

1. B

a-way A-way We're gi-ving it all
- 드 리 - 리 라 - 주 님 의 길로

B

to go Your way
- 가 기 - 위 해 -

B

%
2. B

a-way A-way We're gi-ving it all
- 드 리 - 리 라 - 주 님 의 길로

Go

Words and Music by Matt Crocker
© 2011 Hillsong Music Publishing Australia (admin in Korea by Universal Music Publishing/ CAIOS)

B

438 God Is Able
(능력의 주)

Ben Fielding, Reuben Morgan

God Is Able

o-pen arms He will ne-ver fail is   He will ne-ver fail us   Lift-ed up
리 시 – 네 – 주 님 결 코 우 릴 –   포 기 하 지 않 네 –   죽 음 도

Words and Music by Ben Fielding, Reuben Morgan
© 2010 Hillsong Music Publishing Australia (admin in Korea by Universal Music Publishing/ CAIOS)

B

439 Jesus Messiah
(예수 메시아)

Chris Tomlin, Daniel Carson, Ed Cash & Jesse Reeves

He be-came sin who knew no sin that we might be-come His
bo-dy the bread His blood the wine bro-ken and poured out
죄 없으 - 신 - 우 리 주 님 - 우 릴 의 롭게 - 하
님 의 몸 과 - 그 의 피 를 - 다 내 어 주 신 -

right-eous-ness He hum-bled Him-self and car-ried the cross
all for love The whole earth trem-bled and the veil was torn
시 려 - 고 - 주 십 자 가 를 - 짊 어 지 셨 - 네 - - - -
주 사 - 랑 - 온 땅 은 떨 - 고 - 휘 장 찢 겼 - 네 - - - -

Love so a-maz - ing love so a-maz-ing
- 놀 라 운 사 - 랑 - - 놀 라 운 사 랑 -

Je-sus, Mes-si - ah; Name a-bove all names;
- 예 수 메 시 - 아 - - 뛰 어 난 이 - 름 -

Bless-ed Re-deem - er; Em-man-u-el.
복 되 신 구 - 주 - - 임 마 누 엘 -

The Res-cue for sin - ners, the Ran-som from heav- en;
죄 인 구 하 시 - 려 - - 그 영 광 버 리 - 신 -

Je-sus, Mes-si - ah, Lord of all.
예 수 메 시 - 아 - - 만 유 의 주 -

Jesus Messiah

His All our hope is in You, all our hope
주 우 리 모 — —든 소 망 — 오 직 주

is in You; all the glo — — ry to You, God,
— —께 있 네 — 온 세 상 — —의 빛 되 — 신 —

the Light of the world Je - sus, Mes - si
주 님 께 영 광 예 수 메 시

Je - sus, Mes-si - ah, Lord of all
예 수 메 시 — 아 — — 주 의 주 —

The Lord of all! The Lord of all!
만 유 의 주 — 만 유 의 주 —

O.T. : Jesus Messiah / O.W. : Jesse Reeves, Daniel Carson, Ed Cash, Chris Tomlin
O.P. : worshiptogether.com Songs, sixsteps Music, Vamos Publishing / S.P. : Universal Music Publishing Korea, CAIOS
Adm. : Capitol CMG Publishing / All rights reserved. Used by permission.

B

440 Oceans Will Part

(주의 나라 오리라)

Ben Fielding

If my heart has grown cold, there Your love will un-fold,
Pre-sent suf-fering may pass, Lord Your mer-cy will last.
무 너 진 내 맘 에 주 사 랑 임 하 네
고 난 지 나 가 고 자 비 영 원 하 네

As You o-pen my eyes to the work of Your Hand.
As You o-pen my eyes to the work of Your Hand.
나 의 눈 을 열 어 주 보 게 하 시 네
나 의 눈 을 열 어 주 보 게 하 시 네

When I'm blind to my way, there Your Spi-rit will pray.
And my heart will find praise, I'll de-light-in Your way.
길 잃 은 날 위 해 성 령 간 구 하 사
주 를 찬 양 하 며 기 쁨 의 길 가 리

As you o-pen my eyes to the work of Your Hand.
나 의 눈 을 열 어 주 보 게 하 시 네

As You o-pen my eyes to the work of Your hand.
나 의 눈 을 열 어 주 보 게 하 시 네

O-ceans will part, na-tions come, at the whis-per of Your call.
주 의 나 라 오 리 라 주 께 서 부 르 실 때

Oceans Will Part

Hope will rise, glo - ry shown. In my life,
－ 소 망 과 － 영 광 의 － 주 의 － 뜻

Your will be done.
－ 이 루 － 소 － － 서 －

Words and Music by Ben Fielding
© 2006 Hillsong Music Publishing Australia (admin in Korea by Universal Music Publishing/ CAIOS)

B

441 One Way
(오직 예수)

Joel Houston & Jonathon Douglass

I lay my life down, at Your feet You're the on - ly one I need
You are al - ways, al - ways there eve - ry how and eve - ry-where
주 발 앞 에 나 엎 드 려 주 만 간 절 히 원 해
언 제 나 어 디 서 나 크 고 깊 은 은 혜 로

I turn to You and You are al - ways there
Your grace a-bounds so deep - ly with in me
주 계 신 곳 나 바 라 봅 - 니 다 - -
주 님 항 상 내 안 에 계 - 시 네 -

In trou-bled times it's You I seek I put You first that's
You will ne - ver e - verchange yes - ter - day to -
근 심 속 에 주 찾 을 때 - 모 든 필 요 내
변 함 없 으 신 주 님 - - 어 제 오 늘

all I need I hum-bled all I am, All to You
day the same for - e - ver till for - e - ver meets no end
려 놓 고 겸 손 하 게 모 두 - 드 - 리 리 - -
영 원 히 한 결 같 이 함 께 - 하 - 시 네 - -

One way Je - sus You're the on - ly one that I could live for
오 직 예 수 주 님 만 이 나 의 삶 의 이 유

One way Je - sus You're the on - ly one that I could live for
오 직 예 수 주 님 만 이 나 의 삶 의 이 유

One Way

You are the way the truth and the life we live by faith and not
주 님 은 길 과 진 – 리 생 명 나 는 – 오 직 – 믿 음

by sight for You we're li – ving all for You
– 으 로 – 살 리 – 주 만 – 위 해 – 살 리 – –

You are the way the truth and the life we live by faith and not
주 님 은 길 과 진 – 리 생 명 나 는 – 오 직 – 믿 음

by sight for You we're li – ving all for You
– 으 로 – 살 리 – 주 만 – 위 해 – 살 리

D.S. al Coda

Words and Music by Joel Houston, Jonathon Douglass
© 2003 Hillsong Music Publishing Australia (admin in Korea by Universal Music Publishing/ CAIOS)

B

442

Salvation Is Here

(구원 이 곳에)

Joel Houston

1.God a - bove all the world in mo - tion   God a - bove all my
2.Hear the sound of the gen - e - ra - tions   ma-king loud their

온 세 - 상 위에 계신 - 주 님 - 내 소 - 망 두 렴
이 세 - 대 소리 들어 - 보 라 - 자 유 - 의 노래

hopes and fears   And I don't care what the world throws at   me now
free-dom song   All in   all that the world would know Your name

위 에 - 도 - 다 가 - 올 미 래 두 렵 - 지 - 않 네
힘 차 - 게 - 세 상 - 이 주 이 름 알 - 때 - 까 지

I'm gon-na   be al - right
we gon-na

- - 내 영혼 자유 - 해 -
- - 내 주를

be al - right 'cause I   know   my   God saved the day And I know

찬 양 - 해 - 나의   주   날 - 구 - 원했네 - 주의 말

His   word   ne-ver fails And I know   my   God made a-way for me

- 씀 - 완 - 전하며 - 주 날 위 - 해 - 길 - 만드심 - 아 네

Sal-va-tion is   here

- - - 구 원 이 곳 - 에 -

It's gon-na be al-right 'cause I   Sal-va-tion is

- - - 내 주를 찬 양 - 해 - 나 의 - - - 구 원 이 곳 -

Salvation Is Here

Words and Music by Joel Houston
© 2004 Hillsong Music Publishing Australia (admin in Korea by Universal Music Publishing/ CAIOS)

B

443 Take It All
(받아주소서)

Matt Crocker, Scott Ligertwood & Marty Sampson

Sear-ching the world, the lost will be found. In free-dom we live,
Your sent Your Son, from hea-ven to earth. You de-li-vered us all,
잃 은 영 혼 - 구 원 얻 으 며 - 그 자 유 안 에
이 땅 위 에 - 아 들 을 두 신 - 그 복 된 소 식

as one we cry out You car-ried the cross, You died and rose a-
it's e-ter-nal-ly heard. I searched for truth, and all I found was
- 다 함 께 외 쳐 - 십 자 가 지 신 - 또 부 활 하 신
- 내 게 들 리 네 - 내 가 찾 은 - 진 리 는 오 직

1. gain, My God, I'll on-ly e-ver give my all. You. 2. My God, I'll on-ly e-ver give my all.
주 예 수 내 모 든 것 을 주 님 께 주 예 수 내 모 든 것 을 주 님 께

Je-sus, we're li-vin' for Your Name. We'll ne-ver be a-shamed of You.
주 이 름 위 해 살 겠 네 내 자 랑 되 신 주 예 수 -

Our praise, and all we are to-day. Take, take, take it all. Take, take, take it all.
찬 양 또 나 의 모 든 것 받 아 주 소 서 받 아 주 소 서

Run-ning to the One who heals the blind. - -
주 님 어 둔 내 눈 여 시 니 - -

Flo-low-ing the shi-ning light. In Your hands the power to save
그 빛 따 라 가 리 라 - 구 원 의 능 력 오 직

Take It All

D.S. al Coda

the world, – and my – life.

주 안 – 에 있 – 네 –

Take, take, take it all. Take, take, take it all. Take, take, take it all.

받 아 주 소 서 받 아 주 소 서 받 아 주 소 서

Words and Music by Marty Sampson, Matt Crocker, Scott Ligertwood
© 2005 Hillsong Music Publishing Australia (admin in Korea by Universal Music Publishing/ CAIOS)

B

444 God Is Great
(위대한 하나님)

Marty Sampson

God Is Great

B

445

I Believe The Promise
(믿어요 그 약속)

Russel Frager

I be-lieve the prom - ise a-bout the vi - sions and the dreams
믿 어 요 그 약 - 속 - 비 전 과 꿈 을 주 - 셨 네

That the Ho - ly Spi - rit will be poured out and His po-
- 주 의 성 - 령 - 흘 - 러 넘 치 - 리 - 라 - 주 의 권

- wer - - will be seen Well, the time is now and the place
- 능 보 - - 리 라 - 바 로 지 - 금 여 - 기 이 장

is here and His peo - ple have come - - in faith There's a migh-
- 소 에 - 믿 는 백 - 성 다 모 - 였 - 네 - 강 - 한 소

- ty sound and a touch of fi - re when we're gath-ered in one place
- 리 와 - 성 령 의 - 불 있 - 네 우 리 여 기 모 일 때 -

I be - lieve that the pre - sence of God is here
난 믿 네 주 님 여 기 에 계 - 심 을 -

There's not one thing that can't be changed When the Spi - rit of God is near
세 상 모 든 것 다 변 - 하 네 - - 주 의 성 - 령 임 - 할 때 -

I Believe The Promise

I be - lieve that the pre - sence of God is here
난 믿 네 주 님 여 기 에 계 심 을 –

Where two or three are ga - thered When peo - ple rise in faith
두 세 사 람 모 일 – 때 그 믿 음 모 – 일 때 –

I be-lieve God ans - wers And His pre-sence is in this place
주 의 응 답 믿 – 네 그 분 여 기 에 계 – 시 네 –

No thing on Earth or Hea - ven Can stop the pow'r of God
– 하 늘 과 땅 그 무 엇 – 도 주 님 권 능 – 아 래 –

In - to our hands is gi - ven The call to take it on
주 께 서 우 리 에 게 맡 기 신 소 명 은 –

No o - cean can con-tain it No star can rise a-bove
바 다 도 감 당 못 – 해 별 보 다 더 높 네 –

in - to our hearts is gi - ven The pow'r of His love
우 리 의 맘 에 주 – 신 주 님 의 사 랑 –

Fine

D.S. al Fine

B

Words and Music by Russell Fragar
© 1995 Hillsong Music Publishing Australia (admin in Korea by Universal Music Publishing/ CAIOS)

446

Look To You

(주를 봅니다)

Marty Sampson

So I   look to   You,
주 를   봅 니 - 다

so I   look to   You   No one else will   do   No one
- 주 를 봅 니 다 - 오 직 주 님 - 만 - 오 직

else will   do.
주 님 - 만 -

last time Fine

I know You love me   I know You died for   me   I know You
주 님 의 사 랑 -   날 구 원 하 셨 - 네 - 주 날 다

care.   I know You care   I know You
스 - 려 -   주 날 다 스 - 려 -   부 활 하

live   a - gain   Your life for   all   my   sin   Now I stand
신   주 - 님 - 날 용 서 하 셨 - 네 -   주 님 의

here   in,   in Your grace a - gain   When I
- 은 - 혜 -   안 에   서   있 - 네 -   나 의

look in - to   the sky a-bove   won-der how my   life   has changed
주 님 을 - 바 라 - 볼 때 -   나 의 삶 은 변 - 하 네 -

Look to You

Won-der how Your love it came to me When I
주 님 의 – 사 랑 – 이 다 – 가 와 – 나 의

look in-to the sky a-bove all my fears so far a-way and
주 님 을 – 바 라 – 볼 때 – 모 든 두 – 렴 떠 – 나 네 – 또

all I feel is hea-ven cal-ling me. So I
나 는 주 – 님 만 – 을 느 – 끼 네 – 주 를

D.S.

Words and Music by Marty Sampson
© 2004 Hillsong Music Publishing Australia (admin in Korea by Universal Music Publishing/ CAIOS

B

447

O Praise Him
(주 찬양)

David Crowder

1.Turn your ear to heav-en and hear the niose
2.Turn your gaze to heav-en and raise a joy

저 하늘 – 울리는 소리 – 들어
눈 들어 – 기쁨의 합성 – 주께

in - side the sound of an – gel's awe, the sound
- ous noise the sound of sal-va – tion come the sound

– 보 라 – 주를 – 경 – 외 – 하는 – 천 사
– 울 려 – 구 원 – 받 은 자 – 들 의 – 기 쁜

of an – gel's song, and all this for a King We
of res – cued ones, and all this for a King An

– 의 노 – 래 소 – 리 왕 – 되 신 – 주 께 – 우
– 소 리 – 들 리 – 네 왕 – 되 신 – 주 께 – 천

could join and sing all to Christ the King.
- gels join to sing all for Christ our King.

– 리 도 – 함 께 – 찬 – 양 드 – 리 세 –
– 사 도 – 함 께 – 찬 – 양 드 – 리 네 –

How con-stant how di-vine this song of ours will rise
How in – fin - ite and sweet this love so res- – cu - ing

신 실 – 하 신 – 주 께 – 찬 양 – 을 드 – – 리 네 –
영 원 – 하 신 – 주 님 – 구 원 – 의 그 – – 사 랑 –

O how con - stant how di-vine this love of ours will rise,
O how in – fin - ite – ly sweet this great love that has re - deemed,

거 룩 하 – 신 주 – 님 께 – 우 리 – 사 랑 – – 드 려 –
사 랑 스 – 러 운 – 주 님 – 위 대 하 – 신 그 – – 사 랑 –

O Praise Him

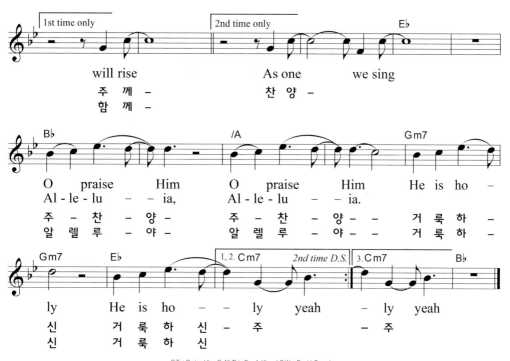

O Praise Him, O All This For A King / O.W. : David Crowder

O.T. : Praise Him, O All This For A King / O.W. : David Crowder
O.P. : worshiptogether.com Songs, sixsteps Music / S.P. : Universal Music Publishing Korea, CAIOS
Adm. : Capitol CMG Publishing / All rights reserved. Used by permission.

B

448

Who Am I

(온 땅의 주인)

Mark Hall

Who am I that the Lord of all the earth
Who am I that the eyes that see my sin
온 땅의 — — — 주 인 되 신 주 – 님 이 –
주 님 은 — — — 나 의 죄 를 보 – 시 고 –

would care to know my name would care to feel my hurt?
would look on me with love and watch me rise a-gain?
내 이 름 아 – 시 며 – 상 한 맘 돌 – 보 네 –
사 랑 의 눈 – 으 로 – 날 일 으 키 – 시 네 –

who am I that the Bright and Morn - ing Star
Who am I that the voice that calmed the sea
어 둠 을 — — — 밝 히 시 는 새 – 벽 별 –
바 다 를 — — — 잠 잠 하 게 하 – 시 듯 –

would choose to light the way for my ev - er wan-d'ring heart?
would call out through the rain and calm the storm in me?
방 황 하 는 – 내 맘 — — — 주 의 길 비 추 – 시 네 — — —
내 영 혼 의 – 폭 풍 — — — 고 요 케 하 – 시 네 — — —

Not be-cause of who I am but be-cause of what You've done
나 로 인 함 이 – 아 – 닌 — — — 주 가 행 하 신 – 일 – 로 –

Not be-cause of what I've done but be-cause of who You are
나 의 행 함 이 – 아 – 닌 – 오 직 주 로 인 – 하 여 –

Who Am I

I am a flow-er quick-ly fad - ing here to-day and gone to-mor-
나 는 오 늘 피었 - 다 - 지 - 는 - 이 름 없 는꽃 - 과 같

- - row A wave tossed in the o - cean a va-por in the wind
- - 네 바 다 에 - 이 는 파 - 도 - 안 개 와같 - 지 - 만

Still You here me when I'm call - ing Lord, You
- 주 는 나 를붙 - 드 - 시 - 고 - 부 르

catch me when I'm fall - ing And You've told me who I am;
짖 음 들 - 으 - 시 - - - 며 - 날 귀 하 다하 - 시 - 네 -

I am Yours I am Yours
나 오 직 - 주 의 것 -

B

449 Majesty

(주 앞에)

Stuart Garrard & Martin Smith

Majesty

fice   Sing-in' maj - es - ty,   maj - es - ty;
네   위   대   한 –   나   의   주

–   Your grace has found me just as I am   emp - ty
–   주 은 혜 의 손 길 안 에 서 –   주 의

hand-ed, but a - live in Your hands.   Sing-in' maj - es - ty,
능 력 으 로 살 아 가 리 –   위   대   한 –

maj - es - ty;   For - ev - er I am changed by Your love
나   의   주 –   주 영 광 의 임 재 안 에 서

in the pres-ence of Your maj - es - ty.
–   주 의 사 랑 으 로 변 화 되 리 –

B

450 More Love More Power

(주의 사랑 주의 능력)

Jude Del Hierro

Mo-re lo-ve,　　　mo-re pow-er,　　　mo-re of You in my　　life.
주 의 사 랑　　　주 의 능 력　　　더 욱 부 - 어 주 소 - 서

Mo-re lo-ve,　　　mo-re pow-er,　　　mo-re of You in my　　life.
내 삶 가 득　　　주 님 으 로　　　더 욱 채 - 워 주 소 - 서

And I will wor-ship You　　with all of my heart　　　And I will wor-ship
주 경 배 합 니 다 - 내 마 음 다 해 -　　주 경 배 합 니

You　with all of my heart　　　And I will wor-ship You　　with all of my strength
다 - 내 뜻 을 다 해 -　　주 경 배 합 니 다 - 내 힘 을 다 해

for You are my Lord　　　　　　You are　my　Lord.
- 오 나 의 주 님 -　　　　　나 의 - 주 님

영어찬양 BEST 450

초판 발행일	2025년 1월 1일
펴낸이	김수곤
펴낸곳	ccm2u
출판등록	1999년 9월 21일 제 54호
악보편집	노수정
디자인	이소연
주소	서울시 송파구 백제고분로27길 12 (삼전동)
전화	02) 2203.2739
FAX	02) 6455.2798
E-mail	ccm2you@gmail.com
Homepage	www.ccm2u.com

CCM2U는 한국교회 찬양의 부흥에 마중물이 되겠습니다.